South Side Impresarios

MUSIC IN AMERICAN LIFE

The Music in American Life series documents and celebrates the dynamic and multifaceted relationship between music and American culture. From its first publication in 1972 through its half-century mark and beyond, the series has embraced a wide variety of methodologies, from biography and memoir to history and musical analysis, and spans the full range of musical forms, from classical through all types of vernacular music. The series showcases the wealth of musical practice and expression that characterizes American music, as well as the rich diversity of its stylistic, regional, racial, ethnic, and gendered contexts. Characterized by a firm grounding in material culture, whether archival or ethnographic, and by work that honors the musical activities of ordinary people and their communities, Music in American Life continually redefines and expands the very definition of what constitutes music in American culture, whose voices are heard, and how music and musical practices are understood and valued.

For a list of books in the series, please see our website at www.press.uillinois.edu.

South Side Impresarios

How Race Women Transformed Chicago's Classical Music Scene

SAMANTHA EGE

UNIVERSITY OF
ILLINOIS PRESS
Urbana, Chicago, and Springfield

Publication of this book was supported in part
by the H. Earle Johnson Subvention Fund of
the Society for American Music, by a grant from
the Henry and Edna Binkele Classical Music
Fund, and AMS 75 PAYS Fund of the American
Musicological Society, supported in part by the
National Endowment for the Humanities and
the Andrew W. Mellon Foundation.

Library of Congress Cataloging-in-Publication Data

Names: Ege, Samantha, author.
Title: South Side impresarios : how race women transformed
    Chicago's classical music scene / Samantha Ege.
Description: Urbana : University of Illinois Press, 2024. |
    Series: Music in American life | Includes bibliographical
    references and index.
Identifiers: LCCN 2024016366 (print) | LCCN 2024016367
    (ebook) | ISBN 9780252046261 (cloth) | ISBN
    9780252088339 (paperback) | ISBN 9780252047534 (ebook)
Subjects: LCSH: African American women composers—
    Illinois—Chicago. | African American composers—Illinois—
    Chicago. | African American musicians—Illinois—Chicago. |
    African American women—Intellectual life—20th century. |
    Music and race—Illinois—Chicago—History—20th century.
    | Music—Social aspects—Illinois—Chicago—History—20th
    century. | South Side (Chicago, Ill.)—History—20th century.
    | South Side (Chicago, Ill.)—Social life and customs.
Classification: LCC ML82 .E34 2024 (print) | LCC ML82
    (ebook) | DDC 780.89/96073077311—dc23/eng/20230412
LC record available at https://lccn.loc.gov/2024016366
LC ebook record available at https://lccn.loc.gov/2024016367

To Sheila Anne Jones

Contents

Acknowledgments

There are mentors who seek to mold your trajectory around their own image, rendering you an extension of their ambitions—a recipe for imposter syndrome. Then there are mentors who seek to shape the path ahead of you in ways that allow you to become your fullest self and find joy in each and every step. I thank Lisa Barg for being one of my earliest examples of the latter. My introduction to Florence Price and Margaret Bonds in Lisa's "Early Twentieth-Century Music" undergraduate course at McGill University set me on my way, eventually leading me to William "Bill" Brooks, my PhD adviser at the University of York. Bill's mentorship unlocked the multifaceted scholarship that I have come to embrace as both a musicologist and a concert pianist. Furthermore, he opened my world to a wider musicological community wherein I met Laurie Matheson.

I thank Laurie for supporting my book, even before there was a book, and for encouraging me further once the ideas for *South Side Impresarios* fell into place. I would not have reached this point, however, without the great deal of feedback and comments I received on earlier versions of this work. So, thank you to Kira Thurman, Sandra Jean Graham, Lucy Caplan, Jeanice Brooks, Gwynne Kuhner Brown, A. Kori Hill, Natasha Lightfoot, Ambre Dromgoole, Marian Wilson Kimber, Douglas W. Shadle, Leah Broad, Kendra Preston Leonard, Liesl Olson, Lee Bey, Tammy L. Kernodle, Matthew D. Morrison, Alisha Lola Jones, Robert L. Kendrick, Mark Hutchinson, and my anonymous reviewers. And thank you to Karla Hartl of the *Kapralova Society Journal*, Emily Wilbourne of *Women and Music: A Journal of Gender and Culture*, and Todd Decker of *American Music* for granting me these platforms to publish the ideas that fed into *South Side Impresarios*.

I would like to give a special mention to the Black Women Researchers in Music group that kept me writing through the height of the pan-
demic. Aaliyah Booker, Uchenna Ngwe, JoAnne Sibanda, Sara Speller, and
Danielle Welbeck: I deeply appreciate the virtual community we fostered.
I also thank Naomi André for gracing us with her presence and encouraging us to push through. Another virtual community from which I drew
support came from the inaugural American Musicological Society (AMS)
Sustainable Mentorship Program. Thank you to mentor Emily Wilbourne
and my cohort of mentees, Anne Levitsky, Alecia Barbour, and Daniel
Castro Pantoja, for dedicating time to my book in our meetings.

I am thankful for the AMS and the Society for American Music (SAM),
both of which Bill advised me to join at the beginning of my academic
career. Receiving SAM's Eileen Southern Fellowship in 2019 for a project
called "Composing the Black Chicago Renaissance" and the AMS's Noah
Greenberg Award in 2021 for "Renaissance Women: Works by Women
Composers-Pianists of the Black Chicago Renaissance" helped me pursue the archival work needed to dig deeper into the topics at the heart of
this book. I also credit the Newberry Library Short-Term Residential Fellowship for Individual Research (which I received in 2019 for "Florence
Beatrice Price and Theodora Sturkow Ryder: A Comparative Study of Two
Prominent Women Composers in Interwar Chicago") for stimulating my
interest in the cartographic side of this work. Having the opportunity to
then deliver virtual lecture recitals on "The Contrapuntal Lives of Chicago's Race Women" at the 2021 AMS conference and "African American
Composers and the Black Renaissance" (also in 2021) at the Newberry
Library provided me with invaluable opportunities to share and refine my
ideas amid communities of caring listeners and awe-inspiring scholars.

I thank the librarians and archivists of the Newberry Library; Center for
Black Music Research at Columbia College Chicago; Special Collections
at the University of Arkansas, Fayetteville; the Rosenthal Archives of the
Chicago Symphony Center; Woodson Regional Library branch of the Chicago Public Library; and the Amistad Research Centre—all of whom made
my in-person visits highly productive and inspirative. I am particularly
thankful for the generosity shown by Frank Villella, Alison Hinderliter,
Bradford D. Hunt, Keelin Burke, Janet Harper, Laurie Moses, Melanie
Zeck, and Heidi Marshall. I also thank Anthony E. Philpott whose personal archives pertaining to the National Association of Negro Musicians
illuminated the names and images of so many in this book.

Many of my research trips were made possible by the funding I received
from the University of York; the Michael Zilkha Trust at Lincoln College, University of Oxford; and my Anniversary Research Fellow fund at

the University of Southampton. My positions as the Lord Crewe Junior Research Fellow in Music at Lincoln College at Oxford (2020–22) and as an Anniversary Research Fellow at Southampton (2022–present) have brought the much-needed grounding of an academic home as well as the resources and networks of support required to complete a project such as this.

Finally, I am indebted to the support of friends and family. My partner, Gregory Booth, has wholeheartedly embraced what this work entails for me; he is my rock and constant reminder to keep dreaming. I thank my wonderful friend Simon Birch for continuing to be such an important part of my journey, for dedicating his time and talents to engraving Price's *Chicago* suite, and for our discussions around Price's approaches and intentions in this little-known, incomplete work. I also acknowledge Miriam Bhimani's and Marianne Parker's generous hospitality during those early Chicago visits, which helped me feel settled and secure as I embarked on my archival projects. Last but certainly not least, I express deep gratitude for the insights of (and ongoing encouragement from) Regina Harris Baiocchi, Renée C. Baker, and Barbara Wright-Pryor and for the advocacy I received from Sheila Anne Jones. Sheila granted me the stage on which I first delivered the ideas for this book; in the manner of the South Side impresarios that I write about, she bridged a young Black woman's ambition with a world of opportunities.

South Side Impresarios

INTRODUCTION

Finding Their Place in the Sun

A new day has dawned for women; a new deal is here. Action has taken place quickly, and women have come into their own. It is fitting at this time that the Negro woman should take her part in the Century of Progress and prove to the world that she, too, is finding her place in the sun.

—Elizabeth Lindsay Davis, foreword to *Lifting as They Climb*, 1933

The Chicago Symphony Orchestra premiered Florence Beatrice Price's Symphony No. 1 in E minor on June 15, 1933, at the Chicago World's Fair Century of Progress Exposition. With this performance, Price became the first woman of African descent to make her symphonic debut with a major US orchestra. In turn, the all-white, all-male Chicago Symphony became the first institution of its kind and caliber to bring the work of a Black female composer into its repertoire. Held under the auspices of the Chicago Friends of Music, the Negro in Music program (to which Price's premiere belonged) unfolded beneath the proscenium arch that "yawned across the orchestra pit" of the Chicago Symphony and faced the "glittering 'diamond horseshoe'" where patrons from both Black and white society could be found (fig. 1).[1]

The concert formed one of the many musical parts behind the Chicago World's Fair, of which the theme was a linearly construed depiction of Chicago's progress, from 1833 to 1933. Belying this narrative, though, was an amalgamation of intersecting and even conflicting agendas housed in the fair—all of which fed into the Negro in Music. From historic firsts for the Race on stage, through white box holders' loud displays of power and popularity, to quiet acts of Black women's patronage behind the scenes, what happened in the Auditorium Theatre on June 15 was, really, a matter of perspective (fig. 2).

Figure 1. Photograph of Auditorium Theatre, Chicago, May 17, ca. 1890, J. W. Taylor Photography. Library of Congress.

As a white society woman, you would have taken your seat in the diamond horseshoe and maybe even found yourself in one of the four center boxes in the lower tier, especially if you were a dinner-concert guest of Mr. and Mrs. John Alden Carpenter and (like the Carpenters) a senior officer of the Chicago Friends of Music. You would have known that black satin was "fashion's latest decree" and adorned yourself in a black satin gown, offset with a short, turquoise-blue velvet wrap.[2] Your choice in attire would have steered you away from the sartorial faux pas committed by Mrs. Carpenter and Mrs. Charles B. Goodspeed, who both arrived in identical black satin Moroccan capes that were lined with white angel-skin material. Embarrassment aside, as a member of this social set, you may have found their capes "reminiscent of those worn so gracefully and romantically by the Italian soldiers."[3] That such soldiers upheld a fascist regime and enacted colonial violence across North and East Africa, presaging the invasion of Ethiopia, would have done little to dim the romance.

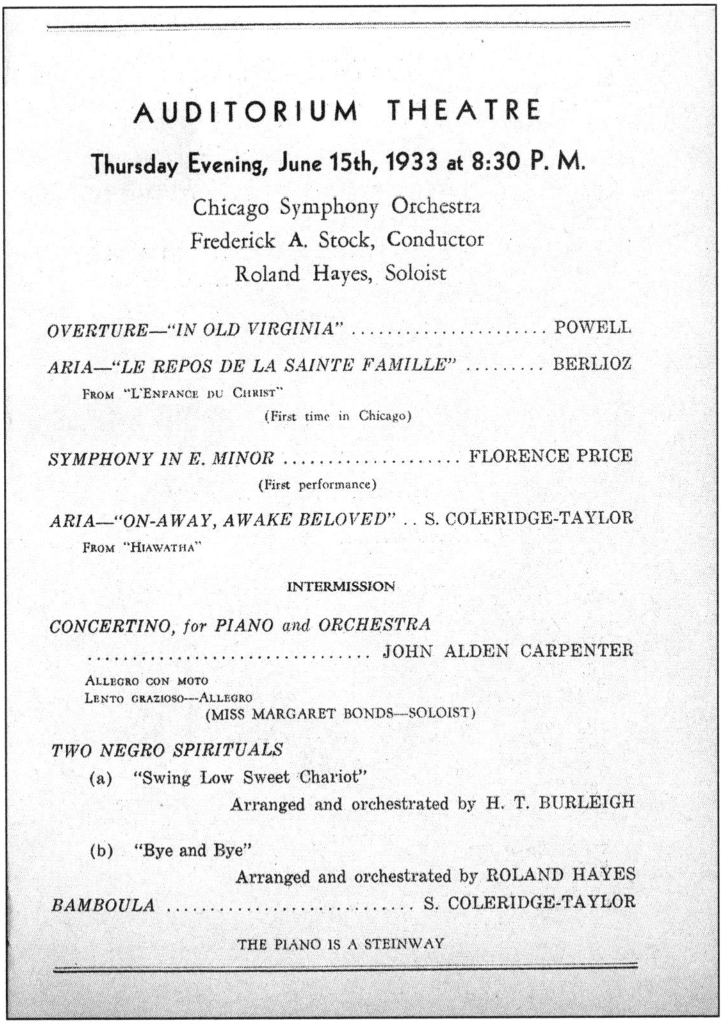

AUDITORIUM THEATRE

Thursday Evening, June 15th, 1933 at 8:30 P. M.

Chicago Symphony Orchestra
Frederick A. Stock, Conductor
Roland Hayes, Soloist

OVERTURE—"IN OLD VIRGINIA" .... POWELL

ARIA—"LE REPOS DE LA SAINTE FAMILLE" .... BERLIOZ
FROM "L'ENFANCE DU CHRIST"
(First time in Chicago)

SYMPHONY IN E. MINOR .... FLORENCE PRICE
(First performance)

ARIA—"ON-AWAY, AWAKE BELOVED" .. S. COLERIDGE-TAYLOR
FROM "HIAWATHA"

INTERMISSION

CONCERTINO, for PIANO and ORCHESTRA
.... JOHN ALDEN CARPENTER
ALLEGRO CON MOTO
LENTO GRAZIOSO—ALLEGRO
(MISS MARGARET BONDS—SOLOIST)

TWO NEGRO SPIRITUALS
(a) "Swing Low Sweet Chariot"
Arranged and orchestrated by H. T. BURLEIGH

(b) "Bye and Bye"
Arranged and orchestrated by ROLAND HAYES

BAMBOULA .... S. COLERIDGE-TAYLOR

THE PIANO IS A STEINWAY

Figure 2. Negro in Music at the Auditorium Theatre, June 15, 1933. From the 1933 Chicago World's Fair Century of Progress Exposition. Courtesy of the Rosenthal Archives of the Chicago Symphony Orchestra Association.

If you were one of Chicago's many Fiskites (i.e., of Fisk University, home of the famed Fisk Jubilee Singers), seated in a box, balcony, or gallery, away from the white glitterati, you would have eagerly awaited your former classmate, the program's headline act, Roland Hayes. If a singer yourself, you likely would have canceled choir rehearsals and postponed your own events for a later date so as to not miss this momentous occasion in which

Hayes would display the breadth of his repertoire, beginning with Berlioz's aria "Le repos de la sainte famille" from the oratorio *L'enfance du Christ*. As the world-renowned tenor closed the first half of the program with Samuel Coleridge-Taylor's aria "On-Away, Awake Beloved" from the composer's enduring *Hiawatha's Wedding Feast*, you would have remembered with pride and warm nostalgia that this number was "a favorite demand during Mr. Hayes' student days" at Fisk University.[4]

By the end of the night, not only would Price become the first African American woman to experience such a high-profile symphonic debut, but Margaret Bonds's performance with the Chicago Symphony as the instrumental soloist for John Alden Carpenter's Concertino for Piano and Orchestra would mark "the first time such an honor had ever been accorded the Race."[5] Bonds's mother, Estella Conway Bonds (a similarly gifted musician, close friend of Price, and steady fixture in Chicago's Black concert scene), would have proudly looked on. From the perspectives of the Bonds matriarch and the *Chicago Defender*'s Nahum Daniel Brascher, you would have felt the historic weight of seeing the Race represented. As Brascher put it, you would have seen in the Auditorium Theatre "the ascending star of our millions in each artist."[6] Predictably, though, such views would be worlds away from the perspective of critic Claudia Cassidy (aka "Acidy Cassidy"). In the typically antagonistic manner of her music journalism, she would, in contrast, frame these historic firsts and their implications for the Race as asides. Cassidy would position Carpenter's Concertino as "[taking] up the white man's burden for the evening." Although she would agree with critics, Black and white, that Bonds had given "a good performance," she would contest that it "would have been more exciting had it not the misfortune to follow on the heels of George Gershwin's miraculous playing" in the American Night program from the evening before. Overshadowing the presence of Bonds, Price, and Hayes were Gershwin and Carpenter, on view in the Carpenter box, "with pleasant smiles covering what must have been page-one ideas about each other's music."[7] *That* was the real story as far as Cassidy was concerned.[8]

Notably absent across the coverage of the Black and white presses, however, was the story of the African American woman who underwrote this historic night: Maude Roberts George. George likely took her "accustomed place" in the diamond horseshoe alongside her husband, Judge Albert Bailey George. After all, they were a prominent couple "in the assemblage of society."[9] Although, given the significance of the occasion unfolding beneath them, this was probably not the time for the *Chicago Defender*'s society columnists to report on Maude Roberts George's gown, wrap, slippers, and jewelry. But where, at the very least, was the story about how

George—president of the Chicago Music Association (CMA), which was a member organization of the Chicago Friends of Music—had sponsored the program at a cost of $250 and, alongside her wider impresarial network of civic-conscious and creatively inclined Race women, helped coordinate the musical content?[10]

As reviews in the white press proliferated for the previous evening's American Night program—reviews that roundly praised Gershwin's jazz-infused orchestral works as "the very essence of Americanism," all the while severing them from the Black origins of their inspiration—some critics made mention of Gershwin's manager, "that good picker" Miss Grace Denton.[11] Glenn Dillard Gunn of the *Chicago Herald & Examiner* wrote that Miss Denton had shrewdly exploited the popularity of jazz and "engaged Mr. Gershwin and his conductor, Mr. Daly, guaranteed their fees and took over the theater and the orchestra from Friends of Music, retaining only their name."[12] Unmentioned in reviews of the Negro in Music program were the details of George's own impresarial work, which were less grounded in popular trends and financial reward (after all, George unlike Denton bore the financial cost for her respective program), and more aligned to the Race woman's calling to lift as she climbed. George and her network seized the opportunity to represent Black womanhood and the Race at large on the world stage. However, their communally driven impetus engendered a communally driven narrative in Black-authored discourse. While the Black press highlighted George's individual role in later, reflective pieces almost a decade on, in the immediate coverage, the moment in question clearly belonged to the collective of Black Chicago.

If the paternalistic overtones of the white press rendered Black participation in the mainstream classical sphere passive, conditional, and anomalous, then the Black press portrayed the participation of its own as active, long overdue, and vicariously felt. Still, the unspoken knowledge of George's role across both realms of coverage leaves us, today, with an incomplete picture of how the Negro in Music came to be. As a result, this impels me to ask, what narratives emerge when we retell progress along the Race woman's timeline and look for the ways in which she, like her white counterparts, took her place in the Century of Progress, rather than waiting for it to be given?

South Side Impresarios moves beyond the gaze of the white glitterati and circle of critics to restore George to her place in the sun. In asking how Race women defined progress, in theory and in practice, the answers neither begin nor end with June 15, 1933. Rather, this date becomes embedded in a much deeper narrative, rife with rhizomatic connections that unfurl through the interwar years and touch on histories even further back, and those more recent. Centered are the perspectives of those who rendered Chicago's South Side geography a key site in early twentieth-century classical music–making—that is, the distinct social set at the vanguard of this activity: Race women. My focus falls on those who were born in the closing decades of the nineteenth century and who made Chicago their home in the early twentieth century, either as the daughters of parents on the move or as independent or (independently minded) wedded women in search of new horizons. It also extends to those born not only in the dawning decades of the twentieth century but also into the ready infrastructure of Chicago's Black concert scene, which had been fashioned by earlier generations of musical South Side residents and visitors.

In their efforts to bridge racial and gender progress with opportunities for creative expression, Race women across these generations nurtured a local (yet widely resonant) Black classical community that entwined with Black civic life. At times, their activity bubbled beneath the surface of mainstream attention, but as we see with the Negro in Music, they also wound their work into the city's white classical music establishments. *South Side Impresarios*, however, is less the story of white validation toward artists of African descent in the American musical landscape and more the story of those who put Black classical Chicago on a cultural map of their own making. Revealed here is the predominantly female-led network that negotiated the restrictive parameters of non- and anti-Black performance spaces and redistributed the balance of power and prestige in the classical realm.

Even though Chicago's Black jazz and blues practitioners outnumbered their classical music counterparts, with the storied trajectories of the former placing the South Side at the heart of some of the most exciting musical developments at this time, in the same geography also existed a Black concert scene whose fruits continue to challenge and transform the global culture of classical music today.[13] Setting George, Price, Estella and Margaret Bonds, and numerous others in the wider cast and context of South Side impresarios, I demonstrate African American women's impact "beyond the blues" (and other popular genres where Black women's contributions are more readily historicized).[14] I foreground the underexamined area of early twentieth-century Black women's classical music performance, production, and patronage in the United States and situate these actors in a Black matriarchal classical counternarrative to Western art music's usual Eurocentric and androcentric whitewash. I challenge their historiographically un- and underdocumented presence and pertinence in the classical music landscape by sounding the unsung voices who set the stage for numerous practitioners of African descent to thrive amid racist and sexist hostilities. In tracing their legacy, I recompose the story of classical music in Chicago, shedding new light on its audiences, supporters, and training grounds, and on the vitality of Race women's cultural organizing and impresarial aptitude.

Positionality, Performance, and Place

South Side Impresarios evinces Eileen M. Hayes's argument that "the history of Western art music would look very different if the literature theorized black feminisms."[15] As Patricia Hill Collins reminds us, "Black women intellectuals have laid a vital analytical foundation for a distinctive standpoint on self, community, and society and, in doing so, created a multifaceted, African-American women's intellectual tradition."[16] What is more, this tradition—one that Collins grounds in the politics of Black feminist thought—extends to every sphere in which historical African American women were collectively active. The realm of classical music is no exception. "Although their contributions are frequently overlooked," writes Teresa L. Reed, "black women have been stakeholders in this artistic tradition at least since the nineteenth century."[17] And in centering historical Black women's agency as concert artists, composers, pedagogues, scholars, and—most pertinently to this book—impresarios, not only does the history of Western art music look different from this vantage point, but as a concert pianist who brings this particular era of music-making to life and puts Black feminisms into performance practice, I find that the history sounds very different too.

Fueling my work is the ongoing dialogue between my research, repertoire, and Black feminism's constant as what Akwugo Emejulu and Francesca Sobande call "a creative and dynamic production of thinking and living otherwise."[18] As a concert pianist, I have performed, recorded, and premiered music by many of the women in this book, such as Price, Margaret Bonds, Nora Douglas Holt, Betty Jackson King, Irene Britton Smith, and Helen Eugenia Hagan.[19] Furthermore, I have performed their music in the same spaces they once inhabited (such as the Chicago Symphony Center and Chicago Cultural Center) and have performed for predominantly Black audiences comprising not only those who knew these women directly but remain, today, members of the clubs and associations that some of Chicago's musical Race women founded around a century ago (such as the CMA, National Association of Negro Musicians, and R. Nathaniel Dett Club of Music and Allied Arts). As a result of engaging in certain spaces as a performer as well as being honored by the presence of so many Black classical music lovers at my concerts, I am drawn to narratives where the scenes and sites of Black women's artistry and intellectuality matter as much as the sounds.

Because my scholarship on collectives and their geographies heavily informs my performances of underrepresented composers (and vice versa), I pursue a line of inquiry that is less about the lives of individuals and the deep musical analysis of their catalog and more about the wider communities and cartographies of Black expressive culture in which they operated. More literature on the former is, of course, necessary and the recent studies of Elektra Voyante, Elizabeth Durrant, and A. Kori Hill, to name a few, signal exciting new developments in this area.[20] Overlapping with their work but departing from a predominant focus on the theoretical analysis of what I might identify as key works, I delve deeper into the sociocultural landscape of interwar Black classical Chicago. I historicize musical Race women's activity, situating it in schools of thought, contextualizing it in wider political currents, and locating it in its specific geography. Even when discussing compositions, such as Price's *Fantasie Nègre* for solo piano or *Chicago* suite for orchestra, what I am interested in are the relationships between musical sound and geographical place, artistic impetus and social influence, the solo callings of the composer and the sisterly responses of her champions. Through this project, a history of Black female sociocultural architects emerges, one that connects interwar Chicago's musical Race women to First Lady Michelle Obama, to the Chicago Symphony's Sheila Anne Jones, and to prolific contemporary composer Regina Harris Baiocchi.

In her memoir *Becoming*, Michelle Obama depicts her early childhood on the South Side and the piano lessons she took as a young girl with her great-aunt Robbie. Obama situates her classical music–making in the realities of Chicago's segregated geography and Black women's enterprise in the face of it all:

> Once a year, Robbie held a fancy recital so that her students could perform for a live audience. To this day, I'm not sure how she managed it, but she somehow got access to a practice hall at Roosevelt University in downtown Chicago, holding her recitals in a grand stone building on Michigan Avenue, right near where the Chicago Symphony Orchestra played. Just thinking about going there made me nervous. Our apartment on Euclid Avenue was about nine miles south of the Chicago Loop, which with its glittering skyscrapers and crowded sidewalks felt otherworldly to me.[21]

Obama depicts her kindergarten-aged self at the pristine grand piano of her downtown concert venue (which was worlds away from the well-worn and much-loved upright that she used at home). Overwhelmed by the change of scene and instrument, the young Michelle desperately searches for middle C. She is, eventually, saved by Robbie, who appears like an angel, and places the young musician's hands in the correct position so that her carefully prepared piece may begin. Through this recollection, Obama reveals how Robbie, much like the women in this book, bridged aspiration and opportunity through her organizing and uplift, and strived to minimize the cultural gulf between the South Side and downtown Chicago. The first lady's Aunt Robbie brings to mind my own impresarial angel, Sheila Anne Jones, whom I first met on April 6, 2017.

That month, I embarked on an archival research trip to Chicago. The Rosenthal Archives of the Chicago Symphony Center were on my itinerary for April 5, where archivist Frank Villella would show me the original booklet for the Negro in Music program and related press clippings. Unplanned, however, were the thirteen hours I spent at Northwestern Memorial Hospital the day before with suspected appendicitis. Fortunately, any serious health concerns were allayed, but I remained exhausted and unwell for the duration of my visit.

Villella had offered me complimentary tickets to the Chicago Symphony Orchestra's Glinka, Dvořák, and Prokofiev program. I was excited to not only witness this world-class orchestra but also to experience aspects of the world to which Price and her network belonged. As I waited in the lobby for my plus-one to arrive, a woman with a kind face and halo of black curls walked toward me. Perhaps she had sensed my feeling out of place and out of sorts. Her name was Sheila Anne Jones. She was the coordinator of the Chicago Symphony's African American Network, a passion project–cum–cultural force that she founded in 2016.[22] Jones's mission was to make the Chicago Symphony Center a more welcoming space for Black audiences. I could not help but notice that the majority of Black employees at the Symphony Center appeared to work in security. There was not a Black artist in sight or in sound on the concert stage that night. The message seemed to be, *we trust you with our lives but not with our music.* As a city that remains highly segregated, these dynamics rang as a vestige of Jim Crow and slavery whereby white individuals and institutions depended heavily on African Americans for their own protections and livelihoods, yet routinely rejected them as intellectual and creative stakeholders in the very spheres in which they labored. Jones's work targeted this chasm, redefining whom this music belonged to, drawing in those that the classical mainstream routinely kept at arm's length, and granting seats for Black patrons, performers, composers, and curious onlookers at a new and inclusive table. Through the African American Network, my cultural horizons would expand to encompass contemporary Black, Chicago-based practitioners, such as Renée C. Baker (the first composer of color to present and conduct two operas at Symphony Center in Chicago, principal violist for over two decades with the Chicago Sinfonietta, artistic consultant for the African American Network, founder of the critically acclaimed Chicago Modern Orchestra Project, and visual artist), Reginald R. Robinson (a ragtime pianist, composer, and 2004 MacArthur Fellow), Norman Malone (a left-handed piano virtuoso and pioneer), and Howard and Darlene Sandifer (directors of the Chicago West Community Music Center, whose mission is "to enhance families and communities through music").[23]

Jones asked what had brought me to Chicago. "Have you heard of Florence Price?" I asked naively. "Of course!" she replied. She broke me out of my shell and a lively conversation ensued. As we exchanged details, another woman walked toward us. From her light caramel cropped hairstyle and regal air, I recognized her instantly: Barbara Wright-Pryor, president of the CMA. A century ago, the CMA's inaugural president, Nora Holt, used to invite Black music students to join her in the first balcony (above where we were standing) and use the ten-minute intermission as an opportunity to "discuss various symphonic works with interested persons."[24] And from the late 1970s to the early '90s, a retired Irene Britton Smith (also a member of the CMA) volunteered her time as a docent for the Chicago Symphony, "help[ing] young students better understand and enjoy the symphony concert experience."[25] I was standing at the transhistorical intersections of Black women's performance, pedagogy, patronage, and philanthropy—intersections that converged even more profoundly in what came next.[26]

On April 12, 2018, Jones and the African American Network hosted my lecture recital, "A Celebration of Women in Music: Composing the Black Chicago Renaissance," which took place in the Richard and Helen Thomas Club (8th floor)—a small, tucked-away space in the Chicago Symphony Center. As I drafted the content, my story developed into a layered narrative that encompassed multiple Black women's voices. Darlene Clark Hine's scholarship had broadened my understanding of the interwar era in question as less a Black derivative of a white and androcentric modernist core and more a sui generis Black Renaissance that was Chicagoan through and through.[27] Furthermore, women were at the heart of its development. I therefore began my presentation with their voices in musical medley.

I opened with the theme and first variation of Irene Britton Smith's *Variations on a Theme by MacDowell* (1947). Its a-minor key allowed me to modulate into the C-major second theme in the first movement of Price's Sonata in E minor (1932). Through a mediant link into the e-minor key of Margaret Bonds's "Troubled Water" (from *Spiritual Suite*, 1967), I dived into the energetic passage that appears toward the end of the B section of this ternary (ABA) form composition—the moment just before the music segues into a recapitulation of the opening. Then, from e minor to the relative key of G major, in which Nora Holt wrote her ebullient *Negro Dance* op. 25, no. 1 (1921), I finished my medley with the closing section of Holt's piece. What followed was the lecture that would go on to form the foundations of this book.

At the end, I gave a full performance of Price's sonata and Bonds's "Troubled Water." Between these works, I addressed my audience, which was largely of African descent and in direct odds with the way I had been socialized to understand classical music as *not for us*:

> I have . . . performed [Price's sonata] a few times now. . . . But the performance that I felt would have the most poignancy is this one here today in the city that Price adopted as her home. Here, countless African American women came together as composers, performers, presidents, promoters, and so much more. Their homes nurtured incredible talents, their newspapers put their pursuits into print for all to see, and their clubs and associations worked tirelessly to break barriers and build platforms for Black artists. Florence Price's achievements certainly catapult her to the forefront of this movement, but this period in Chicago's history is really defined by the community that she was a part of and the *women* at its center.

After my final performance, Jones presented me with a resplendent bouquet and a letter of welcome and recognition from Illinois state comptroller Susana A. Mendoza. Speaking to the audience on the African American Network's import, not to mention echoing the communally driven motives behind musical Race women's work, Jones said,

> Our mission is to knit together and build . . . you might say, a gorgeous quilt of all the talent, of all the love, of all the, you know, passion that exists in the Chicago community in all genres, in all nations. And so, in reality, it is the collective, isn't it? . . . We're living right now [under] hegemony, right? We're fighting for our own selves, and we become sort of separate and individual achievements are overshadowing the collective where our joint talents and gifts really are what matters [*sic*] right now—and the community of music and the community of ideas and the

community of even being able to disagree—right? Conflict is good! As long as conflict isn't mean-spirited, but it's good.... I'm thinking we're on a new footing with the African American Network because of this young ambassador, Samantha, so thank you so much.[28]

But in truth, I was on a new footing because of Jones's and the African American Network's advocacy and affirmation of my work. Many of these composers became a staple in my repertoire. They were not simply linked by gender and race but by the narrative of community and collaboration behind their endeavors. I wanted audiences to not just hear their individual voices but also to get a sense of the wider Black Renaissance era and network in which they operated. That was the impetus behind my program, "Of Folk, Faith, and Fellowship: Exploring Chicago's African-American Composers," performed on April 7, 2019, in the Preston Bradley Hall of the Chicago Cultural Center and hosted by Chicago's Crossing Borders Music. I opened and closed with Price—the sonata and her *Fantasie Nègre* No. 1 in E minor, respectively. (Price dedicated the latter to Bonds, which brought the concert's themes full circle.) Bonds's "Troubled Water" was second in the program, followed by two new works in my repertoire: *Azuretta* by Regina Harris Baiocchi and Toccata by the late Dolores White, both Chicago-born composers.

I had invited Baiocchi and White to attend the concert, and to my delight, they accepted. To me, their life stories and compositional catalogs exemplified the fruits of historical Black women's classical music–making in Chicago. White even revealed, in her address to the audience, that "my mother wanted me to study with Margaret Bonds, but that didn't happen." Even with this missed opportunity, White's anecdote showed the possibilities for connectivity in Black classical Chicago.

Baiocchi's speech broadened the purview, elaborating on themes of restoration, uplift, empowerment, and agency—themes that recur through this book. She said,

> When you go through music school, you study the canon; and a lot of times, for Black women composers, the canon is incomplete because most of the composers that we study are men, or European—most of whom are dead. And so, you rarely get to see the full canon. So what you heard today is a part of the canon that is omitted. It is music written by people who look like Samantha, who look like me, who look like Dolores.

Baiocchi then added in good humor, "And you know, there are Black men composers too—fathom that!" Her closing then brought into focus the significance—and interdependence—of music-making, community-building, intergenerational exchange, and geography:

When you hear Samantha play this music, you hear the spiritual energy of all of the women who she represented here today—all of whom came to this place, which used to be the main public library in Chicago. And all of those women that she played here today studied here, performed here; and it's so great to feel their energy and to feel that another generation has taken that on.[29]

Later that year, Baiocchi invited me to perform *Azuretta* at the National Association of Negro Musicians Centennial Convention. (Over time, the name of this organization has gone from being pronounced with the individual letters of N-A-N-M to *Nam*, the latter of which I use in this book.) With this performance, it dawned on me that I would be playing for the very NANM that Nora Holt cofounded out of her South Side home in 1919 and that Maude Roberts George presided over from 1933 to 1935. I performed at the Legacy Concert, the convention's closing event, which took place on July 19, 2019, at the Studebaker Theater (a familiar performance venue for Chicago's musical Race women and men).[30]

The evening ended with a stirring rendition of the Black National Anthem, "Lift Every Voice and Sing." In this moment, I was reminded that as a Black British woman of Nigerian (Urhobo) and Jamaican ancestries, my points of connection to this history only ran so far. I ultimately felt that this was not my song to sing. Instead, I stood in the transatlantic kinship that my fellow countryman Samuel Coleridge-Taylor must have felt more than a century ago as he, too, found his life's work in dialogue with the politics and artistry of Black world-making across the pond.[31]

I listened, bearing witness to the contemporary display of a historical "Black formalism," which, to cite Imani Perry, describes "the performance and substance" within Black associational and institutional life—that is, the "ritual practices with embedded norms, codes of conduct, and routine, dignified ways of doing and being" and, even more significantly, the "practices that were primarily internal to the black community, rather than those based upon a white gaze or an aspiration for white acceptance."[32] I listened, thankful for the ways in which performance—and particularly Jones's impresarial organizing and Baiocchi's present invitation—had drawn me deeper into this geography and the lives of Chicago's musical Race women.

A Note on Language

Finding the appropriate language to depict the journeys of African-descended practitioners through classical and civic spheres under Jim Crow not only entails an expansive approach to terminology but also necessitates a deep interrogation of the connotations and cultural baggage certain words carry. To begin with, I articulate a capacious definition of the impresario beyond its gendered (i.e., male), geographic (i.e., European), and exploitative connotations to depict the ways in which Black women fostered and patronized local, national, and even international music-making out of their South Side base. Like Ralph P. Locke and Cyrilla Barr, I reread "music patronage" as a "female-centered cultural process" and, in the vein of Doris Evans McGinty, foreground the "music-loving" Race women who "focused their energies on creating institutional structures that responded to the distinct needs . . . of the African-American community."[33] As McGinty illustrates, "The sphere of the black woman in music, as much as in any other field, was large—larger than historians have suggested. From the second half of the nineteenth century to the end of World War II, black women were active professionally not only as performers and teachers, doing work 'that men thought they ought to do,' but also as artist managers and journalists, taking on positions traditionally occupied by men."[34] The "woman's sphere" was, to quote Race woman Fannie Barrier Williams, "just as large as she can make it."[35] And across what Locke and Barr call the "three p's" of "performance, pedagogy, and patronage"—and I will add a fourth: philanthropy—Race women, "whether working as individuals or as groups, on a local or national scale . . . sought and found ways to expand the 'sphere' not only of black women, but also that of blacks generally in music, until it was indeed 'just as large as [they could] make it."[36] As a result, I take an expansive view of the Black female South Side impresario that (a) complicates the connotations of impresarial work and (b) asserts her centrality alongside other kinds of practitioners (e.g., composers, performers, and educators) in narratives of Black women's music-making.

I use "Black" and "African American" interchangeably when identifying practitioners of African descent who were born in the United States and who traced their history through several generations of African-descended people there. I do not make assumptions that every practitioner in this context was a not-so-distant descendent of the enslaved, particularly as this book deals with an elite social class where, for some (such as Florence Price), an immediate lineage of freemen and -women, often with the socially preferred lighter skin complexion, made their upward mobility possible. Out of this arose a class stratum that was as much tied to colorism as it was to financial standing. As a result, "African American" depicts more than skin color; it holds specific cultural heritages and histories, embroiled in the makings of the New World. Therefore, in identifying practitioners as African American, I am voicing their relationships to geographically and culturally specific historical moments.

"Black" bears greater transnational meaning, allowing me to draw connections and distinctions between the African-descended practitioners whom I identify as African American and African-descended practitioners whose lived experiences and lineages extended beyond a US-centric purview. For example, I describe the Canadian-born composer Robert Nathaniel Dett as Black but not as African American. Although he was the son of formerly enslaved ancestors on his maternal side who traveled the Underground Railroad to seek freedom across the border, Dett's formative years were nurtured in a geography and racial climate distinct from that of his maternal ancestors and US-born father. To identify Dett only as African American would therefore be to overlook the role of Canada-bound migration in his narrative and ultimately render "African American" a blanket term devoid of transnational nuances. So, even though I use "Black" and "African American" synonymously at times, I also use them to articulate differences in addition to commonalities.

I am also mindful to not project the politics of the one-drop rule beyond its national borders as "the stubbornness and resiliency of the white/black racial binary in the United States," though pervasive, were not globally ubiquitous. As Allyson Hobbs explains, "The persistence of the 'one-drop rule'; the lack of official categories for multiracial people; the social and economic distance between blacks and whites and the illegality of interracial marriage until the *Loving v. Virginia* case in 1967, and the history of the United States as a white majority/black minority nation until increased immigration led to massive demographic changes in the mid-twentieth century" make up what she calls the "distinctiveness of the bipolar American racial regime."[37] The project of race-making in the United States derived from an idiosyncratic impetus. Although many of its ideas were exported, that is not to say that everything proved translatable.

The mixed-race, mixed-heritage English composer Samuel Coleridge-Taylor, born in 1875, is a case in point. Coleridge-Taylor's father was from Sierra Leone and a descendent of the freemen and -women who had once been enslaved in the Americas. His mother was a white Englishwoman, as was his wife. But these interracial unions would have been illegal in the United States at that time. Ultimately, race functioned differently for Coleridge-Taylor, and even though he felt a great affinity to Black composers on the other side of the pond (which was reciprocated), key to acknowledging his international import is the realization that he was born and raised in a society where the one-drop rule was not baked into its foundations and Jim Crow segregation was not legally enshrined. Because of this, Coleridge-Taylor could develop his craft as a musician, composer, and conductor without enduring the Jim Crowisms many of his African American counterparts faced; he could navigate his US visits with greater ease as a somewhat exotic, curious, and less threatening outsider to the white majority. Following his work closely, revered pedagogue and Race woman paragon Emma Azalia Hackley expressed, "I am convinced that if Coleridge-Taylor had lived in America, much of his music would never have been published."[38] No doubt, a number of his African American colleagues felt the same. In sum, I use language around the race, ethnicity, history, and heritage of African-descended people in a way that reflects the themes and variations among our lives.

I do not use "Negro" of my own accord to describe any African-descended person here; instead, I use it in relation to historically and culturally exact contexts, such as when describing the Negro in Music or discussing the National Association of Negro Musicians. I limit its use to quoted contexts and references to historical documents (e.g., census tracts); historical practitioners' attributions of this word to certain works (e.g., Nora Holt's *Rhapsody on Negro Themes* for orchestra, Florence Price's *Fantasie Nègre*, William Dawson's *Negro Folk Symphony*, etc.); and in relation to the Negro Spiritual—a historical genre that reclaims, restores, and uplifts Black authorship in folkloric expression.[39] I sometimes use "Spiritual" as a shorthand for Negro Spiritual, capitalizing the "s" to distinguish from contexts in which I am discussing spirituality and spiritual affairs more broadly. But at no point do I use "African American Spiritual" as an alternative, as this undermines the historical and cultural reality of the genre.[40]

Following this, I also embrace the archaic adjective of "Race" to index not only race but also sociality and periodization. Brittney C. Cooper frames Race women as "public intellectuals" who nurtured "models of racial leadership and public lecturing" through the second half of the nineteenth century and, in doing so, "created the paradigm for contemporary modes of Black public intellectual engagement" in the decades that followed. Cooper adds, however, that "to talk about early Black women public intellectuals is to talk about a class of elite women with unprecedented educational access."[41] It is to talk about women who did not perform manual labor in white people's homes and institutions (unlike the majority of Black women at that time) and who did not engage in sex work and other "underground economies" to support themselves and their families.[42] It is to talk about women who were, for the most part, light complected, or racially ambiguous, or even white passing, and to recognize that some of these women reproduced racist discourse in work that was intended to racially uplift.

Former soprano and past South Side resident Emma Azalia Hackley is one such example. On the one hand, she wrote, "Colored women have a genius for leadership," but on the other hand, she also reinforced racial stereotypes, positing that the "spots" of African Americans—that is, the features over which they were most ridiculed—could be eradicated with "the inward Sculptor-Thought." "Thought," she argued, could build noses that lacked the "hump" of the more "warlike" Europeans and Indigenous Americans; it could diminish "thick lips" and tighten "leaking mouths." According to Hackley, one could simply think their way out of their "spots" until "the whole expression of the face be changed."[43] Jarringly, Hackley's vision for improving the conditions of the Race perpetuated derogatory caricatures of Blackness as well as other racial stereotypes.

Such contradiction, however, is exactly why I engage the historical "Race" prefix. It reflects the heterogeneity of late nineteenth- and early twentieth-century Black America—of its intraracial class and caste constructs and of middle- to upper-class African American women's complex, even paradoxical, strivings toward racial and gender equality.

Nested Herstories

For all the contradictions and tensions that inhabited their work, *South Side Impresarios* is an ode to the known and unknown Black female practitioners who instilled others with the power and passion to make classical music theirs and to the institutions and associations that these Race women founded and fostered in their collective yet multiplex image. This book recognizes the exceptional feats that they accomplished under the violence of Jim Crow and in a genre that was gendered male and oppressively racialized white—from Holt becoming the first African American person to attain a master of music degree in 1918, to Price and Bonds disrupting decades of racial and gendered exclusion with their 1933 Chicago Symphony debuts, to Maude Roberts George and countless others upholding systems of support and sponsorship through and beyond the interwar period.

I locate the exceptional and extraordinary in what Race women were able to achieve under a white and patriarchal hegemony, rather than locating the exceptional and extraordinary in their drive and ambition. In doing so, I challenge the trope of the exceptional Black woman, whose activity is rendered anomalous for those of her race and gender; detached from the reality of African American women's long-standing intellectual traditions, her contributions, as a result, are imagined as coming from the periphery of society, at best, or a historical and cultural vacuum, at worst.

Tammy L. Kernodle elaborates, "The exceptional woman becomes the rationale for the exclusion of other women and lends support to a narrative of invisibility" that prevails to the detriment of other women in music. "Most important to this discussion," Kernodle continues, "is how this narrative of the exceptional woman has defined common understandings of how these women *worked* and created art."[44] How nuanced understandings and interpretations of brilliant historical Black women become when their intellectual and creative endeavors are framed not as the exception but as the rule—that is, as both necessary factors and inevitable products of the dynamic cultural environments to which they belonged.

In his biography of Madam C. J. Walker, Tyrone McKinley Freeman shows how her moniker as the "first self-made millionaire" generates a "distancing" that "removes her from the broader normative giving structures among black women and African Americans more generally, from which she emerged and alongside whom she gave."[45] A similar view can be held for historical Black women pioneers in the classical realm whose firsts isolate them from broader structures of Black (and female-led) concert life when, in fact, those firsts tend to represent the tip of the iceberg. Price is a prime example.

Almost a decade after the 2009 revelation of numerous manuscripts, previously thought to be lost, Price was then subjected to a rediscovery narrative in mainstream media discourse that musicologists such as A. Kori Hill and Douglas W. Shadle immediately challenged due to the ways in which it divorced Price from the wider and highly active scene of early twentieth-century Black concert life.[46] In Hill's words, "The 'rediscovered' Black composer is a tired, damaging trope." Much like the trope of the exceptional Black woman, "it reflects an active process, where certain histories and cultural memories are not considered 'relevant' to the mainstream until they prove useful." Hill reminds us that "Black musicians kept the name of Florence Price on their lips, in their minds, and under their fingers," and most pertinently, "she was not forgotten."[47] As with Madam C. J. Walker and the Race woman trailblazers in this book, community becomes the focus in a narrative that situates their accomplishments in the many layers of the wholly ordinary, collaborative, and unsung female labor enacted beneath the surface.

Race women's communally driven work resulted in manifold contributions to musical life in Chicago and beyond. With histories of classical music–making extending through the nineteenth century, interwar Black women's activity as composers, performers, pedagogues, patrons, and more was not without precedent. And yet, literature claiming to chart the history of Western art music tends to view their contributions as either marginal or entirely absent. Countering this, I write in response to the evidence of musical Race women's enterprising lives; I use a collectivist storytelling to draw in as many voices as possible, thematizing Black women's collective ambition, strategy, and patronage in the classical realm.

This is not a group biography, particularly as the underrecorded state of this history makes it difficult to present equally detailed life stories for all of the women discussed here. For some of the Race women in this book, theirs is a fleeting presence, briefly captured in meeting minutes, letters, scrapbooks, program notes, Black presses, unbroadcasted performances, and further ephemeral sources. My solution, then, is to present interwar Chicago's musical Race women in a composition of *nested herstories*—my neologized term for the stories within stories that capture the interiority, intricacies, and interconnectedness of their lives. This approach allows me to navigate the silences and "historiographical silencing" I find along the way but still capture something of the multilayered fashion in which Race women worked together.[48]

At times, my focus is on Florence Price, for whom a more detailed portrait can be drawn; this is not the case for a number of women in this book, including Maude Roberts George, Nora Holt, and Estella Bonds. Yet, in centering Price, I do not misidentify her story as the beginning but as one of many beginnings that fed into the tapestry of Chicago's Black classical scene. I situate the extraordinary nature of Price's accomplishments in the ordinariness of her Chicago milieu in which a Black classical community, largely steered by highly educated middle- to upper-class African American women, flourished.

But if Price is only one part of the bigger picture, then how might we conceive of the many more underdocumented and unnamed agents within this realm? How might we override the historiographical silences that surround them to sound the possibilities of their full existences? How might we trace the impressions of their lives, the shape of their discourse, the flow of their activity, and the cartography of their ambition? Put simply, "how do you write the history of a silence?" Well, as Mia Bay resolves, "silences are rarely complete."[49] Just as the Race woman's maxim "Lifting as We Climb" signified a mode of uplift where the individual held the dreams of the collective within her own social, cultural, political, and economic aspiration and ascent, so too do these nested herstories hold the mixture of Race women's firsthand and vicariously felt connections, illuminating and amplifying the hidden layers and hushed evidence of their lives and longings.

Overview

South Side Impresarios unfolds in two parts. The first—comprising chapter 1, "When and Where They Entered," chapter 2, "She Proclaimed a Chicago Renaissance," and chapter 3, "The Black Classical Metropolis"—is an expository sociocultural and geographical mapping of Race women's organizing, leadership, and impresarial enterprise. To find one's place in the sun was to explore new intellectual and creative geographies of the self in antiphonal dialogue with the geography of one's surroundings. As a result, these chapters examine what it meant to be a Race woman in interwar Chicago, how concert music fed into a new era of cultural reinvigoration, and why the South Side itself was such an important site in Black classical world-making. Part 1 is less concerned with a specific chronology (unlike the second part of the book) and revels more in a sprawling temporal and spatial survey of Race women's activity. If the first three chapters provide a lay of the land, with the interludial "Race Woman's Guide to the Realm of Music" and *"Fantasie Nègre"* further illustrating musical Black women's world-making amid Chicago's racially segregated geography, then the second part, told across chapter 4, "Movements of a Symphonist," and chapter 5, "Seizing the World Stage," shows how the themes of the book's first half converged in Price's particular journey as well as in Race women's strategic navigations of the 1933 Chicago World's Fair and its aftermath.

Guiding each chapter is Alisha Lola Jones's argument that "to truly listen to black women's music making is to deeply pursue true sisterhood in the United States."[50] This is what it means to theorize Black feminisms in critiques of Western art music, to recall Eileen M. Hayes's assertion.[51] Pursuing the sisterhood of the South Side impresarios entails listening to how and why the intersections of concert culture, race, gender, class, and geography complicate what we think we know about Black women's collective, transformative impact in the classical world. What I hear amid these nested herstories confronts misconceptions that Black women's gendered and racialized selves render them unnatural protagonists in Western art music's historiography. At the same time, it challenges the notion that the erudite spaces in which their work unfolded (e.g., the conservatory, the clubhouse, the concert hall, etc.) situate their activity on the periphery of Black feminist discourse.

Regarding the latter, a particular passage in Daphne Brooks's *Liner Notes for the Revolution* comes to mind—one that reads rather dismissively of the musical Race woman's position in a Black feminist project. Referring to a handful of Race women who also feature here, Brooks writes, "While the influential legacies of institution-building women such as Ella Sheppard,

Maud Cuney Hare, E. Azalia Hackley, Nora Holt, and Eileen Southern are undeniable, it's worth noting that these were sisters who were situated in academic and classical settings. They were holding it down in the most elegant and elite corners of intellectual life, and God bless them." Brooks then proceeds without them. This particular framing of their contributions (not to mention the briefness with which they are addressed) bares the potential to leave the stories of various Black female classical music–makers and patrons untold, for at stake is the issue of who most authentically represents "the intellectual life of Black feminist sound."[52] Additionally, it overlooks the not-so-elegant backdrops in the cartography of Race women's activity, such as race riots, lynchings, and other forms of terror, which notably come to light in chapters 2 and 4 of this book.

To diminish the role of classical music in Black women's feminist world-making is, as *South Side Impresarios* argues, to perpetuate Western art music's propagandized perception as an inherently white and male genre. It is to reduce African Americans' participation and contributions within this creative site to acts of seeking whiteness, whether in the form of approval, adjacency, acceptance, or assimilation. This book shows, however, that Black concert culture was not intrinsically beholden to a white audience. Although the specifically classical music purview and seemingly minimal presence of popular music in Race women's (and men's) creative pursuits is noticeable, to read their general inclination toward the concert hall over the juke joint as a striving toward whiteness undermines their agency and autonomy. It overstates whiteness as the criterion by which they lived their lives. As Ora Williams writes, "There is this effort to discredit what is considered elitist or 'bourgeois'" when it comes to the recognition of Black artists, an attitude that doubly affects Black women who are all too readily dismissed on the basis of their gender as well. Yet Williams argues that, with regard to any gender, "for a Black person, becoming a trained musician—one who could read and write music—has always been an antiestablishment act."[53] In other words, historical Black classical practitioners—whether operating as performers, composers, pedagogues, or patrons—were as revolutionary as any other.

South Side Impresarios demonstrates how, far from existing in the abstract, classical music was embedded in the community-building mission of Black associational and institutional life in Chicago. Civic work inspired music-making and vice versa. The symphonic, operatic, choral, and salon-esque sound worlds of musical Race women and men were not outliers to Black world-making but integral factors that absorbed and reflected the political spirit of the interwar era. Chicago's Black concert scene largely operated as a "shadow culture" to that of white Chicago, to borrow Naomi André's terminology. It was a shadow culture not in the sense that "the thing illuminated is the true art, and that which is obscured is of lesser importance" but in the sense that the thing illuminated zealously reproduced the hierarchies and hegemonies born out of chattel slavery and Jim Crow, while that which was obscured challenged these oppressive systems.[54] Race women's work, in particular, entailed chronicling, celebrating, promoting, and patronizing Black concert culture as they pursued the interconnected goals of social justice, racial progress, and gender equality.

Put together, then, the chapters and interludes that follow on from here tell the story of how Race women transformed classical music in Chicago (and beyond) from their South Side base. Revealed are the visions and realities that they engendered for themselves and an array of multigenerational Black classical practitioners. Although the historical portrait of their lives remains incomplete, the cartography of their enterprise emerges with brilliant clarity through the extant traces of their multifarious musical journeys, which take us from intimate salons to civic settings, kitchen tables to concert halls, and Spirituals to symphonies. These are the nested herstories of those who came into their own, proved to the world that they too were finding their place in the sun, and simultaneously shone their own light on Black talent, lifting as they climbed and basking in the color and gender barriers they collectively broke.

PART I

Genealogies and Geographies

Colored women have a genius for leadership.
—Emma Azalia Hackley

1

When and Where
They Entered

Before the Negro in Music, there were the Annual All Colored Composers Concerts of 1914 and 1915, which took place in Chicago's Orchestra Hall under impresario and tenor W. Henry Hackney. The *Chicago Defender*—one of the most widely read Black periodicals in the United States—described Hackney as "one of Chicago's energetic young men" whose commitment to "the elevation of musical uplift" exhibited the interconnected discourse of racial progress and creative expression.[1] Hackney was, in essence, a Race man. In fact, the inaugural concert of June 3, 1914, was heavy in Race man representation. Chicago's own Anita Patti Brown was the only female soloist in a program that spotlighted Hackney, Robert Nathaniel Dett, and Ernest R. Amos as the remaining soloists and Dett, Harry T. Burleigh, Samuel Coleridge-Taylor, J. Rosamond Johnson, and Will Marion Cook as composers. Comparatively, the second annual concert of April 23, 1915, shone greater light on the city's Race women musicians, for alongside Hackney, Cook (as conductor), and the two-decade-old Chicago Umbrian Glee Club (founded and managed by Anita Patti Brown's husband, Arthur A. Brown), were Helen Hagan, Maude Roberts George, and Nora Holt—all three of whom resided in Chicago at this time (figs. 3–5). Hagan's, George's, and Holt's presence foreshadowed the gender shift from "energetic young men" to enterprising Race women who would take increasing charge of Chicago's Black classical scene after World War I.

Hagan's portion of the concert included three works from Coleridge-Taylor's *24 Negro Melodies*, Op. 59. As a composer herself, however, she also used the concert to promote her best-known work: the Piano Concerto in C minor. Hagan completed the one-movement piece in 1912 as a student at the Yale School of Music. Soon after, she performed it as the soloist with the music school's student orchestra and New Haven Symphony Orchestra. But in the absence of being able to access such large ensembles on a regular basis, Hagan frequently toured with her two-piano arrangement of the concerto, and at the 1915 All Colored Composers Concert, she delivered her hefty sonata-form, single-movement opus with T. Theodore Taylor playing her handwritten orchestral reduction on the second piano. (These handwritten two-piano arrangements are all that remain of the score today.[2])

Reviews praised Hagan's pianistic skill and compositional prowess. Similar appreciation followed for the other Race women on the program. George's performance of art songs by Coleridge-Taylor, J. Rosamond Johnson, and Holt were enthusiastically received. Evidencing a pattern of collaboration, Holt (who was between marriages and went by Nora Lena James at this time) performed the accompaniment to her art song "Who Knows," while George (as the pre-wed Maude J. Roberts) rendered the lyrics, which derived from the poetry of Paul Laurence Dunbar. "Thou art the soul of a summer's day, / Thou art the breath of the rose; / But the summer is fled and the rose is dead; / Where are they gone, who knows, who knows?" George sang to a now-lost melody as the composition eludes Holt's surviving catalog. But for those in Orchestral Hall who had the honor of hearing it, they met Holt's art song "with genuine applause," suggesting something of its captivating construction and delivery.[3]

The Annual All Colored Composers Concerts seemed to be gaining momentum, with Race women pushing the programs to new, creative heights. As a preview for the next event, set to take place that winter, the 1915 program revealed that it would further showcase Chicago's Race women composers through the works of "Mrs. David Manson." Recognized as the wife of a "devoted husband" and "well-known townsman and clubman" but also as a dynamic classical practitioner in her own right, Elnora Manson of 5816 Michigan Avenue left Black and white music lovers from Chicago and beyond in awe.[4] Various testimonials—from Anne Shaw Faulkner (organizer and director of the Program Study Class belonging to what was then called Theodore Thomas's Chicago Symphony Orchestra) to Harry T. Burleigh—showed the high esteem in which so many (across the color line) held her.[5]

Burleigh, in particular, praised Manson's use of the lecture-recital format in her practice, acknowledging it as "one of the most advanced and educational forms of knowledge . . . entertaining as well as instructive." In this area of her work, Manson likely absorbed the influence of Emma Azalia Hackley, who lived in Chicago around this time (and founded her Normal Vocal Institute there in 1912). Hackley's similarly arranged lecture recitals were known and respected in Black Chicago society and classical communities across the United States. And just as Nora Holt observed of Hackley, it seemed that through her public work, Manson, too, "was dedicated to cultural progress which touched not only music as a high point, but was closely linked to religion, morals and manners of young people as an inspiration towards a more useful and representative place in the social and civic life of the country."[6] That Manson's interests extended from pedagogy and public engagement to musical analysis and composition demonstrates not only the significant scope of her ambition in classical music but an eager audience for her many talents.

In addition to such glowing testimonials, Manson had ready champions in pianist Hazel Harrison and soprano Maude Roberts George, whose programming of the composer's works alongside some of the European giants of eighteenth- and nineteenth-century classical music suggests that Manson might have also possessed an impressively technical and grandiloquent compositional style and would not have been out of place in such musical company.[7] Unfortunately, the 1915 winter program on which Manson was due to appear is presently absent from the public record, as is her full catalog of compositions. Although brimming with great promise and possibility for the continued showcase of Black classical talent—and particularly Race women composers and performers—for reasons still unknown, the Annual All Colored Composers Concerts did not survive beyond their third year. In fact, scant documentation of the third plants doubt as to whether the third concert even transpired at all. Nevertheless, their short run affirms that Black Chicago had both the appetite and aptitude to nurture its own concert scene. Furthermore, George and Holt would decisively take up the mantle of enriching this scene and sustaining its infrastructure. Together, they would build on the educative and community-grounded work of Manson, Hackley, and Hackney, whose civic and musical impact was strongly felt in the years preceding World War I. In the aftermath of the Annual All Colored Composers Concerts and out of the rubble of war, George and Holt would reenter the scene as South Side impresarios.

This chapter situates George's and Holt's sonic and civic expressions of self, sisterhood, and sociality in the endeavors of earlier generations of enterprising Race women who similarly sought solutions and self-help within their own (wo)man-made associations and institutions. I foreground the influence of nineteenth-century Black churchwomen and clubwomen, Talented Tenth ideologies, and the forging of sisterly bonds outside of religious settings. I also examine how World War I, the Great Migration, and industrialization generated demographic shifts in what came to be known as the Black Belt, and how these factors, in turn, spurred

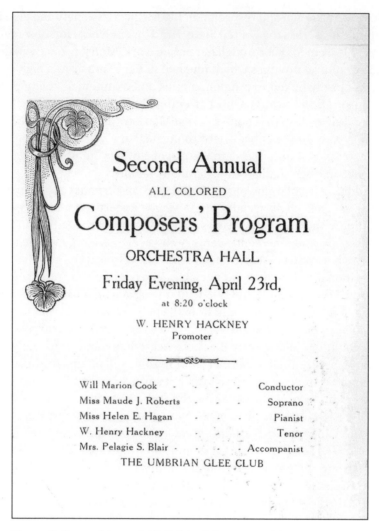

Figure 3. Second Annual All Colored Composers' Program at Orchestra Hall, April 23, 1915. First page. Courtesy of the Rosenthal Archives of the Chicago Symphony Orchestra Association.

Race women to refashion their public lives in service of their city and their people. Then, bringing several other South Side impresarios into conversation with George and Holt, I argue that their impresarial activities sat squarely in the zeitgeist of Race women's intellectual work.

The words of the nineteenth-century foremother of intellectual Race womanhood, Anna Julia Cooper, serve as a motif throughout this chapter: "Only the BLACK WOMAN can say 'when and where I enter, in

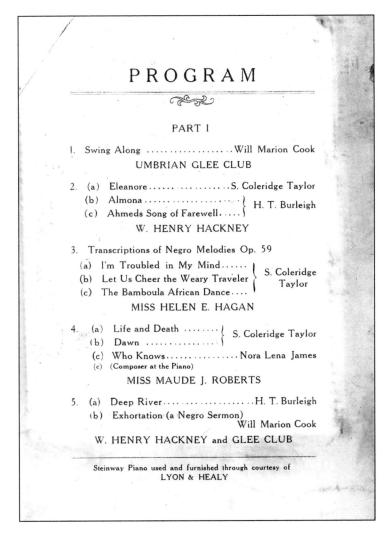

Figure 4. Second Annual All Colored Composers' Program at
Orchestra Hall, April 23, 1915. Second page. Courtesy of the Rosenthal Archives of the Chicago Symphony Orchestra Association.

the quiet, undisputed dignity of my womanhood, without violence and
without suing or special patronage, then and there the whole *Negro race
enters with me.*"[8] The musical resonance of Cooper's "when and where
I enter" proclamation rings in the activity of George, Holt, and others.
Here, I build on the work of Alisha Lola Jones and Tammy L. Kernodle
who similarly identify the overt musicality of Cooper's "when and where
I enter" quotation. Jones, for example, interprets the motif as "a womanist

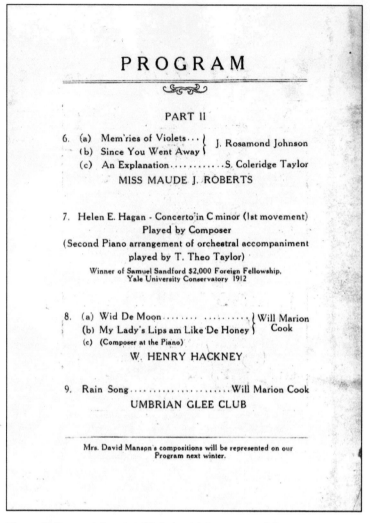

Figure 5. Second Annual All Colored Composers' Program at Orchestra Hall, April 23, 1915. Third page. Courtesy of the Rosenthal Archives of the Chicago Symphony Orchestra Association.

ethnomusicological framework of utterance (say/sing), time (when), space (where) and access (enter)." Recontextualizing Cooper's words in the collaborations of Price and Marian Anderson, Jones reveals their Black sonic sisterhood as a "womanist musical rebuttal of unsisterly white women's movements." Jones unearths an "envoiced" Black women's discourse in Price and Anderson's championing of each other that countered "the concert domains that predominantly comprised white male decision makers, an exclusionist industry bolstered by unsisterly white women patrons that stemmed from a joint colonial past of chattel slavery plantation hierarchy."[9] Like Jones, I use Cooper's words to frame musical Race women's navigations of racial uplift and gendered empowerment within similar spheres.

Another variation on the Cooper motif comes from Kernodle in an essay that considers how the musical daughters of the interwar Race woman generation—such as Undine Smith Moore, Margaret Bonds, and Julia Perry—displayed "eclectic representations of sonic Blackness and narratives of protest and resistance [that] redefined the cultural context of the Black concert milieu in the decade immediately following World War II." She writes that Cooper's words, more than a century on, "can be seen to exemplify the way in which a generation of Black women composers brought the ancestral history and experiences that framed Black life in America to the multivalent contexts of the Cold War–era concert music sphere. It was work that linked them to ritualistic practices that rippled throughout the African diaspora."[10] Although Kernodle's purview extends beyond the largely interwar focus of this book, her scholarship is a necessary reminder of how Black women's sonic expressions and negotiations of the world around them resounded through the second half of the twentieth century and echoed the pertinent words and polyphonic work of their Race women foremothers.

The Contrapuntal Lives of Chicago's Race Women

As 1918 unwittingly ushered in the beginning of the interbellum period, flanked by the Great World Wars, so too did it herald a time of in-betweenness and transition for two of Black Chicago's most influential society women: George and Holt (born in 1892 and 1885, respectively). Coinciding with the year that Arkansan native Florence Price visited her aunt and uncle-in-law (the well-connected South Side residents Olive Gulliver and John Gray Lucas) and made herself known to the musical circles that would eventually become her own, 1918 was a similarly pivotal and portentous year for George and Holt. It was the year that George, on marrying Judge Albert B. George and giving birth to their only child (also named Albert), repurposed her public life away from the spotlight as a "brilliant dramatic soprano" and into the various organizing roles that rendered her a "great factor in the social and civic life" of Chicago.[11] Marriage and motherhood did not limit George's activity in the public sphere; they merely redirected her focus, aligning her with a network of Black women whose leadership was as galvanizing as their musicality (fig. 6). In that same year, Holt became the United States' first "artist of the Race

Figure 6. Judge Albert Bailey George and Maude Roberts
George, National Association of Negro Musicians past president.
Photograph. Theodore Charles Stone Collection of the Center for
Black Music Research at Columbia College Chicago.

[to hold] the degree of M.M. [master of music]."[12] She immediately put to
use her scholarly accolades and social connections, alongside the salon
culture she fostered in her South Side abode, to amass the classical musicians of Black Chicago and beyond. Together, George and Holt drove a
new epoch of brilliant artistry, bold intellectuality, and Black renaissance.

In their capacity as musical trailblazers and community leaders, George, Holt, and their wider cohort of civic-minded, community-conscious Black women worked in intergenerational dialogue with Cooper's "when and where I enter" motif. For this reason, I explore their lives not through their individual biographical strands but through paths that intersect with the deeper history of Race women's work in Chicago. Race women were Black women intellectuals and creatives committed to the entwined tasks of racial uplift and gender equality in their United States. They were, as Tyrone McKinley Freeman illustrates, "agents who staked claims for their own humanity and citizenship in the face of seemingly impossible odds."[13] Collectively and singly, they transformed interwar Chicago's civic and social spheres. Their labor took form and focus in both the communal and intimate geographies in which they moved—from church halls and home salons to school auditoriums and the Wabash Avenue YMCA. Their lives were grounded in their locale and music regularly filled the sites of their activity, acting as a binding agent in the formation of the South Side's associational and institutional structures. Collectively inspired, civically grounded, and often musically inclined, Race women's leadership was inseparable from community-building. Furthermore, their work proved a vital counterpoint to the projected negative images of Black womanhood.

Counterpoint as a general term may depict the ways in which Race women organized both singular and collective livelihoods that rejected discrimination. It captures the dynamics of working *against, in spite of,* and *in contrast to* and finds context in a number of hostile territories, ranging from the general Jim Crowism of the white patriarchy, through the racism of white women's suffrage movements, to the sexism embedded in Race men's Black enfranchisement efforts. This type of counterpoint manifested the counterpublics, counterinstitutions, and countercultures in which Race women worked through the dissonance. The National Association of Negro Musicians (NANM), cofounded by Holt and later presided over by George, is one such example: NANM's inaugural convention unfolded amid the Chicago race riots of 1919, epitomizing the ever-present jarring juxtaposition of white destruction and Black world-making in Race women's endeavors.

This understanding of counterpoint builds on Patricia Hill Collins's assessment that "U.S. Black women participate in a *dialectical* relationship linking African-American women's oppression and activism." Here, Collins's discussion of dialectical relationships refers to two opposite or opposing parties, comprising Black women as an oppressed group versus those that perpetuate their oppression; Collins further elaborates, situating her observations as a distinguishing feature of Black feminist thought,

"As long as Black women's subordination within intersecting oppressions of race, class, gender, sexuality, and nation persist, Black feminism as an activist response to that oppression will remain needed." In addition to responding, however, Collins notes, "In a similar fashion, the overarching purpose of U.S. Black feminist thought is also to resist oppression, both its practices and the ideas that justify it."[14] And this is where a second understanding of counterpoint enters the frame.

Counterpoint as a musical term, conversely, moves away from solely centering violence and trauma in Race women's narratives. It introduces a framework through which to articulate what happened in their social spheres; to consider how Race women's individual voices (encompassing their viewpoints, experiences, actions, and aspirations) sounded simultaneously, diversely, comprehensibly, and coherently; and to grasp the more interior dynamics of working *toward, because of,* and *in concert with*. These dynamics find context in the communities, clubs, associations, and networks that Race women formed around their duties and in the models of Black female leadership, fellowship, and followership that they enacted in those spheres. Along its musical definition, counterpoint becomes a means to interpret what Collins describes as the "distinctively Black and women-centered worldviews" that arose from "Black women's participation in crafting a constantly changing African-American culture."[15] It becomes a means to discern their power vis-à-vis a history of powerlessness and to hear their voices vis-à-vis a history of voicelessness.[16]

On the one hand, Race women worked against the backdrop of their highly segregated living, politically disenfranchised position, and double jeopardized state as women who were not white and African Americans who were not men.[17] On the other hand, their activity took clear definition within their associational and institutional structures, unfolding in concert with a forward-looking sense of social responsibility and indebtedness to the rich Race woman legacies that they had inherited. As with musical counterpoint—technically understood as an "underlying system of rules for the organization of simultaneous voices"—certain rules undoubtedly guided Race women's activity.[18] After all, Race women were, for the most part, society women: middle- to upper-class statuses, marriages to prominent Black male professionals, college-level education, and classical music training were, if not explicitly a must, indisputably thematic. This was a part of the Black formalism that shaped their lives, from their earliest years to adulthood. That is not to say that all Race women voluntarily bound themselves to social strictures. Divorce and scandal were not uncommon in this social set; furthermore, Race women defiantly risked the aspersions of the Black press and society gossip when choosing to leave their marriages in favor of leading more independent and liberated lives, as we see with Holt later in this chapter.[19] However, identifying some of the societal norms and gendered expectations that Race women lived among helps draw together a greater sense of why and how these women functioned and flourished as they did. These "rules," especially when understood as an *underlying* rather than *overriding* system, serve as a starting point for tracing Race women's contrapuntal lives, for deciphering their moments of independence, interconnectedness, and exchange, for hearing and historicizing their covert and overt musicality, and for observing "when and where" they entered.

Sacred Foundations, Secular Flowerings

An important precursor to early twentieth-century Race women's work lay at the intersection of the Black church and the turn-of-the-century woman's club movement. Whereas women's clubs (across the color line) spurred seismic shifts in women's civic participation and political influence, the Black church provided a platform for congregants (male and female) to contest racial discrimination and develop strategies for racial self-help. Early twentieth-century Race women built on the foundations laid by an earlier generation of college-educated Black churchwomen. Born around the mid-nineteenth century, this generation, as Evelyn Brooks Higginbotham explains, "disseminated middle-class morals and values among the masses and, at the same time, generated financial support for the black church and its educational and numerous social service programs."[20] Their influence is apparent in the development of the educational lyceum series that took place at Grace Presbyterian Church, located on the South Side and the church of choice for much of Black Chicago society.

In 1918, a year after assuming the role of the first ever music critic for the pioneering Black periodical the *Chicago Defender*, Holt wrote a column titled "Influence of Lyceums." In the nature of her style—part commentary, part critique, part chronicle—she revealed how Miss Bertha Lee Moseley (a future society columnist for the *Defender* and future wife of the newspaper's city editor, Cary B. Lewis) "gave the community Grace Lyceum."[21] Mrs. Cary B. Lewis, as she became known after her marriage in 1917, was a Race woman through and through. Daughter of one of Chicago's leading Black attorneys (Beauregard F. Moseley), graduate of Englewood High School (where she took a course in journalism), alumna of the University of Chicago, and first president of the Theta Omega Chapter of the Alpha Kappa Alpha sorority, Lewis put her educational background and social advantages to civic use.[22] In Holt's words,

Some three years ago the attendance of the primary Sunday school of which Mrs. Lewis was the superintendent, was unsatisfactory, and the pastor and she formulated a plan to increase and interest the pupils.

The Lyceum was introduced with programs and refreshments after. This proved so successful the social side was eliminated because of increased attendance. It finally attained its present size, which means they turn away eager devotees every other Sunday. Nearly every church in the city now has its lyceum and the good this form of culture is doing is shown by the various types who attend.

The elder members of the church whose existence and the existence of their families depend on the number of days they labor, are refreshed and enlightened by their attendance. The thinking young folk discover an outlet for their artistic propensities. The masses are benefited by association and [contact] with those who have spent years of study in the field of learning.

Civilization needs this growth, and the Lyceum stands superlatively as its sponsor.[23]

Forged in piety, virtue, and uplift, Lewis's Grace Lyceums—of which George was the program chair for the youth division from 1917 to 1930, and for which Holt regularly appeared as a guest speaker and performer—furthered gendered models of racial uplift. Racial uplift itself stood for the elevation of the Race from the lowest rungs of society—in which countless African Americans were politically disenfranchised, socially brutalized, and economically starved—to the level of citizenship enjoyed by the white majority. Church events such as these directly planted Race women's impresarial work in a nonspecialist but music-loving public. Such lyceums became a way to embed music patronage in the wider project of racial uplift as well as in the rituals of Black religious life. They demonstrated the interconnectivity of it all; there, the rigid binaries of the dominant culture (i.e., public versus private, professional versus amateur, white instruction versus Black recipience) were steadily and openly undone.

The earlier generation of nineteenth-century Race women, on which the work of Lewis, George, Holt, and others built, immediately recognized, however, that there was a second imbalance to address, with attendant complexities. Racial uplift was one part of the picture, but the empowerment of their sex was another. Black women contended with an African American patriarchy not unlike the white one; and yet, for the sake of racial unity, they also felt obliged to express solidarity with programs for action dominated by and benefiting men. As Melina Abdullah shows, social movements through the nineteenth century generally focused on race or gender, implicitly requiring Black women to choose—"as if the categories are somehow mutually exclusive," Abdullah notes.[24] Although Black women tended to align with race over gender, they remained as attentive to the sexism embedded in the microdynamics of their community as they were to the racism entrenched in the macrodynamics of their nation. This attentiveness patterned the details of their work.

Evelyn Brooks Higginbotham calls these women the "Female Talented Tenth" in a subtle critique of W. E. B. Du Bois's influential ideology.[25] Du Bois argued in his 1903 essay titled "The Talented Tenth" that racial self-help would arise from the leadership of an elite group: the top 10 percent of the African American population, who were set apart by their education, wealth, and privilege. He posited that "education and work were the levers to uplift a people," proposed "developing the Best of this race that they may guide the Mass away from the contamination and death of the Worst in their own and other races," and offered the solution of the Talented Tenth, emphasizing—not once but twice—"the Negro race, like all other races, is going to be saved by its exceptional men."[26] The phrase "exceptional men" rang as a refrain (he repeated it three times) and his failure to cite Black women intellectuals rings just as loud in light of Race women's progress at the time.[27] The face of turn-of-the-century racial uplift was clearly male; and the Female Talented Tenth, as exceptional as they were, invariably fell short.

Nor did gender bias stop after Du Bois. The new century bore witness to a "New Negro," as Booker T. Washington put it.[28] In the words of Black Renaissance thinker Alain Locke, "The younger generation is vibrant with a new psychology, the new spirit is awake in the masses, and under the very eyes of the professional observers is transforming what has been a perennial problem in the progressive phases of Negro life."[29] But for Locke and his allies, the New Negro emanated from a Black patriarchy.

Therefore, to attend to the activities and accomplishments of intellectual Race women is to supply a much-needed corrective to what Brittney C. Cooper identifies as the "Great Race Man Narrative," in which contemporaneous commentaries and secondary sources have largely formed canons of Black intellectuality around male actors, marginalizing the contributions of Black women.[30] To attend to Race women's thoughts as well as their deeds is to recognize that Black churchwomen supplied their own influential ideology. Their work was not without its controversies, however, for Race women often perpetuated middle-class mores of respectability and propriety, which at times placed them in antagonistic or condescending relationships with the Black working classes. As Jane Rhodes explains, while the "politics of respectability were a response to the racist representations of and routine attacks on black female sexuality, character, and intellect," which enabled "black women to enact subversive strategies of resistance[, they] were also a means for negotiating and managing the class, education, and regional distinctions within African American communities, with an old settler establishment seeking to control what were deemed unruly and uncouth newcomers."[31] Yet it remains that within this complexity, the gendered dimension of Race women's church-oriented activism was a precursor to the increasingly intersectional dimensions of Black feminist thought that arose toward the end of the twentieth century.[32] With the Black church as their base of operations, this earlier generation manifested a "gender consciousness" that, although not without its flaws, took seriously Black women's capacities to change race relations—and their United States—for the better.[33]

Chicago resident and Race woman Fannie Barrier Williams predated Du Bois—a necessary point to make in light of the Great Race Man framework that informs African American intellectual historiographies. Williams was a founding member of the National Association of Colored Women's Clubs (NACW) and the first African American woman to be accepted into the all-white Chicago Woman's Club—a reminder that white women by and large did not regard Black women and other women of color as their equals. In an essay titled "The Club Movement among Colored Women of America," published before Du Bois's much-touted essay on the Talented Tenth, she credited the Black church and women's organizing work within it as essential to the "club work" that she believed was the next phase of Race women's activism:

> The training which first enabled colored women to organize and successfully carry on club work was originally obtained in church work. These churches have been and still are the great preparatory schools in which the primary lessons of social order, mutual trustfulness and united effort are taught. The churches have been sustained, enlarged and beautified principally through the organized efforts of their women members. The meaning of unity for the common good, the development of social sympathies grew into woman's consciousness through the privileges of church work.

The church work they enacted challenged their muted position as, to quote Williams, "the least known, and most ill-favored class of women in this country."[34] Their activities established them as vocal, action-driven, "civically knowable persons," as Brittney C. Cooper puts it.[35] The Black church remained a cornerstone in the lives of interwar Chicago's musical Race women, binding spiritual affairs with civic concerns and music-making with institution-building. Throughout the twentieth century, the scope of Race women's activity and ambition grew into more secular spaces from the religious core of the Black church.

Associated with club life were Black sororities, which furthered a sense of public duty and sisterly connection. Williams described these sororities, which "demand[ed] a higher order of intelligence than is required for church" due to their college and university affiliations, as yet "another school of preparation for colored women." She concluded that "care for the sick, provisions for the decent burial of the indigent dead, the care for orphans and the enlarging sense of sisterhood all contributed to the development of the very conditions that qualify women for the more inclusive work of those social reforms that are the aim of women's clubs."[36] The lettered backgrounds of sorority members were a key piece in the issue of greater institutional access for African Americans, and in the necessary negotiations of a largely anti-Black national (and international) mainstream, as the work of Chicago's Theta Omega Chapter of the Alpha Kappa Alpha sorority shows.[37]

Under founding member Bertha Moseley Lewis and her colleagues Clara Vesta Caldwell, Ida Taylor Jones, Eva Overton Lewis, Geraldyn Hodges Major, and Helen Kathleen Perry, Alpha Kappa Alpha's eighth graduate chapter was established. The date was November 5, 1922, and the address, 5200 South Wabash Avenue. Theta Omega members operated (and continue to operate) on the South Side, though their influence was (and still is) far reaching. From the outset, they raised scholarship funds for students they deemed most promising and sponsored a number of artists, helping to launch some of the most illustrious careers imaginable. One beneficiary was Margaret Bonds, who was a member and received scholarships in 1929 and 1930.[38] Another was Hazel Harrison who was incidentally one of Bertha Moseley Lewis's bridesmaids at her Christmas wedding in 1917.[39]

Theta Omega sponsored Harrison's studies in Europe, where she performed regularly with the Berlin Philharmonic (becoming the first Black female solo instrumentalist to do so) and trained with Ferruccio Busoni.[40] On April 11, 1924, under Theta Omega's management, Harrison gave a recital at the Grace Presbyterian Church; she dazzled her audience with a program of Busoni, Beethoven, Chopin, Alkan, Brahms, Liszt, Weber, and newer works by the South Side's own Elnora Manson.[41] Theta Omega also sponsored the Chicago debut of famed contralto and future honorary Alpha Kappa Alpha member Marian Anderson. On November 18, 1929, under Theta Omega's auspices, Anderson appeared at the Chicago Symphony's Orchestra Hall (fig. 7), achieving, according to the Black press, "one of the most brilliant personal and professional triumphs of her career."[42] Thematic along Anderson's path, as well as the musical paths of so many African American women, were the support and patronage

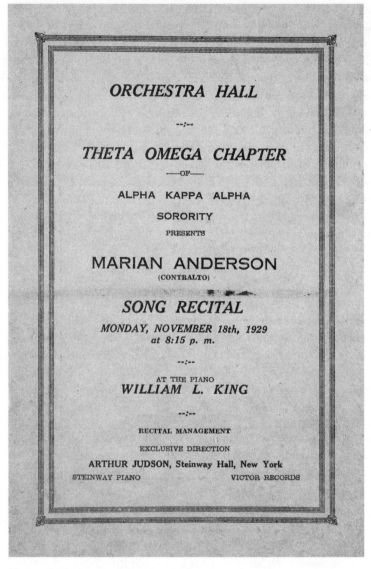

Figure 7. Marian Anderson at Orchestra Hall, concert program November 18, 1929. Manuscript Collection 200, Box 178, Folder 8528, Item 1, Marian Anderson Papers, University of Pennsylvania.

of Black sisterly networks. Expansive in their purview, Race women's sororities (not to mention their church communities) "helped to make colored women acquainted with the general social condition of the Race and the possibilities of social improvement," as Fannie Barrier Williams observed—possibilities that ranged from ballot boxes to orchestra halls.[43]

Williams's words, in conjunction with those of her colleague Anna Julia Cooper, gave new weight to turn-of-the-century Black women's import in the progress of the Race. Lauding Race women as "the first Black women intellectuals," Brittney C. Cooper explains that "as they entered into public racial leadership roles beyond the church in the decades after Reconstruction, they explicitly fashioned for themselves a public duty to serve their people through diligent and careful intellectual work and attention to 'proving the intellectual character' of the race."[44] Race women of the interwar period, bolstered by those who came before, drew on a repertoire of strategies to not only resist erasure from New Negro discourse but also to achieve significant gains for the movement. By the end of World War I, Race women had consolidated their efforts in various local and national networks. They imprinted the detail and design of their work in archives comprising meeting minutes, newspaper profiles, concert programs, self-published volumes, and more. Across these, the rich polyphony of their efforts resounds most brilliantly.

Enter a Prototypical Black Feminist World-Making

What was it about the social and urban composition of Chicago that conduced Race women to lay claim to the city's civic landscape and, with each generation, add new texture to the operations of quotidian life? For one, Chicago was highly cosmopolitan and highly segregated in ways that directly affected how its growing African American populace lived. Migration across different demographics around the turn of the century significantly shaped the city's multiethnic and multiracial makeup. Chicago's booming commerce and industry sectors made it an attractive destination for African American, Mexican, and Anglo-American populations from the southern and southwestern states. Driven by similar factors, continental European immigration—from countries encompassing Czechoslovakia, Germany, Greece, Hungary, Ireland, Italy, Lithuania, the Netherlands, Poland, Romania, Russia, Scandinavia, and Yugoslavia—grew steadily through this time as did the number of Chinese emigrants. Whereas the impetus for moving to Chicago was shared among diverse peoples, Chicago itself was not equally shared. "Race dominated the geographical and social landscapes of Chicago, just as in other industrialized cities," writes

Huping Ling.[45] And this dominance shaped Race women's self-fashioning and world-making amid the deep divisions and disparities of these complex terrains in and around the Black Belt (figs. 8 and 9).

"A city within a city—a narrow tongue of land, seven miles in length and one-half miles in width" was how St. Clair Drake and Horace R. Cayton described it in their 1945 sociological study, *The Black Metropolis*.[46] Its geography bore the tension of progress and prejudice, ever growing due to increasing industrialization and the new arrivals of the Great Migration yet locked into place by Chicago's racially and economically stratified makeup. With the Loop and its commercial high-rises to the north, white working-class neighborhoods to the west, and more affluent Anglo-American and Jewish populations to the east begirding this "narrow tongue of land," the Black Belt gradually extended southward.[47] It appeared on contemporary census tracts as a featureless black block, wedged into the city's segregated composition. But behind the disembodied monolith that stood for the majority of Chicago's Black population, and beneath the surface, were "patterns of life and thought, attitudes and customs" (as Drake and Cayton described) that resisted the restrictive psychology of the Black Belt and embraced the unfettered promise of the Black Metropolis.[48]

Chicago entered the twentieth century as one of the nation's most industrialized and cosmopolitan cities. The resulting prospects for personal economic advancement—amplified in the discourse of prominent Black male community leaders who framed the midwestern city as a veritable promised land—spurred a Chicago-bound Black exodus. Robert Sengstacke Abbott leveraged his position as founder and editor of the *Chicago Defender* to galvanize the "Northern Drive" of the Great Migration.[49] Founded in 1905, the *Chicago Defender* sought to reflect all facets of African American life, from politics and activism to education and the arts. By the 1920s, it had become one of the leading and most far-reaching publications of the wider African American community, maintaining a steady circulation of over 150,000 through the decade.[50] As a result of its influence and ambit, the *Defender* took on a strong didactic, culture-making mantle, printing guides cloaked in uplift and respectability for the city's largely lower-class and lesser-educated newcomers, with instructions such as

> Don't sit out on the front steps in bare feet and undershirt.
> Don't forget to bathe.
> Don't play off the job.
> Don't stand on corners and insult women who pass.
> Don't send your children to school half fed and half dressed.
> Don't forget that you are a citizen and as such are expected to be an
>   active force for decency and welfare.[51]

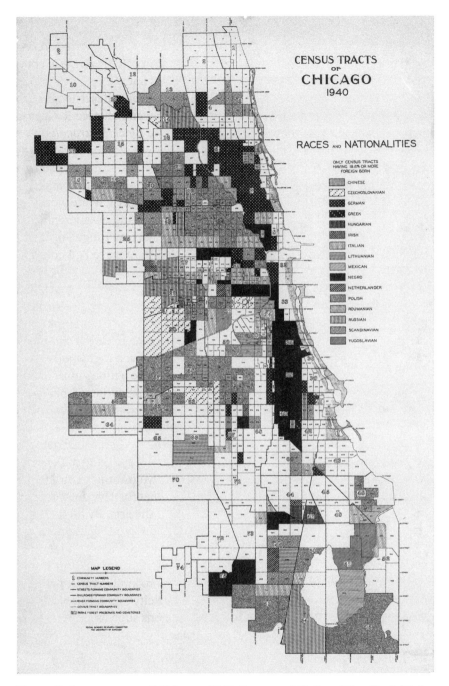

Figure 8. Census tracts of Chicago, 1940. Races and Nationalities (Social Science Research Committee, University of Chicago, 1940). The University of Chicago Digital Preservation Collection and University of Chicago Map Collection, http://pi.lib.uchicago.edu/1001/cat/bib/1586198. Used with permission from the University of Chicago Library.

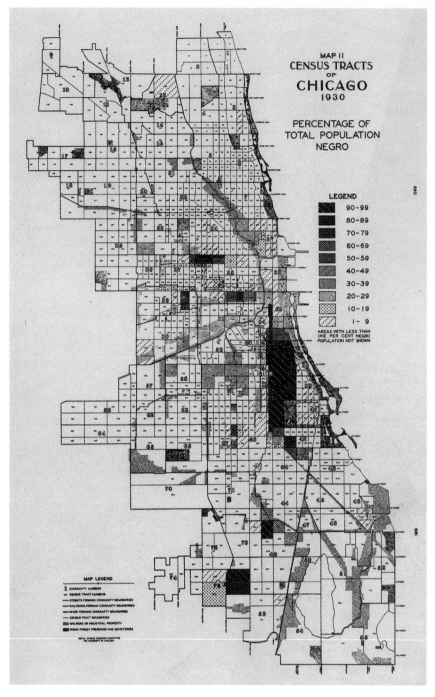

Figure 9. Census tracts of Chicago, 1930. Percentage of total population Negro (Social Science Research Committee, University of Chicago, 1930). The University of Chicago Digital Preservation Collection and University of Chicago Map Collection, http://pi.lib.uchicago.edu/1001/cat/bib/1583690. Used with permission from the University of Chicago Library.

The *Defender* not only helped draw Black southerners to Chicago, but it also played a crucial role in preparing them for the city that awaited. Yet the World War I period in the chronology of the Great Migration housed contradicting truths, as Rima Lunin Schultz and Adele Hast depict: on the one hand, it was a time "of expanded opportunities for African Americans," and on the other, it was "an era of increased tensions and racial violence against Blacks in both the South and in the industrial cities of the North."[52] With World War I creating a dearth of white male labor in the urban north and west, ready to be filled by Black male southerners, sociologists Drake and Cayton observed that following the war,

> for four years the tug of war between northern industry and southern planters, northern Negro leaders and southern leaders continued. The migrants kept streaming up the Mississippi Valley, riding the real trains of the Illinois Central over the same route their forefathers had traveled on the Underground Railroad. When the tide slackened in 1920, Chicago had over a hundred thousand Negroes among her population—an increase of 148 per cent in ten years.
>
> Most Negroes visualized the migration as a step toward the economic emancipation of a people who had been tied to the southern soil and confined to common labor and personal service in the North. The *Chicago Defender* expressed this philosophy in an editorial shortly before the United States entered the war. Declaring that "it is an ill wind that blows none good," Editor Abbott saw the European war not only as "bloody, tragic and deplorable" but also as "opportunity." Coldly realistic, he developed his apologia for encouraging the migration.[53]

World War I generated major shifts in the racial geography of Jim Crow America. Working-class Black men seized on opportunities for economic advancement away from the tyranny of the South. Additionally, southerners of the Black professional class felt the tightening grip of a Jim Crowism that did not care for their education, wealth, or class. They too joined the exodus. Unvoiced in Drake and Cayton's analysis and Abbott's apologia, however, were the journeys and arrivals of Black women migrants. "The very economic diversity—whether real or imagined—that had attracted black women to the urban Midwest," writes Darlene Clark Hine, "also held the promise of freedom to fashion socially useful and independent lives beyond family boundaries."[54] For Black women of all classes, their migrations not only brought opportunities for them to live more liberated lives beyond the color line but to reshape their womanhoods beyond restrictive gendered parameters. In her book *South Side Girls: Growing Up in the Great Migration*, Marcia Chatelain brings another historiographically overlooked dimension to the fore: the ways in which Chicago, and particularly the South Side, similarly posed to Black girls and teenaged women a new landscape of possibility. The Great Migration granted Black girls and women further potential to prosper—materially, politically, and volitionally—in their girlhoods and womanhoods. Although the fight for racial equality and gender progress continued in the North against the backdrop of international and domestic warfare, Black women's and girls' new geographies helped revitalize the ways in which they asserted their place in the world.

Unfortunately, the romance of the migrants' South Side destination soon dissipated. Restrictive housing covenants forcefully redirected Black arrivals (irrespective of their varied class distinctions and financial circumstances) into the tight passageway that stretched southward from the city's center. White flight and redlining maintained the Black Belt's clasp on the city's Black population. Illusions were shattered on arrival as the realities of poverty, squalor, overcrowding, un- and underemployment, riotous violence, white terrorism, and more set in. But for those generations who had lived through these unromantic truths—truths that affirmed, to evoke Saidiya Hartman, that "north and south were just directions on a map, not placeholders that ensured freedom or safety from the police and the white mob"—disillusion had always given way to resolution; and the new influx followed suit, tasked once again with making a way out of no way.[55]

Since the nineteenth century, Race women worked to supply and serve their communities the proverbial manna. And as Chicago's ongoing urbanization through the turn of the century generated a variety of social, cultural, political, and economic challenges for its Black inhabitants, Race women continued to respond to the needs and wants of their locale. The spate of inequalities and injustices that plagued Black lives formed salient impetuses for Race women's organizing and led to what Wanda A. Hendricks identifies as "an unprecedented proliferation of black female clubs" in Chicago and across the state of Illinois.[56] These clubs set the stage for the Black woman to command space and knowability vis-à-vis a national climate in which, Anna Julia Cooper poignantly assessed, "she is confronted by both a woman question and race problem and is as yet an unknown or an unacknowledged factor in both."[57] Caught in the realities that "the average man of our race is less frequently ready to admit the actual need among the sturdier forces of the world for woman's help or influence"[58] (as Cooper voiced) and that the "unsisterly"[59] nature of white women's movements stemmed from their refusal to see Black women's gendered experiences reflected in their own, Race women were therefore compelled to tackle the "woman question," "race problem," and other sociocultural interfaces with intellectual, creative, and ever civically centered fervor.[60] The Black woman's club movement therefore became their conduit for change.

As we have seen, Black churchwomen's work through the latter half of the nineteenth century generated conceptual frameworks that were then transformed more broadly to the secular club movement of the late nineteenth and early twentieth centuries. The latter, in turn, gave rise to the NACW (founded in 1896) and the Illinois Federation of Colored Women's Clubs (IFCWC, founded in 1899), both of which deepened Race women's commitment to public life. The NACW unified and consolidated clubwomen's efforts, bringing organizations at the state and local levels under a single banner.[61] "Thus, for the first time," notes Hazel V. Carby, "Afro-American women became nationally organized to confront the various modes of their oppression."[62] The primary goals of the IFCWC were, as Hendricks explains, "linking the state's women to the NACW, elevating the image of black womanhood, providing social and economic services to blacks throughout the state, and contributing to the welfare of African American women."[63] The NACW's and IFCWC's mottoes—"Lifting as We Climb" and "Loyalty to Women and Justice to Children," respectively— evidenced the congruence of their missions.[64] But from such unifying principles derived, as Anne Meis Knupfer describes, "multiple ideologies, discourses, motifs, and images of womanhood, motherhood, and home life," diversely voiced through the kaleidoscopic range that constituted Black clubwomen's civic activity.[65]

In Chicago, Black women's clubs proliferated through the interwar period. Within its largely middle- to upper-class brackets, members were suffragists, anti-lynching crusaders, matrons, patrons, middle-class mobilizers, and philanthropic aristocrats of color known as the elite Black 400. They were Republicans, Democrats, radicals, and accommodationists. Some were elitist Old Settlers disturbed by the influx of uneducated Black men, women, and children, and even wary of lettered newcomers who might change the order of things.[66] Others were southern arrivals, intraregional incomers, and migrants whose journeys diverged from obvious patterns of Black movement. Gender, race, class, partisanism, and geography shaped Race women's trajectories and emergent narratives in the midwestern city they called home. As Chicago's Race women of the interwar period sought to engender greater possibilities within the stifling parameters of the Black Belt (and the Jim Crowism that continued beyond), they fashioned expansive womanhoods on the legacies of those who came before them. Like their predecessors, they lived and sounded their lives in agitation of racism's and sexism's stifling social, cultural, political, and economic forms.

A Sisterhood in Collage

From 1929 to 1932, the *Chicago Defender* serialized a feature called "A Scrap Book for Women in Public Life." Its coverage portrayed a wide range of accomplished Black women, from the itinerant Merze Tate, whose profile documented the $1,000 foreign fellowship award from the Alpha Kappa Alpha sorority that funded her studies at the University of Oxford, to local heroine Mrs. Grace Wilson, Chicago's sole "Race policewoman on the force."[67] Also featured were the public and highly musical lives of Chicago's Antoinette Cone Tompkins, Gertrude Smith Jackson, Nannie Mae Glasco Williams, Maude Roberts George, Clara E. Hutchison, and Irene Howard Harrison. As the interwar years rolled on, these interconnected figures further defined this era as a time of Race woman–engineered social change and cultural reinvigoration.

Tompkins, Jackson, Williams, George, Hutchison, and Harrison exemplify the ways in which Black women's individual aspirations sounded in tandem with a multigenerational chorus of Race women's collective concerns and ambitions. Through the 1930s, these women worked alongside one another in the contexts of NANM and the CMA, which were the most prominent Black classical music societies at this time in the United States and Chicago, respectively. However, their points of connection, interaction, and overlap neither began nor ended with NANM and the CMA. Collaging the fragments of their activity from the *Chicago Defender*'s "Scrap Book" series, the following demonstrates the contrapuntal nature of their multiplex public lives, as well as their enduring impact on the civic and cultural geography of the South Side.

An unmarried Tompkins (then Miss Crump) arrived in Chicago around 1912 by way of Nashville, Tennessee. She had been a student at Fisk University and a member of the Fisk Jubilee Singers under the direction of John W. Work and alongside Henrietta and James A. Myers. Upon graduating, she received an invitation from Celia Parker Woolley (a white woman who gained recognition for her social reform work on the South Side) to become chair of the Sunday afternoon meetings of the Frederick Douglass Center of which Woolley was president. Located on 3032 South Wabash Avenue, the Frederick Douglass Center was a settlement house, which served to assist the most disadvantaged communities in matters of shelter, education, employment, health care, and more.[68] It ran with the following objectives:

> To promote a just and amicable relation between white and colored people.

To remove the disabilities from which the latter suffer in their civic, political and industrial life.

To encourage equal opportunity, irrespective of race, color, or other arbitrary distinctions.

To establish a center of friendly helpfulness and influences, in which to gather needful information, and for mutual co-operation to the ends of right living and higher citizenship.[69]

The Frederick Douglass Center was a rare instance of interracial cooperation and service in Chicago's white-owned settlements, as most refused to enlist Black expertise or serve Black communities. Tompkins readily accepted Woolley's invitation, which in turn prepared her for her next position as the head resident of the Wendell Phillips Settlement. Like her previous place of employment, the Wendell Phillips Settlement was particularly attentive to the education of young Black girls and boys, to the protection and preservation of their youthfulness, and therefore to "Justice for Children" in reiteration of the IFCWC's motto.[70] As head resident, Tompkins reportedly "conducted and managed this work which developed into the most outstanding of its kind anywhere."

Tompkins continued her musical pursuits alongside her formal employment. To begin with, she remained a dedicated Fiskite, joining the Chicago Fisk Club. She also trained and managed the Illinois Male Quartet, comprising Lemyon Amoureux, Arthur Walker, John Burdette, and John Tompkins. In her work with the quartet, she secured long-term broadcasting opportunities for them on Chicago radio stations such as WBBM, WCFL, and WLS and negotiated other opportunities with stations elsewhere too. Additionally, she organized performance engagements for the quartet in some of the most prominent churches in Chicago and across Illinois; this no doubt included her own Progressive Baptist Church, which boasted a membership of approximately eight thousand. In fact, as the director of her church's choir, which was one of the largest choirs in the city, Tompkins not only built a repertoire of Negro Spirituals and canonic European choral literature, but she also coordinated performance opportunities for the choir that extended beyond their usual church work, and under her direction, the choir fast became "one of the most sought-after church groups in the city." Intersecting with this activity was her two-year tenure with the CMA in a role that entailed coordinating the venues and contents of performances and educational series.

Tompkins's musical life also encompassed the private music studio that she and her husband (possibly John Tompkins from the male quartet) ran for voice and piano. Among her more prolific pupils was Gertrude Smith Jackson.[71] Jackson was born in Chicago and, like Price, Holt, and a number of other musically inclined Race women, first learned music from her mother. Jackson's mother, however, passed away when she was a young girl, which of course brought an end to the formative Race girlhood experience born out of a specific mother-daughter dynamic where music—especially piano lessons in the classical vein—served as a conduit for familial bonding and race-gender-class socialization. After all, classical music study could open the doors to salon culture, to greater participation in church life (e.g., as an accompanist or choir director), a career in music teaching, and wider participation in Black association- and institution-building—all of which made the genteel Race woman. For a time, however, Jackson's progress came to a halt. Upon her mother's death, Jackson subsequently became responsible for her younger siblings and "many adversities, disappointments, and financial trouble" followed. But afterward, Jackson eventually resumed her calling, finding in Tompkins both a maternal and musical role model.[72]

Jackson spent several years under Tompkins's instruction learning piano, pipe organ, and the art of accompanying, "which greatly helped [Jackson] toward her life's work." With further training from music teachers in the Loop who believed more in Jackson's ability than the dictates of the color line, Jackson became an accomplished piano and pipe organ recitalist. She gave concerts "consisting of all Race composers," centering racial uplift in her repertoire. Following in Tompkins's footsteps, she trained and managed vocal groups, such as the Girls Conference Quartet, the Fleur de Lis Choral Club, and the Melody Four Quartet. Jackson also spent several years as an organist and choir director at the Saint Paul Christian Methodist Episcopal Church and three years as an organist and assistant choir director at the Oakwood Boulevard Christian Church, where "many of the leading musicians of the city ... appeared" during her tenure. In 1929, "with the assistance of her husband Rev. F. D. Jackson, she succeeded in organizing the Imperial Opera company." Under (Mrs.) Jackson's direction, they presented three operas in the Loop (including Michael William Balfe's *The Bohemian Girl*) and were engaged to perform at the Chrysanthemum Art and Charity Club (one of the oldest Black charity clubs in the city) at the invitation of its then music chair Nannie Mae Glasco Williams. Evidently, Tompkins's surrogate role in Jackson's life as an "othermother" prepared and propelled her trajectory as a similarly civic-minded, community-conscious musical Race Woman.[73] Jackson in turn nurtured such ethics and interests in her daughters, Catherine and Betty Lou.[74] The latter is better known today as Betty Jackson King, composer, conductor, and NANM president from 1980 to 1985.

Jackson lived by the following motto and no doubt instilled her ethos in others:

> There's only one method for meeting life's test,
> Just keep on striving and hope for the best.
> Don't give up the game and die in dismay
> Because hammers are thrown when you'd like a bouquet.
> Just stick to your work, show the best of your skill;
> Some folks won't like, but other folks will.[75]

Jackson found fellowship in like-minded folks such as Texas native Nannie Mae Glasco Williams. Williams was a consummate society woman. Her parents, Mr. and Mrs. John F. Glasco, were "pioneer Austin citizens"; they belonged to the Black elite and were deeply involved in Black social and civic spheres there. This became Williams's world, and as expected, classical music–making (with a focus on voice and keyboard) was part of it too. A mezzo-soprano, she studied voice under Emma Azalia Hackley and piano with her aunt, Fannie Glasco Madison, who was the "first Race music instructor at the [historically Black] Tillotson College."[76] As a musical Race woman in the making, Williams's training grounds also encompassed the church: "At the age of 16 she was the leading soprano soloist in the Metropolitan church choir of 60 voices and secretary of the Sunday school until leaving for the North." Upon completing her studies—she was an honor graduate of Anderson High School and Tillotson—Williams arrived in Chicago in 1918 and took employment as a specialist typist for the mail company Montgomery Ward on the Near North Side. She simultaneously kept up her voice and piano studies and commitment to church life. Bethel African Methodist Episcopal Church became her spiritual home, where she played as the church pianist.

Williams's social network invariably grew through her many activities, which led to further opportunities and auspicious connections. On the recommendation of her society friends, she became the private secretary of A. L. Williams—"a prominent lawyer, located at 184 W. Washington St." They soon married, and relishing the privileges and responsibilities of Race womanhood, Nannie Williams came to be known as "one of the most prominent young women in the civic, political, religious and club life of Chicago." Over time, she was elected to president of the Chrysanthemum Art and Charity Club (succeeding prominent clubwoman Nannie Reed) and became increasingly active in other types of club work. She was a member of the National Association for the Advancement of Colored People (NAACP) and continued her secretarial work in positions that

ranged from the secretary of the Illinois State Association's budget committee to recording and corresponding secretary of the Douglass League
of Women Voters.

"Few young women can boast of the multiplicity of accomplishments
accorded Mrs. Williams," read the profile of her public life. "The fact that
her talented husband appreciates and makes it possible for her to broaden
her scope of intelligence is worthy of mention."[77] Sympathetic and well-to-
do husbands were a winning combination for the married Race woman.
Those "who married men prominent in their own right," explains Paula
Giddings, "had the latitude to make decisions without reference to dire
economic need, or concern that they might threaten their husbands' self-
worth. It was easier to be a co-equal or partner with a man who had himself
acquired a certain importance."[78]

Although unmentioned in the *Chicago Defender*'s profiles of women in
public life, Holt was another Race woman who was particularly attuned
to the ways in which the stability of marriage could produce a necessary
springboard for her ambitions. Holt supposedly married five times. Yet
rather than being subsumed in the scandal of her relationships (which
sometimes made page-one news), each of her marriages (or terminated
unions) spelled a new era of creativity and self-invention for Holt. For
example, her marriage to hotelier George W. Holt (who was twenty-three
years her senior) led her to acquire a large home out of which she founded
NANM; furthermore, the financial security she enjoyed also made it possible for her to establish her short-lived but popular *Music and Poetry*
journal. Upon her husband's death, Holt became, as Lawrence Schenbeck describes, "a woman of independent means" who "[took] advantage
of this newfound economic freedom [and] engaged in sexual and social
adventures during the 1920s and 1930s that regularly landed her in the
black community's gossip sheets (and on the front page of the *Defender*)."[79]
Additionally, her scandalous divorce from Joseph L. Ray in 1924 catalyzed
a period of international travel and high-profile musical engagements in
New York, London, Paris, Shanghai, and Singapore. But Holt was strategic
all the way: her Race womanhood was conventional in parts, atypical in
others, but ever "fabulous" throughout, as her obituary would state.[80] As
both a classically trained clubwoman and "Jazz-Age Goddess," the complexities and seeming contradictions of her life were key to her continued reinventions through the twentieth century.[81] Although the striking
independence of Holt and her peers cannot be denied, it remains true that
strategic unions with prominent Race men (e.g., lawyers, judges, ministers,
doctors, dentists, hoteliers, etc.) combined with progressive marital politics around gender roles (or generous inheritances, or lucrative divorce

settlements) often meant that Race women could follow their public callings and maintain their musical interests.

Without knowing the professional backgrounds of Joseph H. Roberts
and Alice Roberts, it is hard to specify or speculate what brought them
and their only daughter—Miss Maude J. Roberts (later Mrs. George)—to
Chicago from Jersey City, New Jersey, around the turn of the century. Had
Mr. Roberts been a railroad dining cook like Margaret Bonds's grandfather, Edward W. Bonds, who, with his wife, Mrs. Margaret A. Bonds (her
namesake), and five children (including Estella), moved to Chicago from
New York City around the same time, their move could be situated amid
Chicago's emergence through the nineteenth century as the nation's "railroad capital," the industry's increasing dependence on a Black workforce,
and the South Side's drawing power as a locus of employment prospects.[82]
Without earlier biographical detail to draw on, the reason for the Robertses'
move begins and ends with one word: opportunity. Their journey began
too late for them to identify with Chicago's Old Settlers and too early for
them to belong to the Great Migration, in which the trajectory of Florence
Price neatly fit, as a northbound southern migrant. The Robertses' lateral
movement from the East Coast to the Midwest, in the interstice of two large
chapters in Black Chicago's formation, coupled with a lack of genealogical
detail, obscures Maude Roberts George's early story. Unable to apply to
the musical Race women with scantily documented origins Darlene Clark
Hine's query, "When and by what process did black women come to settle?"
the question therefore becomes "What did they do once they arrived?"[83]

Before marriage, motherhood, and her subsequent pivot during the
interwar years from celebrated soprano to civic leader, Maude Roberts
George followed the familiar path of the Race woman educator in training. Known at this time as Miss Maude J. Roberts, she attended Chicago's
South Division High School and upon graduating completed further study
at the historically Black Walden University in Nashville, Tennessee, and
at Bryant-Stratton Business College in Chicago in 1907 and 1908, respectively.[84] The transcripts of her training are absent from the public record,
but there is little doubt that her college education prepared her for a teaching career, as that is exactly what followed. She taught music and commercial education (a field that drew on her business training) at Nashville's
Walden College from 1909 to 1911 and Lane College in Jackson, Tennessee,
from 1911 to 1913.[85] She returned to Chicago soon after, equipped with the
kinds of experiences and expertise befitting for one who would come to
be regarded as the jewel of Black Chicago society.

As a young unwedded woman, George underwent the rites of passage
associated with her social set, such as the debutante ball, and navigated

these rites with flair, even outshining those around her. At the "coming out" party of Irene Berenice Hudlin (a future NANM and CMA member), which took place on August 31, 1916, at Ogden Assembly Hall on the West Side, Miss Roberts formed part of the receiving line alongside the debutante's mother and Theodosia Brewer (the wife of prominent physician Dr. George Cleveland Hall). Even though the night belonged to Hudlin—"a study in girlish sweetness and artless" on the cusp of womanhood (as the *Chicago Defender*'s society news declared)—Miss Roberts remained as "Chicago's unchallenged favorite; the reigning queen in 'splendid' isolation—having no rivals of the big city's muso-social life; finished; brilliant."[86] Miss Roberts was a paragon of respectability, desirability, and exemplary Race womanhood. Her musical prowess only added to her inimitable virtue.

As a child, George "displayed talent for music."[87] Yet she arrived at the concert hall neither by way of the East Coast conservatory, like Price or the Texan-born musicologist Maud Cuney Hare, nor the midwestern music school, like Holt and Estella Bonds, but by way of Chicago's Herman Devries and his private instruction. Devries, a baritone, was a former soloist and subsequent coach at the Metropolitan Grand Opera. He taught in the Fine Arts Building in the Loop and instructed a number of Black classical singers at that time. He oversaw George's studies in voice, harmony, composition, music history, and pedagogy, as well as French and Italian.[88] Her training under this white instructor evidenced to both Black and white society that hers was a formidable talent—no match for the strictures of Jim Crow segregation.

Recital after recital, Miss Roberts proved her titles as "Chicago's cultured soprano singer" and "Chicago's sweetest opera singer," gaining admiration on "all sides" of the color line.[89] On February 4, 1915, she became the first artist of the Race to perform at Chicago's Abraham Lincoln Center. Enamored with her performance, *Chicago Defender* reader Mrs. E. D. Lindsay of 3233 Vernon Avenue wrote to the press to say,

> Mr. Editor: Permit me through the medium of your valuable columns to compliment Miss Maude Roberts on the solo so beautifully rendered Thursday evening. . . . I wish to express my appreciation for her singing ability and congratulate her on the success which she has attained.
>
> I hear it spoken of with enthusiasm on all sides. . . . she has touched the musical heart and gained a worthy place among the sons and daughters of Chicago. I am sure it is the hope of all her friends that before long they shall have the pleasure of hearing her with some new product.[90]

One of Miss Roberts's new products arrived just two months later in the form of her contribution to the Second Annual All Colored Composers Concert.

As George's subsequent activities show, marriage and motherhood fueled a repurposing of her public life. The identities of wife and mother, as well as the financial stability in which she comfortably sat, spurred on a new path. George began to "[devote] herself more and more to civic work and music promotion," to the extent that her profile in "A Scrap Book for Women in Public Life" read, "Possibly no woman in the country in the musical world is better known than Mrs. George. For many years she has been music critic of The Chicago Defender, and her articles are the source of much valuable information for her many followers." George's premarital livelihood had generated the multifaceted identities of part educator, part socialite, part concert artist, and part community organizer; moreover, these earlier experiences equipped her for some of her most enduring roles yet.

"In addition to her musical ability," the profile continued, "Mrs. George is a great factor in the social and civic life here." Her positions included chair of the YWCA South Parkway branch's management committee, president of the Douglass School Parent Teacher Association, treasurer of the women's auxiliary board for the city's Black-run Provident Hospital, and president of the auxiliary Cook County Bar Association. Within a few years, George would add president of both the CMA (1932–37) and NANM (1933–35) to her list of accomplishments.[91]

George's colleague, NANM historian Clara Hutchison, similarly accrued great accolades. Touted as "one of Chicago's leading musicians," Hutchison's talents came to light at the age of three, when she traveled around her native Springfield, Ohio, and beyond as a "'wonder child' because of her gift of reading any article, no matter how great its difficulty." As a young girl, she moved to Chicago with her mother. She graduated from Haven High School as class valedictorian and then entered South Division High School, where she excelled but was made to cut her education short when her mother fell ill. Nevertheless, a successful musical career soon followed due to Hutchison "being the fortunate possessor of a brilliant soprano voice."[92] In 1920, she graduated from the Chicago Musical College, where she received the Alexander Revell Diamond Medal, which was a "highly merited award" for performers. Just the year before, Hutchison's future CMA colleague Antoinette Garnes received the award "for vocal proficiency in the Post Graduate class," making her "the first Race student to win honors in that class." As Holt explained in the *Chicago Defender*'s coverage of Garnes's accomplishment, the award led to the "successful contestant" also being "given the privilege of representing the class on the graduating program."[93] Hutchison therefore continued this legacy of Race women's accomplishment at the Chicago Musical College. Yet despite the accolades, Hutchison's incomplete high school education evidently stayed with her, and two decades on from her curtailed stint at South Division High School, she enrolled at Englewood High School, graduating in 1922 "with the highest grades." In 1924, she obtained her teaching certificate and immediately thereafter entered a life of educational service as a teacher in the Chicago public school system. And "added to her many achievements" was "the coveted degree of Bachelor of Philosophy at the June [1932] convocation at the University of Chicago."[94] The themes of fortitude and perseverance in Hutchison's narrative, as catalyzed by her mother's illness, echo elements of Jackson's biography—that is, the resolve needed to steadfastly pursue one's calling amid the horrifically disorienting effect of personal tragedy.

Parental health challenges also affected Irene H. Harrison's trajectory. Born in Racine, Wisconsin, Harrison pursued piano and cornet at an early age, learning from locally based German and Danish teachers. The migrant backgrounds of such instructors, notes Kira Thurman more broadly on the nature of these transnational exchanges between European pedagogues and African American students, often "freed them from seeing Black lives and potential careers through the lens of American race relations."[95] As a result, Harrison benefited hugely from this more progressive dynamic. After moving to the Black Metropolis with her family, she enrolled at the Chicago Musical College, studying cornet, harmony, and composition under Emil Kopp and Felix Borowski. She graduated both as an educator and performer. During her studies, Kopp "secured for her the position of cornet soloist with a German band of 50 artists, which she held during their engagement in Chicago." It was also during her time at the Chicago Musical College that "she had the great honor of assisting the late S. Coleridge-Taylor in recital in Chicago." Harrison's musical experiences were vast and varied: she studied at the American Conservatory of Music in Chicago, performed across lyceum, concert, and vaudeville circuits for eleven years, toured the United States and Canada extensively, and shared a program with Sissieretta Jones in New York City. However, when the health of Harrison's father began to decline, she returned to Chicago, entered the medical profession, and upon passing the necessary exams, became only "one of the two Race women in Chicago holding positions as health inspector." Harrison's Chicago return spurred a deeper engagement in civic life on multiple fronts.

She directed the twenty-one-piece boys orchestra of Quinn Chapel Sunday School for seven years, with many members later going on to lead successful careers themselves. She also directed the Chicago Women's Cornet Orchestra for three years. But Harrison left this position to fine-tune her methods in cornet pedagogy, leading to her receiving instruction from

John M. O'Donnel, who had played first cornet with John Philip Sousa's band. Her next appointment was as the director of the twenty-five-piece Chicago Colored Woman's Band, for which Harrison gave "much credit to [Major] N. Clark Smith for [the] orchestral knowledge [she] gained while in his Ladies orchestra."[96] What is significant about Harrison's work is the platform she created for Black women who were less inclined toward the more stereotypically feminine instruments of the voice, piano, and violin.[97] She broadened the definition of musical Race womanhood. Catalyzed by the tragedy of her father's illness, Harrison used her talents to improve both the physical, social, and cultural health of her Chicago.

Although these fragments barely scratch the surface of Tompkins's, Jackson's, Williams's, George's, Hutchison's, and Harrison's contrapuntal lives, they nevertheless leave clear evidence of the ways in which their interwoven musical and civic activity spun out of networks that were themselves patterned with the intricate, interconnected, and intergenerational efforts of countless Race women, beyond those mentioned here. Ashley D. Farmer's metaphor for the simultaneous invisibility and ubiquity of Black women's intellectual work in the United States aptly captures the organizing work of this sisterhood: "Spiderwebs are curious things. They are everywhere, but often invisible to the naked eye. [In] fact, many of us don't even register them until the light hits the strands of the web just right. Only then do we recognize the intricate pattern of the web or the way it connects or bridges structures."[98] There is no truer depiction of Tompkins, Jackson, Williams, Holt, George, Hutchison, and Harrison, of the other named and unnamed impresarios honored here, of the communities they built and bridged, of the art worlds they meticulously structured and sustained, and of the revelatory collage that emerges when we shine the light just right.

Coda

Two decades on from the inaugural Annual All Colored Composers Concert, Charles Clarence Dawson's artwork for the 1934 Chicago World's Fair "O, Sing a New Song" pageant is revealed (fig. 10). Slated for August 25 at Soldier Field, the event will witness an "all colored cast of 5,000 singers, actors and dancers."[99] Their artistry will coalesce in a "dramatic presentation of breath-taking beauty and splendor" that tells a "history of the Black race," from Old World, precolonial Africa to the early twentieth-century United States.[100] The event is Pan-African in its purview and transnational in its modernism, and Dawson anticipates the spectacular breadth and historical depth of it all in his promotional artwork.

At the center of Dawson's poster, a statuesque, copper-hued Black woman stands tall, attired in a black sleeveless gown, hands clasped across her solar plexus, neck elongated by her head's upward tilt, and lips parted in song. She favors Marian Anderson, who is not touted to perform but is an aspirational figure for Black classical communities across the United States. The cultural symbolism that this central protagonist represents—either as Anderson herself or as an allusion—is subtly reinforced by the turquoise adornment below the neckline of her dress, which seems to resemble a pair of wings, as if emblematizing the voice that is about to take flight.

Gathered either side of her base are several Black women in different colored garments that billow around their balletic shapes in possible reference to the Afro-diasporic choreographies of Katherine Dunham that will dazzle and inspire the sixty-thousand-strong audience at Soldier Field. Behind the illustrated dancers, and on the left-hand side of the singer in similar attire, sits a darker-complected Black woman, eyes closed and hands poised as she plays on a full-mast grand piano. Might she be Margaret Bonds, who will perform at the pageant as the soloist in Price's Piano Concerto in One Movement?[101] Or is she an amalgamation of prodigious Black "piano girls" turned Race women virtuosos, blending Bonds, Hazel Harrison, Helen Hagan, and others?[102] Whoever the pianist in Dawson's iconography stands to represent, her role is one of uplift and her instrument is a conduit for the long history of Black expressivity. In Dawson's image, the piano lid falls on the right-hand side of the singer and, due to its dimension and perspective, appears simultaneously as a path that connects past and present, continent and diaspora.

A group of men congregate behind the pianist on the left; they are of a different time and place: the Antebellum South. One man sits with a banjo in hand, while another man, wearing a hat, appears as the lead singer. A few men to his right seem to respond to or harmonize around his folk melodies, while others form an engaged audience. The scene snakes around to the right behind the piano lid and back even further in time and place to precolonial West Africa. A male and female dancer perform amid a collection of talking drums and a semicircle of male and female players.

The farthest scene is in ancient Egypt, challenging that which white supremacist dogma tells the Race they are without: history. Tucked behind the southland forest that forms a backdrop to the African American folk musicians and the tropical flora around the West African performers, African antiquity is where the story of the Race begins in the manner of Black American pageantry.[103] A sphinx and two pyramids rise out of the desert. In the left corner are a small cluster of Egyptian royals (as their attire

Figure 10. Charles Clarence Dawson, "O, Sing a New Song," ca. 1933. 2024
© The Metropolitan Museum of Art/Art Resource. Photo Scala, Florence.

suggests) with a harpist in front of them, stooped at his instrument. In the right corner stands a sculpturesque woman, self-assured in her femininity, and an ancient forerunner of the modern Race woman who stands at the edge of this history.

Dawson ascribes heritage and hope to the nested narratives of the Race around an expressive and featureful Black chanteuse. Black music-making and community-building live in every scene. The central Race woman's clasped hands evoke the bringing together of it all. Her bodily gestures signal readiness and arrival. Her entry is posed to initiate a grand fugue—fugue meaning, in its original Italian *fuga*, "flight" or "escape"—sounding a new song in the key of liberation for all. She is Maude Roberts George, Nora Holt, Anita Patti Brown, Helen Hagan, Hazel Harrison, Elnora Manson, Emma Azalia Hackley, Mrs. Cary B. Lewis, Antoinette Cone Tompkins, Gertrude Smith Jackson, Nannie Mae Glasco Williams, Clara E. Hutchison, and Irene Howard Harrison. She is all of the musical Race women in this book. And as she begins her new song, so too do the collective past, present, and future of Black lives enter with her.

2

She Proclaimed a Chicago Renaissance

Chicago was on the cusp of a new era. The discerning audience that eagerly awaited Roland Hayes was, from Nora Holt's perspective, evidence that the city was "awakening to the cultural as well as social and civic trend" of its Black populace. This was how Holt opened her review for the famed Boston tenor's local recital, which took place on the evening of November 27, 1917, at the South Park Methodist Episcopal Church (fig. 11). According to Holt, Hayes's warm welcome signaled Chicago's transformation into the cultured metropolis that it purported to be. Ever evocative and incisive with her language, she wrote of how his recital proved that the city was "rapidly recovering" from its earlier "cultural aphasia." Rooted in the subtext was how the concert's South Side location only affirmed the transformative impact of the social, civic, and cultural trends that took shape within this geography and its communities.

Holt observed that in the past, visiting artists tended to not take their engagements in the Windy City as seriously, "placing a light valuation upon Chicago's technical efficiency and art interest" and, as a result, delivering programs that were "positively trite." Audiences were perceived as less discerning than those of, say, New York or Boston. However, the tide had turned, and Holt was delighted to see that Hayes brought to his Chicago audience—and, even more significantly, this South Side venue—a near replica of the program he had given at Boston's Symphony Hall almost two weeks earlier. Hayes did not underestimate Black classical Chicago in the slightest.

With his "lyric voice, mellifluous and resonant," he delivered an engaging program that "upheld his reputation as one of the greatest tenors." To those who beheld his artistry from the church pews, "his interpretation

Figure 11. South Park Methodist Episcopal Church, Chicago, ca. 1922. 740 Rush Street, Chicago, Illinois: Committee on Conservation and Advance, The Methodist Episcopal Church. Special Collections 4th floor; VAULT Case folio E185.6 M48 1922. Newberry Library, Chicago.

of [Louis Campbell] Tipton's 'Spirit Flower' and Coleridge-Taylor's 'On, Away, Awake, Beloved' was a revelation, while his pure, shaded legato singing of [Gaetano] Donizetti's 'Una Furtiva Lagrima' characterized him as the embodiment of tonal perfection," Holt raved.[1] In awe must have been a young Margaret Bonds, alongside her mother, who never missed a

Hayes concert when he was in town.[2] Bonds adored the way he closed his recitals with Spirituals (as Abbie Mitchell and Marian Anderson would go on to do), so much so that it inspired her own Spiritual arrangements later. Holt was similarly captivated by Hayes's programming, but for her, his magnetism also lay in his "presence and poise," devoid of pompous theatrics. Holt saw in Hayes a self-possession that evoked "that musical savant, Mr. H. T. Burleigh, whose wonderful personality and glorious voice held an envious place on the concert stage for many years." Hayes's performances exuded a certain nostalgia even as he advanced a new era of Black classical artistry.[3]

Many decades later, Earl Calloway of the *Chicago Defender* would write in a profile of Holt's life that "when Roland Hayes made his appearance at the South Park Methodist Episcopal Church, she proclaimed a 'Chicago Renaissance.'"[4] Although Holt's original review did not use the term "Chicago Renaissance," she certainly felt it.[5] Her writing conjured up themes of rebirth and revival as she articulated the city's "awakening" and resurgence during this period. Through such vivid language, she voiced her detection of a changing current, one that historians would later term the Black Chicago Renaissance.

If Hayes's South Side recital was the product of a shifting climate, then what were some of the cultural, social, and civic trends occurring behind the scenes, perpetuating change, and bringing such musical events into being? Put another way, if his concert was proof of a public sphere aflame with intellectual and artistic curiosity, then what was the fuel? Holt's professional life stands as a reminder of the curatorial, impresarial, and institutional influence that Race women exerted in the public sphere. Their work interwove culture-making, social justice, and civic leadership, rendering classical music a site of Race woman–engineered revolution. This chapter therefore delves deeper into the trends that Black women spearheaded—trends that gave rise to the city's concert scene, renaissance era, and flourishing Black Metropolis (to reinvoke the language of St. Clair Drake and Horace Cayton).

I begin with an overview of the Black Chicago Renaissance, which Darlene Clark Hine depicts as "a dynamically prolific period of African American creativity in music, performance art, social science scholarship, and visual and literary artistic expression."[6] I then journey through the modernist aesthetics of composers from this time to establish more of the wider cultural backdrop in which practitioners such as Holt and Hayes were operating. I draw various social and civic trends into the conversation as I turn to the development of Black concert life in Chicago. The discussion here encompasses the visits of the Fisk Jubilee Singers in the late nineteenth century, the turn-of-the-century founding of the Chicago Choral Study Club (one of Black Chicago's pioneering music associations), and the subsequent establishment of the Chicago Music Association (CMA) and National Association of Negro Musicians (NANM). In observing the ways in which Race women operated as culture-makers, social architects, and civic leaders across these areas of activity, Holt emerges as a driving force behind the very renaissance that she proclaimed.

Composing the Black Chicago Renaissance

Like Harlem's New Negro movement, the Black Chicago Renaissance celebrated Black diasporic folklorism, epitomized Afro-modernism, fueled race-conscious feminism, and galvanized civil rights activism. Yet it also rivaled the cultural contributions of Harlem and maintained its own distinctiveness as a result of the specific ways in which Black Chicagoans, both newly arrived and previously settled, engaged in geographically grounded, intellectually vitalized, and artistically inspired methods of self-actualization and collective uplift.[7] Unlike the majority of Chicago's Black inhabitants, New York's Black population was scattered over five boroughs, as Helen Walker-Hill observes, with its Black cultural renaissance experiencing greater input from white patrons across its artistic realms.[8] This contrasted with the Black concentration and self-sufficiency of the South Side—an ecosystem that produced a multitude of Race women impresarios and a distinct flavor of Black Renaissance intellectuality and artistry.

Yet, just as it was in the Black Mecca of New York, so too was it in the Black Metropolis of Chicago that thinkers and visionaries of African descent—encompassing all shades, from working classes to society folk, itinerant visitors to rooted residents, Caribbean and Canadian arrivals to intranational migrants—similarly pushed for self-definition beyond the constraints of the old, the traditional, the rural, and the stereotypical. They breathed new life into their pasts, asserting the wondrous depths and breadths of Black history, heritage, and humanity in the face of a white supremacism that sought, routinely and violently, to deny these truths. They imbued their present with renewed hopes and aspirations, and from there emerged revitalizations of self as these thinkers and visionaries reckoned with what it meant to be Black in the United States at this time.

The zeitgeist of the era exteriorized in prose, poetry, and plays; radio programs, periodicals, film, and photography; paintings, linocuts, and sculptures; ballet, neo-folk choreographies, and contemporary dance; and any other media through which Black artistry, intellectuality, empowerment, and uplift could be realized. The revolution unfolded across churches, nightclubs, ballrooms, auditoriums, community centers, kitchenettes, and dining tables. Its impact burst Chicago's Black Belt open, giving way to what Drake and Cayton conceptualized as the "Black Metropolis"—a geography undeterred by the limitations imposed on it, a geography whose chromatic cultural composition would bear both national and international import.[9] But the South Side was its home and Bronzeville was its capital.

The expressive arts functioned and flourished as vehicles for change, and artists provided some of the most essential forms of activism in the Black Metropolis. Darlene Clark Hine explains that "artists comprised the vanguard of the struggle to fashion new expressive sites for contesting racial, class, and gender hierarchies and reshaping public culture."[10] Numerous Race women were actively involved in these reshapings, bringing such critical issues to the fore in their nurturing of Chicago's Black classical community. Anne Meis Knupfer documents more broadly that during the Black Chicago Renaissance era, African American women—as "artists, writers, theater directors [as well as] schoolteachers, clubwomen, founders and administrators of community institutions, activists, volunteers, and caretakers"—"were largely involved in promoting the expressive arts, sustaining community institutions, and fostering black solidarity through social protests."[11] Such creative identities and civic roles formed the multifaceted backgrounds of musical Race women and coalesced in the classical strand of the Black Chicago Renaissance.

This strand has been overshadowed, both in its own time and ours, by the literary and popular music innovations of the era—innovations that not only gripped the imaginations of wider Black America but also lodged themselves firmly in the cultural consciousness of the white majority. This included the culture-shifting authorial contributions of Richard Wright, Gwendolyn Brooks, and Lorraine Hansberry that illuminated modern Black life in Chicago; as well as the explosion of distinct Chicago blues, jazz, and gospel sounds forged by figures such as Thomas A. Dorsey, Earl Hines, and Mahalia Jackson.[12] And yet, the formation of Chicago's Black concert scene predated their contributions and the broadly accepted 1930–50 periodization of the Black Chicago Renaissance.[13] In fact, it predated the Harlem Renaissance, which was said to have started it all.

Samuel A. Floyd Jr. reveals that Black classical community-building toward the end of the nineteenth century and in the dawning decades of the twentieth "had no parallel in literature or the arts." He therefore asks, "Was it the example of music that gave initial impetus to the Renaissance's artistic philosophy?"[14] The classical strand leads to this very possibility and, combined with a greater attentiveness to musical Race women's capacious identities along this thread, offers another perspective through which to interpret the origins of the Black Chicago Renaissance.

The Black Transnational Modernism of African American Concert Culture

In addition to complicating the intraracial dynamics of Black cultural production in the first half of the twentieth century, the classical strand of the Black Chicago Renaissance inspires a rethinking and reframing of music historiographies that overstate the themes of white male sonic world-making (i.e., post-tonal idioms, dissolution of form, and detachment from the musical past) as the dominant means through which to hear this modernist period. Understated is the regenerative work of Black sonic world–makers who expanded tonal palettes with Black diasporic color, revised classical forms, and reconnected with a breadth of musical pasts. Set against the backdrop of impending war, the Great Depression, and domestic terrorism, their modernism responded to the violence of their surroundings not with further dissonance (as many of their lauded white counterparts did) but with Black folk melodies, sonata forms, diasporic dance rhythms, and a language of uplift. Their modernist foundations arose out of the intersections that comprised their lived experience.

When Margaret Bonds opined in later life, "It has to be human . . . and people have to like it; it has to move them spiritually and intellectually. I don't think the atonal and serial music has much to do with human emotion—it's so contrived," she was speaking about the significant and interlinked functions of heritage, history, *herstory*, and humanity in her craft.[15] Although Bonds's Black postmodernist peers such as the Kentucky-born Julia Perry and Virginia's Undine Smith Moore would embrace atonal and serial influences, that Bonds generally kept her distance was evidence of the ways in which this early twentieth-century Black, and notably Chicago-influenced, concert aesthetic shaped her compositional outlook. Bonds's words affirmed the ideologies of Black Renaissance modernism, invoking the spiritually and intellectually guided work of earlier generations of Race women and men who galvanized a Black classical sphere around their own modernist narratives.

This sphere emanated from a history that encompassed the moment the African diaspora made its musical mark on the New World. From the artistry of the enslaved emerged a musical lexicon of pentatonic scales and minor modes, blue notes and bent tones, call-and-response patterns and pendular third motions, dance syncopations and tapestry-like vocal textures. Banjos, fiddles, foot stomps, hand claps, hums, hollers, cries, and shouts filled the plantation sound world. Improvisation abounded. But enslaved music-makers worked with a shared understanding of form and function, never notated but always studied, practiced, and refined with each performance.

Over time, Black practitioners gained access to classical music study at national conservatories or with European pedagogues in private studios. Their works decomposed color lines, exhibited expansive modes of expression, and fed into the projects of empowerment and uplift. When Antonín Dvořák declared to white America in 1893, "I am now satisfied that the future of this country must be founded upon what are called the negro melodies. . . . These beautiful and varied themes are the product of American soil. They are American," the descendants of the diaspora were already at work, finding beautiful cohesion and powerful conversation between the folkloric idioms of early diasporic Africans and the conventions of their classical training.[16]

Two decades before Dvořák's proclamation, the famed Fisk Jubilee Singers stepped out onto the world stage in the early 1870s, "fastidiously dressed in Victorian finery and singing 'spirituals' in a muted pianissimo," as Jennifer Lynn Stoever evocatively portrays.[17] They awakened global audiences to a concertized genre of Black American folk songs that, in the words of Black Chicago Renaissance literary figures and chroniclers Arna Bontemps and Robert Lucas, "had a strange, haunting quality" and "contrasted vividly with the popular minstrel music."[18] W. E. B. Du Bois recalled that "the world listened only half credulously" to the Spirituals "until the Fisk Jubilee Singers sang the slave songs so deeply into the world's heart that it can never wholly forget them again."[19] The Fisk Jubilee Singers changed the course of Black classical life in the United States.[20] Their performances housed the transformation of the Spiritual and of its public perception, which resonated deeply with Talented Tenth ideology, the politics of respectability, and racial uplift. The metamorphosis of vernacular traditions into a widely recognized and celebrated art form became a metaphor for the transformation of the race, from the dehumanizing thralls of slavery to the rehumanizing ambitions of freemen and freewomen. The concert Spiritual reified the aspirations of classical practitioners such as Maud Cuney Hare—who believed, "with all people, folk music goes out as art music comes in, and spontaneous expression gives way to studied and purposeful use of artistic expression"—and New Negro thinkers like Alain Locke—who put forth that the Spiritual could "undergo without breaking its own boundaries, intricate and original development in directions already the line of advance in modernistic music."[21] Hare's and Locke's writings stemmed from their knowledge that classical music had famously absorbed so many other folk languages—Russian, Turkish, Hungarian, Bohemian. And so, why not African American? For these two Black Renaissance figures, the folk songs of the enslaved, combined with the studied approach, produced the ideal vehicle for contemporary practitioners to articulate a spirit of resilience, rebirth, and reconnection for a new, modernist era.

If the Fisk Jubilee Singers represented one pillar of the Black concert aesthetic, then Samuel Coleridge-Taylor represented yet another. In fact, for early twentieth-century Black classical composers, the example of Coleridge-Taylor arguably resonated more deeply across the Atlantic than that of Dvořák. As Walker-Hill affirms, "His example as a black musician and composer, respected by whites in his own land, impressed the black audiences and communities [in the United States] and gave new impetus to their classical music activities."[22] As a symbol of racial uplift alongside his music, Coleridge-Taylor wrote the many shades of Blackness into his scores, drawing on African folk melodies, Caribbean songs, Negro Spirituals, and Moorish dances across his vast compositional catalog. At the same time, however, Coleridge-Taylor claimed European conventions (devoid of African continental and diasporic influences) as his voice too—just as Helen Hagan would several years later with her German-inspired piano concerto. Coleridge-Taylor's musical relationship with his African and European ancestry was not prescriptive; no aesthetic shade was more or less authentic to his artistic and intellectual being than the other. His African-descended North American contemporaries and successors took note. Performers made his music a part of their repertoire. Where Negro Spirituals were concerned, composers like Margaret Bonds studied his scores but substituted the stoic Victorian aesthetic of his arrangements with more of what Bonds called that "'American Gospel' feeling," reinterpreting his approach through transnational, modernist vistas.[23]

Although Coleridge-Taylor's life was short, his legacy endured, especially in Chicago. As *Chicago Defender* critic Nahum Daniel Brascher would later write, "Coleridge-Taylor was a charming person to know; he had a dream of music for us, all too soon ended by his early death."[24] Soon after his untimely demise, the Coleridge-Taylor Music School of Chicago blossomed out of the homes of a few Black classical musicians (likely including that of the school's cofounder Estella Bonds), before establishing its headquarters at 3618–3628 South State Street in 1913 and then, in 1916, moving to Thirty-Sixth Place and South State Street.[25] By this time, the school could boast of "a faculty of Negroes prominent in the world of music," such as pianist T. Theodore Taylor, organist Walter E. Gossette, soprano Martha B. Anderson, composer and author Herbert H. Byron, baritone Theodore Bryant, pianist and organist Estella Bonds, and pianist Nannie May Strayhorn (later Reid).[26] More than Dvořák's, Coleridge-Taylor's voice lived on in Black Chicago, the wider renaissance, and its distinctive concert aesthetic.

Within this aesthetic, many composers made the Negro Spirituals and wider array of African American vernacular idioms central to their craft. However, practitioners were also energized by the possibilities for new creative expression in art songs, chamber works, ballets, opera, symphonies, and concertos. Their compositional homages to Black folkloric pasts were examples of what A. Kori Hill calls "New Negro modernism," with Afro-modernist approaches including reinterpretations of Black vernacular idioms (e.g., call and response, pentatonic scales, pendular thirds, etc.) in classical forms.[27] The aesthetics of African American folk song were heavily disparaged in white American mainstream culture, warped to grotesque distortion through the wildly popular institution of Blackface minstrelsy, and, as Stephanie DeLane Doktor observes, funneled through "a voyeuristic lens into the white imaginaries of so-called African primitivity" by various white American and European practitioners who advanced modernism's primitivist vogue with problematic gusto.[28] However, African American folk song aesthetics simultaneously reemerged in a twentieth-century narrative of Black renaissance and in classical music genres that were propagandized by a white patriarchy as beyond the intellectual reach of African Americans, of white women, and thus of Black women, further marginalized at this intersection.[29] Despite racist propaganda and sexist prescriptions, many African-descended classical composers of this time unapologetically drew their modernist narratives from the folk songs of the enslaved and from twentieth-century Black collectivist visions of uplift, rebirth, and liberation.

Their compositions encompassed Spiritual arrangements with uncomplicated harmonies to complement the modal contours and lyrical content of Black sacred song. Sometimes composers even rendered their own arrangements on the stage, like Burleigh, Hayes, Robert Nathaniel Dett, and Will Marion Cook. There were also transcriptions born out of ethnographic studies, such as the Creole song collections of Maud Cuney Hare and Camille Nickerson, and the Negro Spiritual volumes of brothers James Weldon and J. Rosamond Johnson—both of whom gifted Black America with "Lift Every Voice and Sing," which came to be known as the Negro National Anthem by 1921 and was later absorbed into the opening rituals of CMA meetings.[30]

In addition to utilizing creative sources from a more distant past, Black Renaissance composers also looked to a contemporary Black literary canon for inspiration. Paul Laurence Dunbar and later Langston Hughes were firm favorites of Price, Holt, Margaret Bonds, and other Black Renaissance composers. In fact, Cook brought Dunbar, alongside the Black concert aesthetic and vernacular tradition, to Broadway, blurring highbrow and lowbrow and spotlighting the splendor of all-Black casts. In dialogue with the latter were folk ballets and operas that dramatized the lore and landscape of the Black diaspora. As genres known to venture into the abstract and mythical, composers used these large-scale vehicles to reimagine Black folkloric pasts, as witnessed in the Deep South settings of Scott Joplin's *Treemonisha* (1911) and Harry Lawrence Freeman's *Voodoo* (1928), the Caribbean conjurings of William Grant Still's *La guiablesse* (1927) and Clarence Cameron White's *Ouanga* (1928), and the transatlantic geography of Shirley Graham's *Tom Tom* (1932). In a similar vein, grandiose orchestral works and chamber suites drew primary themes out of plantation songs and lively movements out of juba dances. As symphonists, Price, Still, and William Dawson paved the way with a national sound unafraid to claim the Black cultural foundations of the United States.

Unlike the music of the enslaved, these compositions were notated. Most remained in manuscript form while a few were published in their respective composer's lifetime and therefore made more widely available. However, the culture of community inscribed in earlier cultures of Black music-making remained. The names given here do not represent all of the composers who shaped a Black transnational modernism, but they do represent an intergenerational cohort through which ideas were passed down, in which composers championed one another, and behind which a network of Black patrons, promoters, clubs, churches, and other institutions gave their support.

Since the late nineteenth century, Black classical Chicago had exhibited these dynamics of exchange, advocacy, and patronage. They transpired in the visits of nineteenth-century touring jubilee singing groups and societies whose concertized Negro Spirituals reclaimed Black vernacular narratives, in the prototypical Black music clubs of the 1900s, in the founding of the Coleridge-Taylor School of Music and Holt's initial institution-building through the 1910s, in NANM's and the CMA's deepening commitment to composers and artists through the 1920s, in Price's folk-infused symphonies of the 1930s and '40s, and in Margaret Bonds's emergence as a purveyor of all that had come before her. In the making of a Black transnational modernism, all roads led to Chicago.

Sounding Black Classical Chicago

Classical music's firm entry into Black associational and institutional life in Chicago and wider Illinois toward the end of the nineteenth century was inextricably tied to the musical development of the Negro Spiritual from its folk origins to a concertized genre, as well as to the emergent genre's increasingly commercial performance contexts and growing cultural capital. Its journey from "the riverboats, fields, praise houses, and camp meetings" of its folk origins to the concert hall "required considerable musical and cultural translation," notes Sandra Jean Graham—a feat embedded in the legacy of the Fisk Jubilee Singers.[31]

In 1886, the Fisk Jubilee Singers performed at Central Music Hall in downtown Chicago to a large audience. With their hugely popular tours, not only in the United States but also overseas, the Fisk Jubilee Singers extended the frontiers of sociocultural possibility. Deeply inspired by their impact and reach, a number of new jubilee singing groups subsequently formed across Illinois and other states, with the Negro Spirituals constituting the bulk of their repertoire and Chicago proving a popular destination on national tours. Behind such local events lay the impresarial advocacy of Black classical Chicago. As recorded in Arna Bontemps and Robert Lucas's contributions to the mid-twentieth-century study *The Negro in Illinois*, "Concerts sponsored by churches and other organizations were commonplace." For example, "in 1875, Bethel A. M. E. Church sponsored a 'grand jubilee concert and tableaux' at Burlington Hall in Chicago," another downtown location, and "the Louise Cowen Concert Combination, 'a troupe of colored singers,' was presented at Quinn Chapel on Fourth Avenue in 1879."[32] As some of the earliest cornerstones of Black civic and musical life in Chicago, Bethel African Methodist Episcopal Church and Quinn Chapel (of the same denomination) were forerunners of the ways in which an increasing number of Black churches on the South Side (which would come to include South Park Methodist Episcopal Church, Grace Presbyterian Church, etc.) could be counted on as dependable spaces or sponsors in the Black concert circuit for international stars (e.g., Roland Hayes and Hazel Harrison) as well as local artists in need of a platform.

A mix of home-grown talents and high-profile visitors shaped Black concert culture in Chicago through the second half of the nineteenth century. Out of this climate grew the Chicago Choral Study Club, which was, alongside Arthur A. Brown's Chicago Umbrian Glee Club, one of Black Chicago's earliest music societies. Founded somewhere between 1895 and 1898, the Choral Study Club at Olivet Baptist Church "was organized to create a desire for better music among Chicago Negroes and to render musical numbers of a higher type." The "higher type" referred to the classical tradition, as opposed to popular or vernacular music genres, and distinguished the club as a purveyor of "high culture" in keeping with the entwined rhetoric of respectability and racial uplift. The Chicago Choral Study Club sought to perform "some of the most difficult pieces of music including Handel's 'Messiah' and [Albert Robert] Gaul's 'Holy City,'" showing its readiness to compete with the classical mainstream. However, members of the club were not mere imitators. They were innovators as one of the first organizations to champion the music of Coleridge-Taylor. Their repertoire included his *Bon-Bon Suite* as well as "The Death of Minnehaha" and "Hiawatha's Wedding Feast" from the composer's hugely popular *Scenes from the Song of Hiawatha by Henry Wadsworth Longfellow*, op. 30.[33] Furthermore, the club brought Coleridge-Taylor to Chicago to direct their performance of *Hiawatha*.[34]

The club was largely credited as the creation of its inaugural director, Pedro T. Tinsley, overshadowing the contributions of its less publicized cofounder Mattie Johnson Young. Remembered in her obituary as a "widely known clubwoman and widow of the late George H. Young, pioneer barber of the South Side," Young had been a fixture in Black Chicago's music and society circles. Born in Nettleton, Mississippi, and educated both in her home state and neighboring Tennessee, Young made her way to Chicago in May 1893.[35] This was the same month and year that Tinsley, as a member of the Apollo Music Club of Chicago, performed at the World's Columbian Exposition in a program called "Chicago Day."[36] Young's and Tinsley's paths quite possibly crossed there or, at the very least, immediately after because once Young settled in Chicago, she "soon became widely known in church and society circles."[37] Although underdocumented in the public record, Young's influence as a founding member of the Chicago Choral Study Club rippled through the South Side and beyond.

Over the next two decades, the Chicago Choral Study Club profoundly shaped the city's musical landscape, giving Black Chicagoans "opportunities that would have been lacking without its help," and exerting "an educational influence of great value."[38] The club performed throughout Chicago, not only in the local venues of the Black Metropolis but also in the downtown halls that they rented out when funds permitted. Entering white spaces was as essential as engaging Black civic spheres. This was one of the ways in which Race women and men strived to bridge the gulf generated by Chicago's segregated geography. They operated with the hope and belief that music could fill this void.

Among the Choral Study Club's members were "Old Chicago's most prominent musicians," including Gertrude Smith Jackson, John Gray Lucas, George W. Duncan, Martha A. Cole, Anita Patti Brown, Arthur A. Brown, Blanche Wright Page, Mabel Burton, Maude Roberts George, and Estella Bonds.[39] This was not a complete list but one that certainly represented "some highly musical people" on the South Side (as the Race scholar James Monroe Trotter might have put it).[40] As the collage of musical Race women presented toward the end of the previous chapter shows, Jackson had been deeply involved in Chicago's Black concert life since girlhood, blossoming into an active performer, churchwoman, and community organizer through the interwar period and shaping a similar path for her daughters Betty and Catherine. John Gray Lucas, aside from being Florence Price's uncle-in-law and one of Black Chicago's top practicing lawyers, was also a tenor. He performed in a variety of programs on the South Side as a soloist and choir member. He also organized programs, presented artists, wrote music criticism, and took on administrative roles in the CMA. Then there was "Chicago's noted prima donna" and "credit to her Race" Anita Patti Brown, and her husband, Arthur A. Brown, who "arranged and managed her concert tours [and] was founder and organizer of the famous Umbrian Glee club, one of Chicago's pioneer musical organizations."[41] As for George and Bonds, their paths as artists, advocates, and community-builders would remain intertwined through the years that followed. Unfortunately, the historical portraits of Duncan, Cole, and Burton are faintly drawn in the public record, but their Chicago Choral Study Club membership alludes to the breadth of these social networks. These members likely went on to join NANM and its local chapters, given the unifying and consolidatory purviews of the association and its regional branches. This was certainly the case for Jackson, Lucas, the Browns, Page, George, and Bonds.

Black concert life in turn-of-the-century Chicago coalesced around Race women's and Race men's collective ambitions to excel in the classical realm and exceed the limitations of Jim Crow. The Fisk Jubilee Singers signaled an important turning point in the presentation and reception of Black American folk song, while an emerging generation of African-descended composers and performers shaped their catalogs and repertoire to uplift the Race. The Chicago Choral Study Club, alongside other singing societies, performing arts schools, and music associations, provided much-needed platforms for local talent, of which there was a great deal. The South Side was a magnet for Black classical music–makers of all ages. But what this ever-growing community of practitioners needed now was an umbrella organization, comprehensive in scope, national in reach, and lasting in infrastructure. It also needed a larger-than-life character to lead the way.

A Renaissance Woman at Work

As she proclaimed a Chicago Renaissance, Nora Holt began to position herself at the crux of African American concert culture, not only in the Black Metropolis but in the wider United States. She was already known as a music critic, composer, performer, and scholar, but with the founding of NANM, Holt established herself as a clubwoman and community leader. Traces of her multifaceted path linger across the articles that she wrote for the *Chicago Defender* and her own *Music and Poetry* journal, charting the development of the association and her involvement in it. Holt believed that documenting NANM's early progress was paramount; she knew that "with the onward march of human progress, incidents both accidental and prepared come and go so quickly that the memory fails to accurately serve when a review of facts is needed."[42] As a result, she wrote to preserve a history of the behind-the-scenes activity that propelled so many early twentieth-century Black classical practitioners into the spotlight; it was a record of the unglamorous, even dangerous, but wholly necessary organizing work that is all too easily forgotten in favor of more public-facing individual, celebrity narratives. Holt's chronicles reveal the extent of her influence during this era, and when entwined with the contemporary commentary of Chicago residents and prominent NANM members Clara E. Hutchison and George Howard Hutchison (relation unknown), Marian Anderson's autobiographical reflections, and Doris Evans McGinty's documentary history of NANM, it becomes clear that Holt not only proclaimed a Chicago Renaissance but that she was one of the most influential voices of the movement.[43]

Through the 1910s, Black classical practitioners across the country had been crystallizing their vision for an institution that unified and uplifted their interconnected artistry and activism on a national scale. This materialized through the early organizing work of a cadre that represented a microcosmic who's who of the Black concert scene. On March 3, 1916, Clarence Cameron White called on Black composers and musicians across the United States to form a National Association of Negro Music Teachers. In the July 1921 issue of her *Music and Poetry* magazine, Holt documented that White envisioned the association as a means of "race unity and advancement" that would "[raise] the musical standard of the teaching profession of our race throughout this country" and offer "better instruction in music and a systematic means of improving the musical taste of the public." World War I temporarily halted White's efforts, but on October 22, 1918, Robert Nathaniel Dett picked up the cause and sent letters to interested parties explaining that unfavorable conditions had interfered with the proposed inaugural convention for the National Association of Negro Music Teachers; he wrote that it would therefore take place at a later date. There remained, however, a persistent need for a national organization.

Taking action three years on from White's initial meeting, Holt hosted a gathering of musicians at her home on 4405 South Prairie Avenue on March 12, 1919. She chronicled, with third-person critical distance in the pages of *Music and Poetry*, "In the spring, 1919, Nora Douglas Holt sent out letters to many prominent musicians in Chicago to attend a meeting at her home in honor of Clarence Cameron White, visiting artist, and to perfect plans to form a national, also a local organization of musicians. Sixteen famous artists of the city were present and Mrs. Holt presented her plans to hold the first annual convention in Chicago, which was heartily accepted by all present."[44] NANM historian McGinty writes that "the chief topic of conversation was the desirability of cooperation among black musicians over the nation." "Musical Unity" is what Holt called it in a *Chicago Defender* article that implored her colleagues across the country to join forces. Holt cautioned, "Two or more societies for the same purpose is perilous to the progress of each body, and the Race, being limited as to finished artists, cannot survive a division."[45] Knowing the stakes, Holt, during the meeting at her home, established a date for the first annual convention of what was to be known as NANM and cofounded the association in the process. Her columns gave necessary amplification to the ideas she had long sewn in her social spheres as an organizational leader.

Consistently proactive with her institution-building, Holt had, by 1918, already founded the CMA. She was its inaugural president, and under her leadership, the organization played a key role in establishing NANM. In her own words, "By personal letters, announcements through the *Chicago Defender*, and help from the Chicago Music Association, the plan [for NANM] was supported and financed."[46] McGinty further documents that the CMA had already "been promoting the idea of forming a national association" and that under Holt, the organization worked alongside a nascent group called the Temporary Organization of Negro Musicians and Artists "to take the necessary steps to set up a permanent organization."[47] According to CMA board member and NANM historian Clara E. Hutchison, "this temporary organization met in conjunction with the Chicago Music Association in the city of Chicago. I hear you say, 'I wonder why?' Well, the C.M.A. had themselves already begun a similar movement and were therefore quite eager and wholly willing to unite with other musicians in carrying forth this project."[48] Across the records of Holt, McGinty, and Hutchison, the portrait of Holt and the CMA spearheading efforts becomes increasingly apparent.

The elected officials of the temporary organization that Hutchison described included Henry L. Grant of Washington, D.C., president (and a past student and future director of Harriet Gibbs Marshall's Washington Conservatory of Music); Holt, vice president; Alice Carter Simmons of Alabama, secretary; H. P. B. "Fred" Johnson of Tennessee, treasurer; and T. Theodore Taylor of Chicago, publicity chair.[49] Although, absent from both Hutchison's and Holt's chronology, as McGinty points out, was the role of Harriet Gibbs Marshall. This omission was probably not a deliberate one but, perhaps more likely, evidence of the multiple and sometimes little-known threads that could be traced even further back through the type of big-picture retrospection that McGinty enacts.

In June 1906, Marshall voiced to pianist Gregoria Fraser Goins "a plan she had of having an association of Negro musicians who had had conservatory training." At Marshall's request, Goins wrote to a handful of the nation's most prominent practitioners, including Harry T. Burleigh, Maud Cuney Hare, and Emma Azalia Hackley, but to no avail. It took almost a decade for Marshall to find an enthusiastic audience and for a meeting to take place that would propel her vision into reality.

Around the time that White sent out letters to interested parties, Henry Grant called a meeting at Goins's home in D.C., but again, the attempt to galvanize a national association faltered. Goins sent out further letters and kept track of her progress, writing, "Spring of 1917, same notices went out; no answer. 1918; same notices, no answer. Spring 1919—They came!" Present at the meeting were concert artist Sidney Woodward of Florida; choral director J. Wesley Jones of Chicago; Robert Nathaniel Dett of Hampton, Virginia; soprano Florence Cole Talbert of Tennessee; father and son (and violinist and organist, respectively) Edward Hill Sr. and Edward Hill Jr. of Philadelphia; and several local artists from Washington, D.C., that included Mary Europe (the sister of bandleader James Reese Europe).[50] This cohort spanned vast geographies and varied accomplishments; such variety was exactly why a consolidation of efforts was needed.

Chicago held the solution. McGinty asserts, "If it was the Washington initiative that succeeded in setting the stage of the new organization, it was in Chicago that the first act opened." Chicago was not only the birthplace of NANM; it was also the host of the first annual convention; and as a result of the CMA, the Black Metropolis played a major role in shaping NANM's formative years.[51]

Figure 12. Wabash Avenue YMCA. Schomburg Center for Research in Black Culture, Jean Blackwell Hutson Research and Reference Division, New York Public Library. "Wabash Avenue Y.M.C.A." New York Public Library Digital Collections, https://digitalcollections.nypl.org/items/510d47de-4d77-a3d9 -e040-e00a18064a99.

The inaugural convention took place at the Wabash Avenue YMCA, also known as the "Y" (fig. 12). Located on 3763 South Wabash Avenue and built between 1911 and 1913 with the philanthropic boost of Julius Rosenwald, the Wabash YMCA became a vital part of community life in the Black Metropolis; its large assembly hall hosted a variety of events, meetings, and programs in aid of its surrounding neighborhood.[52] The CMA regularly assembled there. Additionally, it was the first home of the Chicago University of Music, founded in 1920 by Race woman and "protégé of the incomparable E. Azalia Hackley," Pauline James Lee.[53] The school later moved to Michigan Avenue and appears to have become the National Conservatory of Music, but its early history shows the extent to which the Wabash YMCA was integral to a number of musical enterprises on the South Side in the early decades of the twentieth century.

The inaugural NANM convention took place on July 29–31, 1919. Henry L. Grant was the founding president (serving from 1919 to 1922) and Holt

Figure 13. A street view of the aftermath of a bomb thrown into a building on 3365 Indiana Avenue. Schomburg Center for Research in Black Culture, Jean Blackwell Hutson Research and Reference Division, New York Public Library. "Damage done by a bomb, thrown into a building at 3365 Indiana Avenue, occupied by Negroes." New York Public Library Digital Collections, https://digitalcollections.nypl.org/items/510d47df-1efc-a3d9-e040-e00a18064a99.

was the organization's first vice president. The convention, however, ran through the Red Summer of 1919, so called after the spate of white terror that claimed countless Black lives across numerous cities and towns, including Chicago, Washington, D.C., and Elaine, Arkansas, reaching devastating pinnacles nationwide.

In Chicago, violence erupted following an incident on July 27 during which a seventeen-year-old boy named Eugene Williams waded into the so-called whites-only section of Twenty-Ninth Street beach. A white mob pelted Williams with rocks until he drowned; that he transgressed this watery color line warranted punishment, as far as his attackers were concerned. Williams's death blew the lid off the already simmering racial tensions between Black and white Chicagoans. But in the subsequent protest, the South Side suffered a great deal further; many died, many more were injured, and Black homes and businesses went up in flames at the hands of torch-wielding and bomb-throwing white rioters (figs. 13 and 14).

Figure 14. An interior view of the aftermath of a bomb thrown into a building on 3365 Indiana Avenue. Schomburg Center for Research in Black Culture, Jean Blackwell Hutson Research and Reference Division, New York Public Library. "Damage done by a bomb, thrown into a building at 3365 Indiana Avenue, occupied by Negroes; a six-year-old Negro child was killed." New York Public Library Digital Collections, https://digitalcollections.nypl.org/items/510d47df-1efd-a3d9-e040-e00a18064a99.

Two days after Williams's murder, race riots raged on near NANM's point of assembly, which, Earl Calloway writes, "prevented most of the musicians from getting through from the Dearborn Street Station."[54] Numbers were affected; some attendees were delayed, while others were absent altogether.[55] It was a reminder of the violence and terror that loomed over Black lives, regardless of intraracial class distinctions. But could NANM afford to delay any further? Three years had already elapsed since the idea was first discussed, with seismic events such as World War I stalling efforts toward its formation. The gravity of the 1919 Chicago race riots could not be underplayed. But NANM's organizers resolved to push through because if not now, then when?

A decade on, Clara Hutchison reflected, "Those of us who were fortunate enough to be present at this joint meeting can recall the din and uproar of a city shaken and torn by rioting that prevented many of the musicians who were in the city from attending the sessions at the Y.M.C.A., which was located in the midst of the turbulent section. However, all musicians who were enabled to reach the 'Y' were pressed into service."[56] Further echoing the great sense of duty that members felt in pressing forward were the remembrances of CMA and NANM treasurer George Howard Hutchison: "They met at the Wabash Avenue YMCA during the hectic days of a riot at the close of the war, yet they, like brave soldiers, had courage and faith that all would be well with them, and carried on in the name of music and formed the NATIONAL ASSOCIATION OF NEGRO MUSICIANS."[57]

Holt similarly recollected, "Despite chaotic conditions and complete suspension of surface and elevated service, Chicago and the visiting musicians met at the Y.M.C.A. and perfected the organization of a National Association of Negro Musicians." She continued, "Lack of transportation caused all social and entertainment preparations to be abandoned so the concert planned by the Chicago local [i.e., the CMA] to be given on Wednesday evening at Grace [Presbyterian] church was presented in the assembly hall of the 'Y.' Those fortunate enough to be present enjoyed a concert which has no precedent in the history of Negro musicians. Each participant was a star and each star an artist." And amid the calamitous violence that raged in the streets, was a contralto voice that cut through the riotous noise—that of Marian Anderson's.

As Holt recalled, "The greatest height was reached when Marian Anderson, a high school girl, exhibited a voice equal to that of Rosa Raisa, the wonderful contralto of the Chicago Grand Opera Company, and every one stood and acclaimed her with cries of bravo and *bis*, while tears of joy were in the eyes of many of the musicians who felt that the dawn of a new era in music has arisen for our people."[58] Such was the grand impression made by the young Anderson that Holt, chair of the NANM scholarship fund, awarded her as its first and highly deserving beneficiary. Clara Hutchison was "one of the association's first contributors to the scholarship fund"; she recalled how Anderson "made history at this Convention":

> Her singing was met with such an ovation that the walls of the Y.M.C.A. reverberated the echo. Miss Anderson was at once elected to be the recipient of the first scholarship. In less time than it takes to tell it, pledges reached the amount of $155. Nora Douglas Holt led the list with a pledge of $50. Over twenty dollars in cash was collected.[59]

Despite a notable variation in the purported funds raised, George Hutchison also recalled how "among the trail-blazing delegates was an unassuming girl choir member from a Philadelphia church." With the first note, it seemed, "her exceptional talent was at once recognized and the neat sum of four hundred dollars was quickly subscribed to help further her studies."[60] Whether it was $155 or $400, NANM's scholarship fund was supposed to set Anderson on a similar path to that of pianist Helen Hagan; members hoped that Anderson would attend the Yale School of Music. This would therefore allow Anderson to move on from the private studio of Giuseppe Boghetti in her local Philadelphia and into the prestigious heights of an Ivy League education. But evidently, this was not meant to be. In fact, NANM's limited finances would serendipitously set the contralto on another path, leading to prestigious heights of her own making. As Anderson reminisced,

> I might not have spent so much time with [Mr. Boghetti] if a plan projected in Chicago had worked out. I happened to be in that city during a convention of the National Association of Negro Musicians, a rather strong organization with branches in some twenty-five states. One afternoon I sang. As soon as I finished—indeed, while I was still in the room—someone rose to make a motion that the association should help me with my musical education. The motion was seconded. People began raising their hands and pledging certain sums. Soon there were pledges of about a thousand dollars. . . . It was agreed that I should try for the Yale School of Music. I went back to Philadelphia and filled out an application, which was then forwarded to a member of the organization who had been assigned to complete the arrangements. Yale accepted the application. Unhappily, not all of the pledges were redeemed, and at the start of the school term there were not enough funds in hand to pay the tuition. Whatever was raised was turned over to Mr. Boghetti. It seemed to be ordained that I should remain with him.[61]

Anderson studied under Boghetti until his death in 1941, with NANM's well-intentioned efforts inadvertently affirming the trajectory that she was already on. In her autobiography, Anderson emphasized that she would not have had it any other way.

For all its shortcomings, NANM was a project in posterity—a factor that fueled its formation against the harrowing circumstances of the 1919 Chicago race riots. Holt reiterated NANM's commitment to generational uplift in her assessment of the association two years on, writing,

> The national [i.e., National Association of Negro Musicians] today extends its arms to all sincere musicians to join with us in our effort to build a sound foundation for our music and musicians. This we must do in order to leave monumental examples for coming generations.[62]

On the one hand, the organization, as McGinty recognizes, "could not avoid being considered an elitist organization" given its focus on classical music and affiliation with high-profile musicians from the outset, such as Clarence Cameron White, Robert Nathaniel Dett, and Harriet Gibbs Marshall. However, NANM was deeply rooted in on-the-ground engagement and community-building. According to McGinty, "Close observation would probably show that the ordinary musician, the teacher in a small studio or the church organist, actually gave as much or more to support NANM in its early period of growth than did the prominent artist or academician." McGinty argues further that "the opportunity for participation by musicians on several different levels and in different spheres was a crucial factor in the support and nurturing of NANM."[63] Although complicated by NANM's financial shortcomings, Anderson's involvement and experience with the organization as an up-and-coming artist (rather than as a honed professional) was a case in point.

Holt paved the way for her peers and future generations as "the most visible and influential woman in early NANM leadership." Her engagements through the 1910s and '20s across the multiple facets of Black classical Chicago—as a composer, performer, promoter, public scholar, critic, founder, president, administrator, and more—helped centralize and consolidate a community of African-descended practitioners. Moreover, her foundational work with NANM and the CMA, along with the subsequent wave of African American female leadership, helped institutionalize Black women's activity and influence in the classical music sphere.

McGinty observes that "the twenties saw a general trend toward more participation by women in public life, and on the whole NANM was neither a leader nor an exception in this movement." She notes, nevertheless, that "it is rather remarkable that of the five NANM presidents who served between 1930 and 1942, four—Lillian LeMon [1930–33], Maude R. George [1933–35], Camille Nickerson [1935–38], and Mary Cardwell Dawson [1940–42]—were women. Among the NANM pioneers, the other woman who stands out is Harriet G. Marshall, a driving spirit behind the founding of the association." But it was not until Holt's involvement that Marshall's initial vision for a national association for conservatory-trained musicians and wider communities of classical music–makers was realized.

As an itinerant renaissance woman, however, Holt was regularly on the move. In 1922, she withdrew from her position at NANM and discontinued her role at the CMA, citing the death of her husband (George W. Holt) and other personal reasons for her departure.[64] New adventures beckoned, but in the years that comprised her Chicago era, Holt more than made her mark in the city and beyond, with her influence rippling through the careers of Philadelphia's Marian Anderson and Chicago's innumerable adopted and homegrown talents. To trace these trajectories is therefore to identify Holt's foundational work—especially the reception she hosted at her South Side home on the March 12, 1919—as a time and space in which the past, present, and future of African American concert culture coalesced. As Holt herself reflected, no doubt with these events in mind, "In a musical way, the year 1919 has been, and bids fair to be, one of Chicago's most progressive, because of many new ventures, successfully launched, and a growing interest of music givers, music venders and music lovers."[65] Chicago's renaissance was well underway.

Coda

The year 1927 witnesses the well-earned recognition of Black classical Chicago in a volume titled *The Negro in Chicago, 1779–1927*. Its pages chart and celebrate almost a century and a half of Black "educational, economic, social, civic and commercial life" on the South Side and beyond. Facilitated by the "encouragement and unstinted support" of the Wabash Avenue YMCA, familiar Race women such as Ida B. Wells-Barnett and Elizabeth Lindsay Davis, and prominent Black publications like the *Chicago Defender* and *The Crisis*, the volume illuminates the shifting cultural composition of the Black Metropolis, encompassing the transformative work of its key players and the political functions of its Black-built institutions.[66] The past documented in this tome underpins the future that Florence Price, upon her Chicago arrival, will create thereafter.

In the same year that *The Negro in Chicago* is published, Price and her family prepare to join the city's influx of southern newcomers, riding the wave of the Great Migration. Price additionally embarks on summer courses in orchestration and public school music methods at the Chicago Musical College, deepening her commitment to a life of composition and pedagogy and steadily rooting herself in the city's classical music scene.[67] With the growth of her social circles and artistic networks, Price is likely aware that Holt is also in town that summer.

Fresh from her studies at the American Conservatory at Fontainebleau as well as from her induction into Parisian nightlife as a performer and hostess orbiting the same venues as Josephine Baker, Holt returns to Chicago in the midst of a new and even more glamorous era.[68] Gone are her darker tresses in favor of a blonde look that allows her to falsely brand herself as Creole and play up her exoticism to European audiences who are none the wiser (fig. 15). "These French are too excitable to be stable," she writes in a letter to confidant and Harlem Renaissance patron Carl Van Vechten, as if laughing through the page at the ignorance of her French devotees.[69]

Figure 15. Nora Douglas Holt, October 1926. Photographs of Prominent African Americans, James Weldon Johnson Collection in the Yale Collection of American Literature, Beinecke Rare Book and Manuscript Library. Used with permission of the Carl Van Vechten estate.

Holt's time away only enhances her celebrity at home, making her the ideal personality to launch "the finest club, white or colored, in the city of Chicago." Situated on Thirty-Fifth Street—"the heart of the nightlife district" with which Forty-Seventh Street will later compete—the Apex Club opens on July 8, 1927. Holt's affiliation with Van Vechten helps drum up the predominance of white attendees. But her own star power shines just as bright. She is "resplendent in jewels and untiring in her attention to the scores of guests" that pour through the doors.[70] She performs this role with ease, making it all the more remarkable how over the course of her career, her identities never displace one another. She remains a non-conformist renaissance woman in her ability to move so fluently back and forth between clubwoman and club hostess, Creole chanteuse and Race composer-pianist-critic, and erudite scholar and outgoing socialite.

Although another multifaceted renaissance woman, George continues to cultivate her influence behind the scenes rather than in the spotlight compared to Holt. Several months after Holt's club opening, George coordinates the music program for a cultural series called Negro in Art Week—an event that, as Race man E. Franklin Frazier retrospectively boasts, would show Chicago's "cultural rival" of New York "what her artists could do."[71] With the Art Institute of Chicago as its venue, the exhibition spans from November 16 to December 1 and includes the works of Charles C. Dawson, Henry Tanner, Edmonia Lewis, William A. Harper, William McKnight Farrow, William Edouard Scott, Hale Woodruff, Arthur Diggs, Edward A. Hadeston, and other Black Renaissance artists.[72] Held under the auspices of the predominantly white Chicago Woman's Club, Negro in Art Week materializes out of "the belief that a knowledge of the accomplishment of the Negro in various forms of art would improve the relations between the two races."[73] In this sense, George's endeavors are not so different from Holt's hostess role at the Apex Club. Whether engaging patrons in concert halls or nightclubs, the intersections of both George's and Holt's lived experiences compel them to foster a more harmonious social sphere in all that they do.

George extends the event's artistic purview with a riveting showcase of Black classical talent and Race women's contributions. The "climax of the week," according to Cary B. Lewis's newspaper report, is "Friday night [December 2] at Orchestra Hall where the wealth of the city" will hear the Fisk Jubilee Singers, pianist Hazel Harrison, violinist Clarence Cameron White accompanied by T. Theodore Taylor, and soprano Lillian Evanti accompanied by "Chicago's own brilliant young" Race woman pianist Goldie Guy Martin.[74] After the concert (for which tickets may be purchased from the Orchestra Hall box office or from George directly at her home on 3231 Vernon Avenue), George will host a reception for the artists involved at the New Vincennes Hotel of which Race woman Mrs. Elizabeth Barnett Lewis is the proprietor.[75]

Pulling together Black and white patrons—such as the Abbotts, James A. Mundy, Mr. and Mrs. J Wesley Jones, Mr. and Mrs. Herman Devries, Dr. and Mrs. C. George Hall (of the South Side's Provident Hospital), and Mr. and Mrs. Harold L. Ickes (soon to be of the Franklin D. Roosevelt administration)—George exercises her social and civic influence to produce a program that will be roundly praised across the city's Black and white presses.[76] However, if the Negro in Art Week is somewhat undermined by its fleeting presence as a relatively short affair with no sign of recurrence, as well as by the overarching framework of white women's paternalism and patronage, then *The Negro in Chicago* offers a substantial and enduring counter with a document that restores Black authorship of Black accomplishment.

The volume spotlights a number of nationally known artists, such as Burleigh, Cook, Coleridge-Taylor, Dett, Clarence Cameron White, Melville Charlton, Carl Rossini Diton, J. Rosamond Johnson, Alice Carter Simmons, Camille Nickerson, Lillian Evanti, Henry L. Grant, and of course, Roland Hayes—the tenor whose mellifluous tones and aspirational aura led Holt to proclaim a Chicago Renaissance a decade ago. However, a great deal of space is dedicated to Black classical Chicago and the institutions and individuals that make it.

Listed are the Coleridge-Taylor School and Pauline J. Lee's National Conservatory of Music (formerly the Chicago University of Music), both of which go on to inspire Estella and Margaret Bonds's Allied Arts Academy (founded in 1938) and Herman Billingsly's Clarence Cameron White School of Music (founded in 1941). Also cited are organizations such as the Chicago Umbrian Glee Club, the Choral Study Club, and the CMA. Mentioned, too, is the R. Nathaniel Dett Club of Music and Allied Arts, founded on February 5, 1922, by a group of young female Chicago Musical College students. The Dett Club—named so with the composer's blessing under the condition that members "pledge themselves to always uphold the standards of good music"—is born after its founders have their applications to the more socially exclusive CMA rejected on account of their age, inexperience, and apparently, unsatisfactory preparation for the life of a professional concert artist. But they soon disprove these claims, especially when the Dett Club becomes a chartered member of NANM in 1922, makes its mark in this monumental 1927 volume, attracts the membership of Price in 1928, and wins the approval of the CMA's future president, Maude Roberts George.[77]

George is named under "Celebrities in Chicago's Old Musical World," a section that includes "old-timers" like Pedro T. Tinsley, Gertrude Smith Jackson, Martha B. Anderson, and Anita Patti Brown. Other noted fixtures of the city's classical music scene are Hazel Harrison, J. Wesley Jones (Holt's CMA presidential successor), Florence Cole Talbert, Estella Bonds, and Nora Douglas Holt, who is described as the first president of NANM—a detail that is not entirely accurate but nevertheless acknowledges her foundational role. Further names from this South Side network are listed too, such as pianist Goldie Guy Martin, bandleader Major N. Clark Smith, choral director James A. Mundy, violinist Walter Dyett, and Dyett's future wife, pianist Neota McCurdy—many of whom will become close collaborators of Price.

But what of Black classical Chicago's future? Margaret Bonds appears under the subheading "Promising Young Artists." Her generation represents the sons and daughters of the Black Chicago Renaissance—that is, those who will aspire toward Price's compositional accomplishments, absorb the nurturing energies of Estella Bonds's salon, advance under the patronage of Maude Roberts George, and bask in the legacy of the itinerant Nora Holt. These are the sons and daughters who will write the next chapter of the "Negro in Chicago" and inherit this Black classical metropolis, built on the cultural, social, and civic enterprise of those who came before.[78]

3

The Black Classical Metropolis

The Negro in Music, the Annual All Colored Composers Concerts, and the Roland Hayes recital that led Nora Holt to proclaim a Chicago renaissance were not only reflections of aesthetic currents in the art world at large but also demonstrative of the ideologies and institutions that stimulated public culture on the South Side. And Ballet Night was no exception.

Ballet Night took place on June 16, 1933. It was the third event in a series of "notable programs" under the Chicago World's Fair that set out to "epitomize in clear outline the progress of our musical culture from 1833 to 1933."[1] Unlike the Negro in Music that took place the night before, Ballet Night was less an overt showcase of the Race and more a potpourri of musical styles, genres, and eras. But if the program was supposed to sound a chronology or cartography of American musical progress, it certainly fell short. In fact, Ballet Night's critical reception in Chicago's white press reflected the doggedly colonial ways in which Eurocentric agents of the classical mainstream largely saw and heard their United States. To them, the South Side—and Black America at large—was as remote and exotic as the mythical Martinique portrayed in Ballet Night's finale: William Grant Still's *La guiablesse*.

From its interracial cast to its cinematic score, almost everything about the closing item seemed to break the mold. In this Chicago premiere of Still's ballet, Ruth Page—a white choreographer in the midst of her "Black period"—performed as the fair siren, *la guiablesse*.[2] Page's text on Still's piano reduction of the score describes *la guiablesse* as "a devilish creature who appears in the guise of a beautiful woman for the purpose of luring the man susceptible to her charms to his death."[3] African American dancers comprised the remaining ensemble. Jack Smith played Adou, the male victim. In the role of Adou's lover, the village maiden Yzore, was Katherine Dunham. Multifaceted in her practice, Dunham was not only a dancer, but (in the words of her daughter, Marie-Christine Dunham Pratt) an anthropologist, scholar, author, activist, humanist, and "innovative choreographer" as the "creator of the Dunham Technique, which changed the world of modern dance."[4]

In working with Dunham and Still, whose African- and Caribbean-inspired choreographies and compositions (respectively) stemmed from the Black transnational modernism of their craft, Page evidently strived to steer her vision away from the dangers of minstrel-esque caricature. Yet, given the modernist zeitgeist, not all would have picked up on the nuances of her project. As Glenn Dillard Gunn and Herman Devries showed through their criticism, white mainstream audiences would have largely heard and seen *La guiablesse* through primitivism's reductive lens.

Gunn remarked, "The music possesses what sounds to Western ears to be authentic African flavor. It is surprisingly rich in melody, realizes the expected rhythmic impulse, is cleverly set for the orchestra and was eagerly yet seriously translated into the dance by the Negro ballet."[5] That rich melodies in a Black diasporic work—not to mention under the hand of a composer and conductor who had more than made his mark in classical music by this time—could be a surprise to Gunn evidences the ways in which Blackness remained an othering criterion, constantly having to prove itself and drawing astonishment each and every time it did.

Similarly othering overtones characterized Devries comments on the Black dancers, all of whom hailed from the South Side. He wrote, "The ballet is danced well by trained members of Chicago's literary and 'dance-minded' Negro colony, and very well too, with remarkable understanding of the African atmosphere intended by the composer and the choreographer."[6] The "Negro colony" to which Devries referred was Bronzeville, the heart of the Black Metropolis. And what "Western" (read white) ears heard was not the "authentic African flavor" or "African atmosphere" but a Black Renaissance imaginary—a *Fantasie Nègre*, as some of Price's compositions put it—where African-descended practitioners reclaimed the vastness of their heritage with imaginings and reimaginings that possessed both forward-looking creative flair and reverence for the past.

Page knew to look beyond her northside neighborhood to realize her modernist vision for *La guiablesse*, as Liesl Olson observes. Page recognized that "the creative ferment of the city could be found in Bronzeville," a place, Olson describes, where inhabitants "were emboldened by their community's quest for economic and cultural self-determination" and "ran key institutions like the newspapers, the library and a hospital [i.e.,

Provident Hospital]."[7] Dunham and her fellow dancers were not passive individuals plucked by Page out of Chicago's Black colony of artists. They were agents of the Black Renaissance and their artistry and activism—just like that of their musical counterparts—were steeped in the geography of the Black Metropolis.

This chapter therefore nuances Devries's depiction of a "Negro colony," building on the work of St. Clair Drake and Horace R. Cayton to conceptualize and map what I call the Black classical metropolis. In articulating a Black classical metropolis, I am departing from analyses of Black intellectual and creative life in Chicago that focus almost exclusively on popular culture. My insertion of "classical" between "Black" and "Metropolis" reinforces the way in which I conceive of Black concert culture's integral function in the making of this geography. The Black classical metropolis did not exist in the shadows or on the periphery of a Black public sphere. It operated at the heart of it.

I use this term to reflect a geography that existed at the intersections of concert artistry and social advocacy, in the stifling parameters of the Black Belt, and along the liberatory lines of musical Race women's endeavors. This is the perspective from which I think through the Dunham-Still-Page collaboration in Ballet Night and through which I examine the sites, systems, and of course, sisterhoods that shaped and nurtured public culture on the South Side. Engaging Martha S. Jones's framing of "public culture" as "an expansive rubric that encompasses the deliberations of African Americans within their own institutions and their engagements with overlapping publics," I am therefore interested in the "public culture of institutions and ideas" that comprised the Black classical metropolis.[8]

Drawing in a greater cast, I interweave the dance ambitions of Dunham and the political journey of Marjorie Stewart Joyner with the work and worksites of the South Side impresarios. Joyner offers somewhat of a detour. Although a graduate of the Chicago Musical College, she was not an active practitioner in the arts, but she certainly knew the power of those who were. And as a Race woman beautician campaigning to become the mayor of Bronzeville, it was to this community—specifically Maude Roberts George and the Chicago Music Association (CMA)—that she turned for support. Her story therefore illuminates more of these overlapping publics and the interconnected areas of Black womanhood, beauty culture, classical music, and political autonomy.

Like Dunham in the realm of dance and George in the realm of music, Joyner drew on her expertise in the realm of beauty (which, like dance and music, was also a traditional area of feminine agency) to enact greater societal change. Bringing Joyner into the fold, then, I challenge the ways in which Gunn and Devries positioned artists and activists of the South Side as siloed "others." Moreover, I argue that the physical and psychic spaces of the Black classical metropolis empowered an array of Race women to assert their right to the wider city.

Recovering Realms of Institutions and Ideas

Undergirding the so-called Black colony and its intellectual and creative cultural outputs—whether staged in South Side venues or downtown concert halls—were realms of ideas with boundless potential and realms of institutions with bounded realities. Devries alluded to the ideological strand when he spoke of "Chicago's literary and 'dance-minded' Negro colony." This description acknowledged Black Chicagoan's intellectual and creative cultural production (albeit through a reductive lens); and in citing the *mindedness* of a Black culturati, it also touched on an aspect of African American public culture that Martha S. Jones calls the "realm of ideas." This was a realm in which overlapping ideologies, energized by "a collective understanding of the issues of the day," generated "a community of interpretation." This was nowhere more salient than in the converging artistic- and political-mindedness of those who fueled the Black Chicago Renaissance. But what Devries barely scratched the surface of was the realm of institutions—that is, what Jones identifies as "bounded spaces whose parameters were defined to a significant degree by racism."[9] In addition to platforms like the Black press, political organizations, and other clubs, these institutions also encompassed the physical spaces that African Americans shared (e.g., the hospital, churches, schools, clubhouses, private homes, etc.).

Concerts such as Ballet Night signal deeper clues about the realms that flourished behind these programs, evidencing not only the nested narratives and intersecting ideologies of Black Chicago Renaissance agents but also revealing the topography of sites underlying their agency. Take, for example, Dunham, her company (the Negro Dance Group), and a particular program that took place on March 2 and 4, 1934, in which a variety of nested narratives, intersecting ideologies, and institutional sites could be found (fig. 16).

To begin with, Dunham founded and formalized the group "for the purpose of bringing to the concert stage not only the highest developments of classical, modern and character dancing, but also to express the folk themes and folk ballets."[10] Her interests in the latter—as both a scholar and performer—stemmed from her explorations into the expressive cultures of the African continent and diaspora, drawing many significant ideological

Figure 16. The Negro Dance Group 1934 promotional ephemera. Ann Barzel dance research collection Series 1: Subject Files, 1890s–2010, Dance-MS-Barzel, Research Special Collections, Newberry Library, Chicago.

parallels with the classical strand of the Black Chicago Renaissance, such as its uplift of Black vernacular traditions and its forging of a welcoming Black space on hostile terrain.

Dunham recalled, "Black dancers were not allowed to take classes in [white] studios in the '30s. I started a school because there was no place for blacks to study dance. I was the first to open the way for black dancers and I was the first to form a black dance company."[11] In 1933, after an unsuccessful start downtown on Michigan Avenue (due to the racism of a building manager who did not want African Americans occupying the space), the school found its subsequent home in what Joanna Dee Das describes as "the 57th Street artists' colony in Hyde Park." But despite a successful launch party, which was attended by members of Black society and covered in the Black press of the *Chicago Bee*, its South Side geography ultimately cast Dunham's school in an inferior light, even to other Black Chicagoans. Das explains, "African American parents had been willing to take their children to classes on Michigan Avenue but not to the Hyde Park artists' colony on the South Side. Dropping their children off in the Loop was a status symbol and also a political statement, a challenge to white supremacist notions of who belonged on the Magnificent Mile. The Hyde Park artists' colony, a neighborhood of bohemian whites and a growing African American population, did not make the same statement."[12] But Dunham persevered with her South Side base. What is more, in entering interracial collaborations, Dunham could push through systemic barriers to gain greater access and opportunity for herself, her dancers, her students, and future generations of Black dancers. Dunham did not shrink her authority within these interracial collaborations; rather, she used them as stepping stones toward the realization of a vision without borders. These collaborations furthered Dunham's ambitions to, in her own words, "create a dance with an authentic base for black people" and to develop her anthropological work on continental and diasporic African dances into what would be known and internationally celebrated as the Dunham Technique.[13]

On the evening of March 2 and in an afternoon matinée on March 4, 1934, Dunham and her troupe performed at the Abraham Lincoln Center, under the direction of Russian ballet instructor Ludmilla "Luda" Paetz Speranzeva (fig. 17). This was the same venue where Maude Roberts George broke the color barrier with her vocal recital two decades earlier and similarly leveraged the support of her white instructor (Devries) to claim this downtown space.

The music for the dance program resembled the recitals of Black concert soloists who would often mix contemporary repertoire by African-descended composers with Spiritual arrangements and familiar names from the European canon. Samuel Coleridge-Taylor's "At the Dawn of Day" and "The Bamboula" (from *Twenty-Four Negro Melodies*, op. 59) accompanied the opening performances, followed by Margaret Bonds's art song "To a Brown Girl Dead" (from Countee Cullen's eponymous poem). Opening the second half of the program were arrangements of "Go Down Moses" and "Swing Low Sweet Chariot," Stravinsky's Berceuse from *L'oiseau de feu* (*The Firebird*), and Debussy's hugely popular "Golliwog's Cakewalk." If Dunham's other documented performances of "Golliwog's Cakewalk" were anything to go by, for which it was noted that the dancers wore

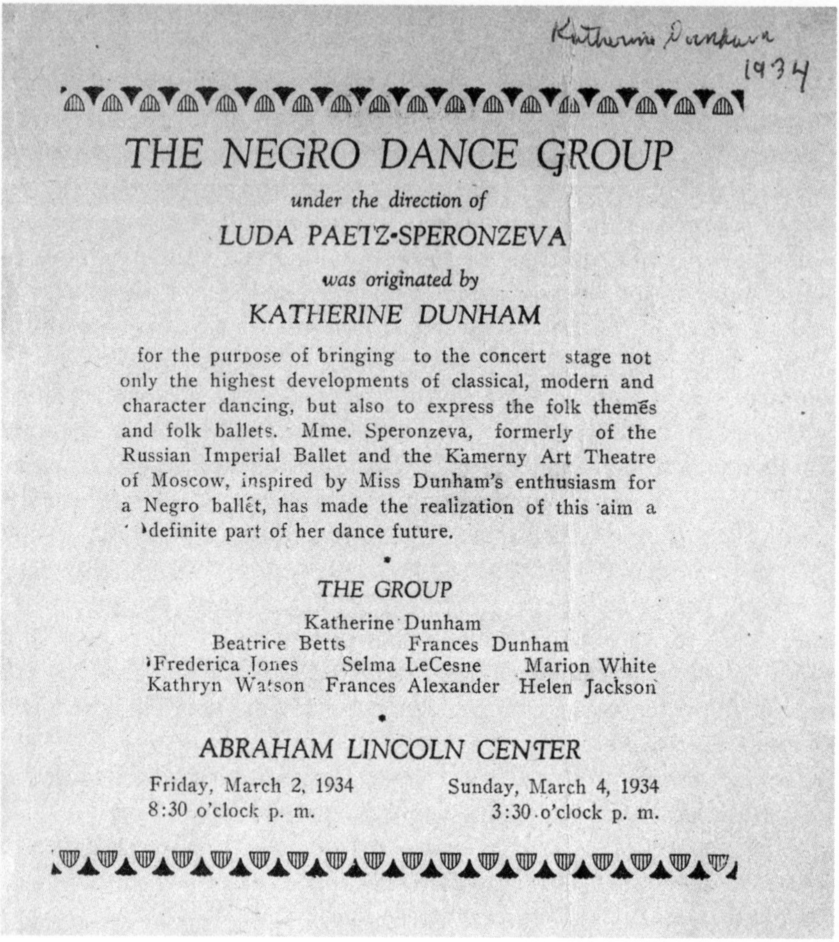

Katherine Dunham
1934

THE NEGRO DANCE GROUP

under the direction of

LUDA PAETZ-SPERONZEVA

was originated by

KATHERINE DUNHAM

for the purpose of bringing to the concert stage not
only the highest developments of classical, modern and
character dancing, but also to express the folk themes
and folk ballets. Mme. Speronzeva, formerly of the
Russian Imperial Ballet and the Kamerny Art Theatre
of Moscow, inspired by Miss Dunham's enthusiasm for
a Negro ballet, has made the realization of this aim a
definite part of her dance future.

•

THE GROUP

Katherine Dunham
Beatrice Betts   Frances Dunham
Frederica Jones   Selma LeCesne   Marion White
Kathryn Watson   Frances Alexander Helen Jackson

•

ABRAHAM LINCOLN CENTER

Friday, March 2, 1934   Sunday, March 4, 1934
8:30 o'clock p. m.   3:30 o'clock p. m.

Figure 17. The Negro Dance Group 1934 program. Cover page. Ann Barzel
dance research collection Series 1: Subject Files, 1890s–2010, Dance-MS-
Barzel, Research Special Collections, Newberry Library, Chicago.

"grotesque costume" when performing it, then this choreography may
have also subverted Debussy's musical minstrelsy. Here, the dancers may
have similarly drawn on the language of Signifyin(g), as they did for other
performances, engaging in what Henry Louis Gates Jr. theorizes as the
rhetorical tropes of irony, parody, and hyperbole in African American
expressive culture, as they revised and satirized Debussy's composition.[14]

In challenging primitivist projections, Dunham and her colleagues
aligned themselves with their composer and concert artist counterparts.
Furthermore, the connectivity across artistic spheres did not end there.

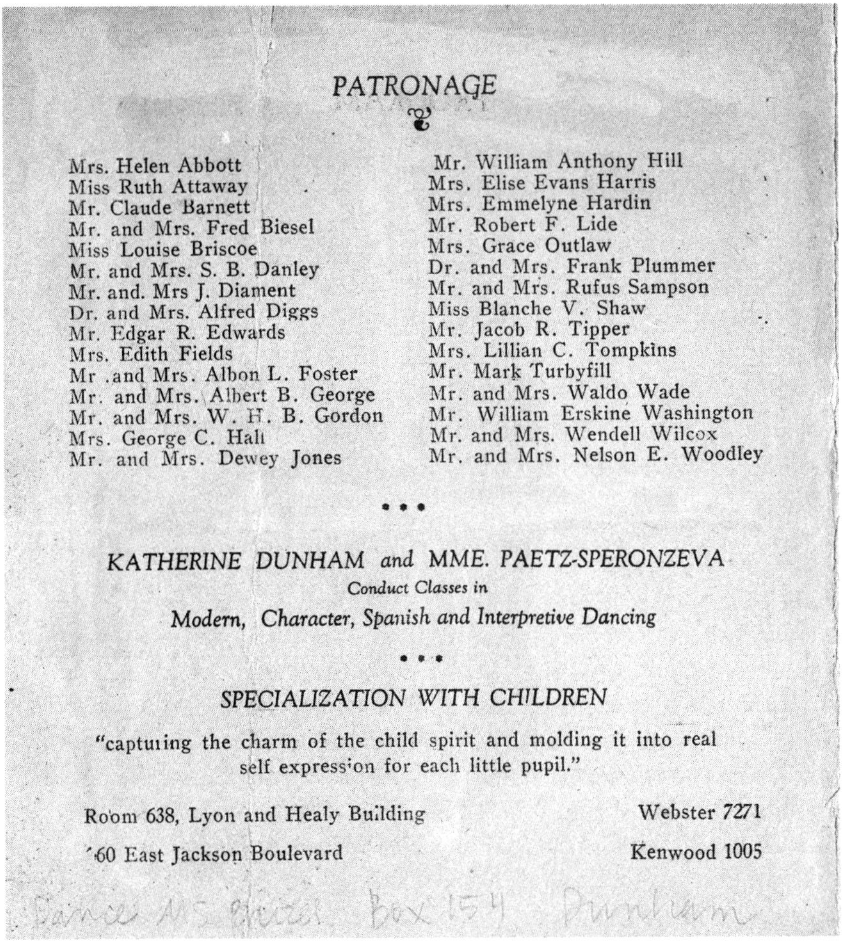

PATRONAGE

Mrs. Helen Abbott
Miss Ruth Attaway
Mr. Claude Barnett
Mr. and Mrs. Fred Biesel
Miss Louise Briscoe
Mr. and Mrs. S. B. Danley
Mr. and. Mrs J. Diament
Dr. and Mrs. Alfred Diggs
Mr. Edgar R. Edwards
Mrs. Edith Fields
Mr .and Mrs. Albon L. Foster
Mr. and Mrs. Albert B. George
Mr. and Mrs. W. H. B. Gordon
Mrs. George C. Hall
Mr. and Mrs. Dewey Jones

Mr. William Anthony Hill
Mrs. Elise Evans Harris
Mrs. Emmelyne Hardin
Mr. Robert F. Lide
Mrs. Grace Outlaw
Dr. and Mrs. Frank Plummer
Mr. and Mrs. Rufus Sampson
Miss Blanche V. Shaw
Mr. Jacob R. Tipper
Mrs. Lillian C. Tompkins
Mr. Mark Turbyfill
Mr. and Mrs. Waldo Wade
Mr. William Erskine Washington
Mr. and Mrs. Wendell Wilcox
Mr. and Mrs. Nelson E. Woodley

• • •

KATHERINE DUNHAM and MME. PAETZ-SPERONZEVA

Conduct Classes in

Modern, Character, Spanish and Interpretive Dancing

• • •

SPECIALIZATION WITH CHILDREN

"capturing the charm of the child spirit and molding it into real self expression for each little pupil."

Room 638, Lyon and Healy Building   Webster 7271

60 East Jackson Boulevard   Kenwood 1005

Figure 18. The Negro Dance Group 1934 program. Back page. Ann Barzel dance research collection Series 1: Subject Files, 1890s–2010, Dance-MS-Barzel, Research Special Collections, Newberry Library, Chicago.

The intersections between Black concert music and dance continued through to the event's sponsorship. Thirty names were listed in the program booklet under the title "Patronage." Sat among several luminaries of Black society and the wider art world were a cohort of South Side impresarios who knew Black Chicago's overlapping performance scenes well: Mrs. Helen Thornton Abbott, Mrs. Dewey Roscoe Jones (aka Faith Eleanor Jefferson Jones), Mrs. George C. Hall (aka Theodosia Brewer Hall), and Mrs. Albert B. George (aka Maude Roberts George) (fig. 18). Their listing bespoke the realms of ideas and institutions across Black Chicago, while also evidencing how Race women embraced the spotlight that their marital associations afforded them and yet redirected its focus to advance their own interests in arts, culture, social work, and patronage.

Mrs. Hall's and Mrs. Abbott's sponsorship of causes and concerts were part of a history of the two women upholding artistic life on the South Side and making newsworthy displays of it as society women. But with Dr. George Cleveland Hall being the chief of staff at Provident Hospital on the South Side, the largest Black hospital in the United States, and "Abbott" being synonymous with the *Chicago Defender*, Mrs. Hall and Mrs. Abbott were, by virtue of their names, inevitably tied to two cornerstones of Black institutional life in the city.[15] The same could be said for Mrs. Jones, whose husband was the *Chicago Defender*'s managing editor, but additionally Jones (a graduate of the University of Chicago, like Dunham) was known for her Alpha Kappa Alpha sorority membership and her vocation as a social worker with the United Charities of Chicago; evidently, the impetus for her patronage also stemmed from other institutions of giving and organizing that formed her own life's work.[16] And of course, Mrs. George, wife of the much-revered Judge Albert B. George, also embodied institutional affiliations by way of the patriarch as well as by way of her own social and civic engagements.

Race women's endorsements and sponsorships played significant roles in facilitating and securing Black artists' performances in Chicago's historically white spaces, as the careers of Dunham, Bonds, Price, and others show. But the nexus of their operations was the South Side. And even though its inhabitants had to contend with the mark of inferiority that stained even self-held perceptions of their geography, Black women persevered in building realms there, knowing that their perseverance would beget greater pride, and pride would lead to empowerment. These realms were an investment in themselves, their communities, and in the physical space that was, for better or for worse, their home. On the surface, concerts within and beyond the Black classical metropolis said little of Race women's movements and meeting points across this geography. But Dunham's stagings, Bonds's recitals, and Price's showcases were not born out of thin air or white imaginations. They were rooted in the physical and philosophical cartography of Black concert culture on the South Side; they bloomed from Race women's bounded institutions and boundless ideas. These concerts were proof of Race women's impresarial lives but were a drop in the ocean of activity that comprised their work across this geography.

Recovering the realms of institutions and ideas at the heart of Race women's work therefore necessitates tracing the sites where they came together. Before reaching concert halls and other performance spaces, it was out of homes and civic buildings (e.g., churches, schools, the Wabash Avenue YMCA, etc.) that networks of sponsorship and sisterhood took shape. These were the realms in which Race women formed committees and clubs at the service of their people, where they hosted teas and charity balls to raise awareness and funds for social concerns, and where they met or furnished the burgeoning and finished artists who would further uplift the Race and prove worthy of their patronage. And key to the communication and documentation of their efforts were the forms of printed media—club circulars, meeting minutes, newspaper columns, magazine articles, concert programs, music scores, and more—that charted the who, what, when, and where of musical Race women's influence in the Black Metropolis.

From News Columns to Clubs and Congregations

Formalized, improvisatory, enduring, and fleeting, musical Race women's hubs of activity were kaleidoscopic in range. But running through as common threads were their proclivities for public education, Black formalism, spiritual and religious grounding, and close sisterly support and bonding. These threads took further shape in the edifying music columns of the *Chicago Defender*, the founding and flourishing of music clubs, the steadfast nature of the Black church, and the intimate space of the home. What emerged was a prismatic tapestry that reworked the social image and cultural impression of the musical impresario and cultural tastemaker. Doris Evans McGinty observes, "The patronage of the press was all-important" and "the support and exposure given to artists by the black press and the black church made possible their development into mature artists and, for some of them, led to careers of national acclaim."[17] But if Race women's work in the press and church offered support via exposure, then their activities in the club and home offered support via shielding—that is, protecting artists from the harsh realities of Jim Crowism (as well as classical music's institutionalized white supremacy), and bolstering self-esteem with an interior personal and professional network of Black care and encouragement.

In addition to sponsoring programs on the South Side and beyond, music clubs like the National Association of Negro Musicians (NANM), the CMA, and the R. Nathaniel Dett Club turned their giving inward, with a philanthropic arm that embraced all members. This aspect stemmed from the influence of African American fraternalism, an early example of Black formalism that dated as far back as the eighteenth century. Over time, Black fraternalism grew to "enhance economic, philanthropic, and civic participation for their members." Tyrone McKinley Freeman explains, "The mutual aid fostered by black fraternals was substantial and grew out of their pooling of weekly membership dues. . . . They offered social insurance, an important asset during a time when white insurance companies regularly denied black people coverage. Such social insurance—which could have provided for burial expenses, payouts to . . . survivors, and benefits in case of inability to work due to sickness—were of particular interest to black women because of their economic roles in their families."[18] Fannie Barrier Williams documented how Black sororities drilled these aspects into their foundations. And Freeman shows how Madam C. J. Walker built these models into her profoundly matriarchal institution in which many of its agents were the primary breadwinners. Although not all of the CMA's female members were the economic heads of the household, the precarity of Depression-era Chicago made the absorption of Black fraternal and sororal practices a necessary part of its operations. Furthermore, that the CMA had a designated Sick Committee, which under the direction of its chair sent flowers, cards, and funds to unwell members and led visits to those whose illnesses placed them in Provident Hospital, reveals even more of who the South Side impresarios were in each other's private company.

The home was the least public area across Race women's sites of activity, but open invitations and the ready publication of private addresses in the Black press gave the home a community-facing dimension, therefore firmly locating it in the complex of African American public culture. Like the church in miniature, congregations of faith-filled, civic-minded folks drew great strength from the home as a tightly bound social space. Nevertheless, setting the home further apart from the newspaper columns, the club, and the church was the fact that the home was a space that was typically gendered female and pejoratively so. The home was supposed to function as a suppressive mechanism and "for many women, especially [middle- and upper-class] white women, the home became the space of deferred dreams and muted voices." However, for Black women, Tammy L. Kernodle observes, "the home and domestic sphere represented so much more." Race women's homes echoed the uplifting overtones of the Black press, embodied the fluid functions and significations of the Black church as a site of refuge and respite for those in need, and mirrored the camaraderie of the music club. But the home was also a site that nurtured more interior strategies of self-help and community-building. As Kernodle explains, "It was in living rooms and at kitchen tables that black women transferred the knowledge that was key to their survival and negotiation of white and male-centered spaces. Knowledge transference also extended to the work of cultivating and preserving different forms of cultural expression. In time, the poetry, art, dance and music they created and nurtured migrated beyond the walls of these homes, entered mainstream America's consciousness and radically redefined expressive culture." As sites of creative expression and intellectual discourse, many of these homes drew influence from nineteenth-century European salon culture. Black women, however, repurposed the culture to their own ends, fostering new definitions of what—and whom—the creative and intellectual space of the home salon could represent.[19]

Together, the institutions of the Black press, club, church, and home—though not the full extent of the impresarial landmarks and hallmarks that shaped the geography of this Black classical sisterhood—formed the cornerstones of musical Race women's organizing. During her Chicago years, Nora Holt cultivated and consolidated a civically engaged Black concert sphere across these four sites. As music critic for the *Chicago Defender*, Lawrence Schenbeck remarks on how her "pioneering music journalism combined reviews, encouragement of young artists, educational outreach, and coverage of both local and national events of interest to Chicago's black classical musicians," in conjunction with her further pioneering efforts (i.e., "the first to cover classical music on a regular basis for a black newspaper" and "the first woman to become part of that paper's regular writing staff"), ultimately "set the tone for classical-music coverage in the *Defender* for years to come."[20] That her first music column was published on the "Woman's Page" but her subsequent reports—often under the banner "News of the Music World"—appeared in the regular news pages is indicative of the kinds of cultural conversations and shifts she enacted.[21] Holt's reviews ranged from recitals in Black concert venues on the South Side to performances by the Chicago Opera Association and Chicago Symphony Orchestra, which, as Lucy Caplan observes of the latter, were "nominally open to black audiences but had very few black attendees in practice." Holt therefore claimed these predominantly white cultural spaces, not only for herself but on behalf of a Black readership that was unable to access these domains, yet eager to learn more. She also broke ground in the cultural institution of classical music criticism itself. Noting that "classical music criticism is often perceived as a male domain, and scholarship on this topic focuses almost exclusively on the contributions of white men," Caplan rightly puts forward that "Holt's status as a black female music critic" challenged and continues to challenge "dominant narratives of musical life in the United States on several fronts."[22] Without a doubt, Holt's music criticism rewrote the script of Western classical music and placed Black artists front and center.

Further extending her mission were her engagements (i.e., lectures and recitals) with Black churches on the South Side, most notably Grace Presbyterian Church. But in the necessary manner of shielding, Holt also brought the club and the home into the mix—building a "sound foundation for our music and musicians" with the former and offering "the hand of fellowship to members of the art world" in the latter through an open invitation that she published in the *Chicago Defender*.[23] Although 1930s Chicago was largely without her physical presence, Holt's earlier impact at the intersections of contemporary African American public culture, concert life, and music criticism remained. Her monumental examples of situational advocacy and binding were, by this time, baked into the fabric of the Black classical metropolis due to the work of those who followed in her wake.

When George became the *Chicago Defender*'s main music critic in 1922, she inherited Holt's "News of the Music World" columns.[24] By the 1930s, George's columns had started to include her home address and the instruction to "mail all articles for this column to 3231 Vernon Ave., Chicago." Her home could not hold all of Black Chicago's growing classical community, but through inviting practitioners to share their stories with her directly, George, like Holt, similarly extended the hand of fellowship to the art world, rendering the domestic sphere a site for "the community of music and the community of ideas," to quote Sheila Anne Jones.[25]

The growing popularity of "News of the Music World" paved the way for greater music coverage in the *Chicago Defender* and another themed feature, titled "In the Realm of Music." Neota L. McCurdy Dyett authored many articles under this banner. Like Holt's and George's pieces, Dyett's writings were a fascinating survey of the goings-on in the Black classical metropolis. And like that of Holt and George, Dyett's commentary stemmed from her own experiences at the heart of this activity. Dyett was president of the R. Nathaniel Dett Club, first from 1925 to 1927 and later from 1933 to 1937. During her first term, she made her home an official place of meeting to save on costs as the burgeoning club took flight.[26] Known for her "cheerful disposition," Dyett strived to be a firm friend to all of Black classical Chicago: "There was never any Chicago program when this unusual young woman failed to respond to an invitation for co-operation, personally, as an accompanist or arranging for the members of the Dett club to assist with numbers."[27] One such example of the latter is in her musical contribution to a reception that was held at the clubhouse of the CND Women's Club (or Chicago and Northern District Association of Colored Women's Clubs, in full) in honor of Beulah Mitchell Hill, another contributor to the "In the Realm of Music" columns.

Less is known about Hill, but it can similarly be assumed that her music columns reflected a world she knew intimately. Described as "an outstanding musician," Hill was also a seasoned journalist. Her earliest newspaper articles unfolded under the journalistic work of her late father. She then joined the newly founded *Chicago Bee* as a music critic. After its demise, she wrote for the *East Tennessee News* and later became society editor for the *Atlanta World* and *Scott Newspaper Syndicate*. She returned to Chicago in the summer of 1934 to join the *Chicago Defender*, and it seems her presence was greatly cherished because later that year, the CND Women's Club recognized her with a widely attended reception.[28] Led by the club's music committee chair (and former CMA president), Martha B. Mitchell Parks, the program featured mezzo-soprano Nannie Mae Glasco Williams and the CND Women's Club chorus under Parks's direction.[29] Maude Roberts George, Nannie Reed, Nannie Mae Strayhorn Reid, Major N. Clark Smith, and others "brought greetings from their various organizations" and "others who spoke briefly" included Anita Patti Brown, Margaret Bonds, Theodore Charles Stone, pianist T. Theodore Taylor, and Neota McCurdy Dyett. Toward the end of the reception, Ruth Henderson "presented flowers to the honored guest."[30] Held in high regard in the intersecting circles of musical and club life, it may be deduced that Hill, too, was deeply involved in the binding mission of the South Side impresarios. The work of George, Dyett, and Hill across the realms of institutions and ideas that underpinned the Black classical metropolis positioned them as some of the many inheritors of Holt's vision. Another inheritor was Estella Bonds.

Blest Be the Tie that Binds

"Bonds" by name and "bonds" by nature, Estella was, for many, the heart and soul of the Black classical metropolis. As Theodore Charles Stone reflected, "one could hardly think of music in Chicago without thinking of the Bonds family."[31] At one point, the Bonds family home on 6652 South Wabash Avenue comprised four generations of women: Mrs. Margaret "Mima" Bonds (also a musician and owner of their residence, widowed around the year 1910); Mrs. Bonds's foster mother; Mrs. Bonds's daughters, Estella (born in 1882), Victoria, and Helen; and her granddaughter, Margaret. The younger Margaret's father, physician and civic leader Dr. Monroe Alpheus Majors, moved into the Bonds family home for the brief duration of his marriage to Estella. As the author of *Noted Negro Women: Their Triumphs and Activities* (1893), he similarly reiterated the public uplift of Race womanhood (even though he was, in spite of his civic image, a polygamist with four wives, whose reputation as a "ladies' man" earned him the moniker "Big Daddy").[32] Helen Walker-Hill notes, "That Margaret chose her maternal name, Bonds, instead of her father's name, Majors, is an indication of the strong female influences in her family."[33] And with Estella being an engineer of dynamic sociocultural crossings both at home and in key local institutions, and Margaret a prodigy proudly claimed as "Black Chicago's own," the Bondses fostered a definition of family that encapsulated every deep and meaningful connection made in their South Side abode.[34]

The hand of fellowship was readily found in the Bonds family home. It extended to artists across various backgrounds, disciplines, and generations. Stone remembered the Bondses' home as "the only place where young black students could meet major international celebrities such as Roland Hayes or Lillian Evanti."[35] It was a hub of musical activity—"the meeting place for many of the aspiring young musicians and persons interested in other fields of endeavour," as well as an intimate venue for highly anticipated and hugely enjoyable Sunday afternoon musicales, some of which featured Evanti.[36] Estella was not especially well-off, but through extending the hand of fellowship across Chicago's artistic and intellectual scene, she created for Margaret an upbringing that was culturally abundant and educationally rich. As reported in the *California Aggie*, Estella "surrounded her child with almost every black musician of any importance. The Bonds circle of intimates included such august names as R. Nathaniel Dett, Camill[e] Nickerson, N. Clark Smith, Clarence Cameron White, William L. Dawson, and Florence Price. The latter two composers became Margaret Bonds' early teachers," as did Abbie Mitchell under whom, said Margaret, "I learned the importance of the marriage between words and music" and "had close analysis of the works of all the composers."[37]

In keeping with Stone's recollection of how the Bondses' home brought together those from all walks of life, the article also remarked that "the Bonds household, completely unbiased racially, entertained humanitarians of all racial and religious groups and the family of limited financial affluence gave Margaret—child prodigy—every opportunity for the study of music with the most eminent."[38] This, too, was Margaret's recollection of her childhood:

> From my mother, a church organist, Estella C. Bonds, I had actual physical contact with all the living composers of African descent. My mother had a collector's nose for anything that was artistic, and, a true woman of God, she lived the Sermon on the Mount. Her loaves and fish fed a multitude of pianists, singers, violinists and composers, and those who

were not in need of material food came for spiritual food. Under her wings, many a musician trusted, and she was my link with the Lord.[39]

Estella's was a life scantily documented despite her centrality to the making of the Black classical metropolis. But what is known is that her "cheery smile and pleasing disposition" drew so many in and as a passionate churchwoman, "modest and retiring in person," her spirituality guided her in all matters.[40] As Margaret reminisced, "Many a time when I would compete in a contest I'd say, 'Oh, God, please let me win. I know I'm not much good, but my mother is so good; please good God, let me win for her.' And generally I won." For Margaret, as well as countless others, Estella was a symbol of piety and goodness with her home rather like the church in microcosm.[41]

A poignant detail in her otherwise vague biography is how, during her term as CMA president (succeeding George in 1937), Estella introduced a new ritual to the proceedings. As was custom, members began with the Black National Anthem, "Lift Every Voice and Sing"—a means to orient the association in a grander, patriotic purpose and purview. Afterward, under Estella's direction, meetings adjourned with members rising to sing the hymn "Blest Be the Tie that Binds."[42] Similarly anthemic and inspirative, this hymn reminded members of their more localized, day-to-day interactions and of the spiritual resonances and implications reflected in their self-conduct. The hymn's opening verse showed how the hand of fellowship and realm of ideas (i.e., "kindred minds") mirrored a higher plane:

> Blest be the tie that binds
> Our hearts in Christian love;
> The fellowship of kindred minds
> Is like to that above.

The third stanza reinforced the interconnectivity of their inner lives, their empathy for one another's circumstances, and their vicariously felt experiences:

> We share our mutual woes,
> Our mutual burdens bear,
> And often for each other flows
> The sympathizing tear

The final verse depicted transcendence, from a binding that subjugated through "sorrow, toil, and pain, and sin" to a binding that liberated through "perfect love and friendship":

From sorrow, toil, and pain,
And sin we shall be free;
And perfect love and friendship reign
Through all eternity.

Estella's hymn epitomized all that the Black classical metropolis aspired to be: compassionately driven, collectively inspired, spiritually uplifted, and of course, musically filled. This is not to suggest that its various sites of activity were conflict-free zones; "the community of even being able to disagree," as Sheila Jones identifies, was inevitable and even alluded to in various minutes of meetings.[43]

In one instance, the CMA minutes for May 29, 1937 (under the term of outgoing president George) captured that Ruth Henderson "took issue" with Estella (who was chair of the board). A heated argument followed, which precipitated further disagreements between several other members, "who for the time disregarded all the parliamentary rules and ethical social conduct." Elections for the new president, which were supposed to take place on that night, had proved a source of contention, resulting in Estella being told by George (at the request of Martha B. Mitchell Parks) to temporarily vacate her position as chair. Estella agreed, and Parks assumed the role of chair, but tensions continued to run high and some members reached breaking point.

According to the minutes, George unsuccessfully tried to restore order. Another member, Iceler Petty Tittle, "expounded parliamentary usage to no avail." John Gray Lucas "sought to reason the matter out" with Theodore Charles Stone, the latter of whom "was considerably wrought up." Doing little to allay the growing resentment among members were the words of Louise Simmons who "eloquently yet firmly admonished some of the members for their unseemly behaviour" and antagonistically compared their conduct to "antics becoming monkeys rather than intelligent human beings." For all her eloquence, Simmons weaponized the rhetoric of Black inferiority and subhumanness against her own colleagues. Unsurprisingly, some "left the room amid the loud harangue" of the evening's affairs. The meeting subsequently came to a close, and the election was postponed to July 6 of the coming week.

By July 6, the dust had settled. Countering Simmons's invectives from the previous week, "Mrs. Estella Bonds spoke of the 'spirit of divine love'" and the election for the next CMA president went ahead. Bonds won the vote and before the meeting adjourned, she "called a special meeting of new elected officers and extended an invitation to the two past presidents"—Maude Roberts George and Martha B. Mitchell Parks—"to meet at her home" on July 13 at 9:00 p.m. And in that special meeting, she named Ruth Henderson as chair of the Social Committee. The Social Committee organized parties on the South Side, inviting jazz musicians and dancers as guest performers. These events involved social dance and games; they foregrounded pleasure, lightheartedness, and communal bonding. As a result, Henderson would be responsible for ensuring the spirit of "love and friendship reign" in the Black classical metropolis.[44] For all their disagreements, Chicago's musical Race women worked toward a common goal. The press, the club, the church, and the home were their domains. Moreover, the binding work they enacted in these spaces resonated with various others. Because of their work, many more artists and activists of the Black Metropolis—especially women—were emboldened to lay claim to the wider city.

Parallels in Political Arenas

It was perhaps inevitable that Marjorie Stewart Joyner's political journey would bring her to the Black classical metropolis. Joyner would have seen parallels between the philanthropic and community-building ethos of the Madam C. J. Walker Company, of which she was president, and that of the CMA. In turn, the CMA's notably matriarchal structure would have led members to deeply identify with Joyner's Black womanhood. Chicago's musical Race women would have greatly empathized with the systemic racism and sexism that Joyner faced along her trajectory. Moreover, they would not have thought twice about using their finances, press columns, and other available resources to support her campaign for the mayor of Bronzeville.

Bronzeville materialized from individual and collective desires for autonomy and agency. The *Chicago Bee* (comprising a majority-female writing staff under prolific businessman, former municipal judge, and founding publisher Anthony Overton) coined "Bronzeville" in the early 1930s, conjuring up a place-name for the cultural capital of the Black Metropolis that was inspired by the complexions of the people within it. The impetus for the name was the newspaper's sponsorship of a local mayoral contest.[45] "Bronzeville" stuck, and the elections, although technically unofficial, allowed its residents to take the systems that governed them into their own hands. Peter M. Rutkoff and William B. Scott write of how these elections allowed, "black Chicagoans to participate, even symbolically in their own political world," several decades before the election of Chicago's first Black mayor, Harold Lee Washington.[46] The exigency with which Black Chicagoans sought self-sufficiency grew out of the necessity

of Jim Crow resistance, as well as the pride in the progress and promise
of their own communities.

There was a readiness for the CMA, under Maude Roberts George's
presidency, to endorse Bronzeville's first female mayoral candidate in
the 1936 elections: Marjorie Stewart Joyner. Joyner was an Old Settler, an
alumna of the Chicago Musical College (graduating in 1924), and a more
recent graduate of Northwestern University's School of Speech.[47] She was,
as Toni Costonie describes, "deeply involved in what could best be titled
the Chicago Renaissance." In a piece titled "Profiles of a Legend: The
History of Dr. Marjorie Stewart Joyner," Costonie sheds further light on a
woman who, in the words of the author, "pioneered in the fields of beauty
culture, education, community service, organizational development, and
political and social activism":

> Dr. Joyner started her career as a beautician. She opened her first beauty
> salon in Chicago's south side in 1916. In the same year she began to work
> and travel with Madame C. J. Walker. When Madame Walker died in
> 1919 Dr. Joyner continued on as National Supervisor for the Madame
> C. J. Walker Beauty Colleges, a national chain of beauty culture schools.
>
>   In 1929, Dr. Joyner moved the businesses to 47th and South Park (now
> King Drive). Soon she was in the heart of a booming Black metropolis.[48]

Over the course of her career, Joyner transformed Black beauty culture, building on the work of her predecessor, Madam C. J. Walker, to
challenge the industry's superficial connotations and further the Walker
enterprise as one that would benefit and empower Black women more
holistically. As Davarian L. Baldwin asserts, "Joyner became a model figure
through whom the profession was catapulted from just 'doing hair' to the
ascendancy of women into public positions through beauty culture. Joyner
became not just a beautician but an inventor and public advocate for the
black metropolis and beyond."[49] Joyner's pivot to mayoral candidate was
therefore a logical progression for someone whose professional world
was already grounded in the politics of place, race, and resistance. That
Joyner's transformative work centered on Black womanhood, however,
also brought the intersectional dimension of gender to the fore, making
her an important representative for those yet to see their womanhoods
reflected in this area of political leadership. Her life's work particularly
resonated with the musical matriarchs of the Black classical metropolis.
What is more, such reverence was reciprocal as this was the community
to which Joyner turned in order to launch her mayoral campaign.

On August 4, 1936, exactly one month after the *Chicago Defender* (as
the new custodians of the elections) launched Bronzeville's third mayoral

elections, Joyner attended one of the CMA's regular meetings, held at the Wabash Avenue YMCA. As usual, the proceedings began with all members singing the Black National Anthem. On this occasion, Ophelia Welch conducted as Theodore Charles Stone accompanied at the piano. Reports from senior administrators followed, along with remarks of welcome to Clara Hutchison who had been absent for a time due to illness. George then presented Joyner "as a special guest who had come to visit and make an important announcement." Joyner "was warmly received and spoke appreciatively of the opportunity to again come into intimate contact with the musicians, and voiced hope to, at a near future date, to [sic] join the CMA as a regular member."[50] The political dance of canvassing votes was in full swing. She reminded members of her Chicago Musical College affiliation and her $5.00 contribution to last month's CMA party at Poro Gardens (on 4415 South Parkway), which was a highly strategic move to ensure the CMA's endorsement, especially considering that the garden party took place on the site of Annie M. Malone's Poro College of Beauty Culture.[51] Poro was a long-standing supporter of NANM and the CMA, but Malone was also one of Madam C. J. Walker's earliest competitors. However, Joyner was prepared to forsake historical rivalries to demonstrate her support toward the CMA too. She therefore pledged future donations and reminded members that "she could always be relied upon as an interested friend."

Then the announcement came: "There would be a meeting at Roseland Hall on Aug. 11 sponsored by the CND Women's Club on behalf of partly hosting her candidacy for Mayor of Bronzeville and collecting contributions for support of the club."[52] The CND Women's Club was a subsidiary of the Illinois Federation of Colored Women's Clubs and affiliate of the National Association of Colored Women's Clubs (NACW), the League of Women Voters, and other federations that championed women's progress. Enacting its motto—"From Possibilities to Realities"—the CND Women's Club assisted thousands upon thousands of individual charity cases and donated to numerous institutions and causes, from the Frederick Douglass Center, Wendell Phillips Settlement, and Provident Hospital to the Equal Suffrage Association, Illinois League of Women Voters, and the National Association for the Advancement of Colored People. They operated out of "a commodious Woman's Club House" on the South Side but opted for a grander stage on which to present Joyner.[53] As a venue that hosted an array of public-facing events (e.g., exhibitions, concerts, and townhalls), Roseland Hall was the ideal space for Joyner to draw in the wider South Side community and move them with an impressive display of her oratorical skill, political acumen, and civic care.

After Joyner's announcement, circular letters from the CND Women's Club were then distributed to CMA members. The circular began with the formal invitation to "you and your friends to a Public Mass Meeting" at Roseland Hall in honor of "our candidate for the Mayor of Bronzeville—Marjorie Stewart Joyner, the only woman candidate and the people's choice." The endorsement was unapologetic about Joyner's gender, framing the intersections and experiences that shaped her life and livelihood as significant assets for the role of mayor.

> We feel that in honoring Marjorie Joyner we reflect credit upon Negro Womanhood. Mrs. Joyner has been the manager of the Chicago Branch of the Mme. C. J. Walker Company for a number of years and has made an enviable record for herself in the business world. She is aggressive, courageous, and possesses the qualities which fit her for this office.

Describing Joyner as "aggressive" and "courageous" was a powerful move. It reclaimed characterizations that were favorably attributed to men but not women (regardless of racial background). Yet it also rewrote a narrative of Black womanhood beyond the interlocked racial and gendered stereotype of the dominant matriarch (or, as we know this trope today, the "angry Black woman"), who is labeled emasculating, "unfeminine," and "too strong" in a way that is designed to "undercut U.S. Black women's assertiveness." Joyner's Black womanhood was proudly assertive, brave, enterprising, and a reflection of the autonomy Race women exercised around their self-definition in the face of hegemonic systems that, since the slave era, sought to discredit them.[54]

The circular came with the instruction for recipients to mail copies of the document to their friends and wider networks. Joyner had already mailed one thousand copies, stating that "the CMA would receive all money collected over $90.00."[55] These were not huge sums, especially compared to that which could be provided by the Carnegies, Rockefellers, Rosenwalds, and Wanamakers of the world. However, as Tyrone McKinley Freeman argues, limiting Black women's patronage and "philanthropy to specific financial examples prevents us from seeing the whole because, although money was important, it was not the full extent." Race women's "gospel of giving," as Freeman terms it, "found expression through a medley of channels because of an expanded definition and practice of what constitutes giving."[56] And these channels—such as the provision of music programs at fundraisers and various forms of communion at Black civic spaces and institutions like the Wabash Avenue YMCA, Poro College, and Roseland Hall—were inextricably grounded in their geography due to the immediacy of the needs that Race women served.

The CND Women's Club circular evidenced the ways in which a conflu-
ence of channels worked to bolster Joyner's campaign, for it was noted that
as part of the mass meeting at Roseland Hall, a "splendid program" had been
arranged by a cohort that included Maude Roberts George, Nannie Mae
Glasco Williams, Helen O. Brascher, Nannie Reed, Irene McCoy Gaines, and
Carrie B. Horton.[57] Like George and Williams, these Race women saw no
demarcation between music and politics. Staunchly grounded in club life,
Brascher was the president of the CND Women's Club at this time.[58] Reed
was the president of the Illinois Association of Women's Clubs (IAWC), an
incorporation of the NACW, while Gaines served as vice president under
Reed. Horton was a former president of both the CND Women's Club
and IAWC. Together, they coordinated a program that simultaneously
embodied and enacted the continuous dialogue between concert culture
and civic life on the South Side, utilizing a breadth of sites (i.e., the CND
Women's Club, Wabash Avenue YMCA, and Roseland Hall and Ballroom)
to house these conversations. Joyner tactically alluded to this dialogue
when reminding CMA members of her musical ties, civic contributions,
and institutional support. The contents of her circular further echoed the
necessary reciprocity, interconnectedness, and geographical anchoring of
Race women's impresarial and socially uplifting work.

Before Joyner's portion of the meeting agenda closed, George affirmed
that "a creditable music program would be furnished by the CMA." Ruth
Henderson volunteered a further contribution with the Apollo Ensemble
under her direction. Gertrude Smith Jackson followed suit, offering the
Elsie Breeding Chorus of which she was the conductor, and Theodore
Charles Stone put forward his pupil Harmon Johnson, who would perform
a piano recital. The exact repertoire of the program remains unknown, but
these performers undoubtedly represented some of Black classical Chicago's best. The Apollo Ensemble was a "prize-winning group of women,"
established by Henderson on July 17, 1933, "for the purpose of stimulating
interest in the higher type of music." The ensemble subsequently went on
to appear "in all of the leading churches of the city and suburban towns"
and additionally performed at settlements and women's clubs; "their well-
trained voices, rich in artistic beauty, their beautiful costumes and their
pleasant personalities soon won the attention of outstanding organizations
and clubs." The Apollo Ensemble first sang for the CND Women's Club at
their clubhouse on March 18, 1934, to an overflowing audience. Two years
later and once again under the auspices of the CND Women's Club, they
would likely be just as well received at Roseland Hall.[59]

The Elsie Breeding Chorus arose earlier that year in 1936 in the wake
of Elsie Breeding's death at the age of thirty-five. She was survived by

two sons for whom a memorial scholarship fund was established and to which the CMA contributed in the manner of Black fraternal and sororal giving. Breeding, herself, had been a CMA and NANM member as well as a celebrated soprano, appearing "in the capacity of soloist on many South [S]ide music programs."[60] The ensemble that carried her legacy forward was evidently a relative newcomer to the Black concert scene, but its director was not. And under Jackson's helm, the singers of the Elsie Breeding Chorus were sure to make a galvanizing contribution to Joyner's campaign. Although even less is known about Harmon Johnson, his instructor, like Henderson and Jackson, was another fixture in the Black classical metropolis. Stone was a baritone and music critic and served as president of the CMA from 1954 to 1996 and NANM from 1968 to 1975; his recommendation of Johnson would have certainly reflected his acute ear and eye for local talent. This was a creditable program for a creditable Race woman whose life's work similarly sat at the intersections of artistic expression, political ambition, racial uplift, gender equality, civic consciousness, and South Side institutional rootedness.

But despite promise and progress, Joyner lost the election to physician Dr. I. H. Holloway. Even though she was one of the most qualified out of the thirty hopefuls (twenty-nine male, one female), as only one of two on the ballot who had been a cabinet member for the previous mayor (W. T. Brown), her experience in conjunction with the backing of some of Chicago's most prominent musical networks and women's clubs was evidently not enough.[61] Bronzeville as a whole was not ready for its first female mayor. And yet it clearly could not do without Race women's civic presence. Even Drake and Cayton observed that "Bronzeville is somewhat suspicious of its Race Men, but tends to be more trustful of the Race Woman," which suggests that Joyner's loss was, in part, the result of a Black patriarchy that almost always prevailed in spite of its flaws.[62] But from the outset, Bronzeville bore Black women's imprint. Both Bronzeville and Joyner's campaign evidenced that the "evolving cultural apparatus of the Black Metropolis" (i.e., the newspapers, clubs, and communal buildings of this geography), to cite James N. Gregory, not only "depended upon entrepreneurship in the linked worlds of business, politics, and culture" but also on Race women's active input. Joyner's candidacy epitomized Bronzeville's promise and prejudice. And in seeking to overcome the latter in favor of realizing the former, she not only sought endorsement from Race women's more sweeping bureaucratic associations like the CND Women's Club and IAWC, but she also engaged a "unique" and woman-made "'counterpublic' with mature institutions of communication" located in the Black *classical* metropolis.[63]

Coda

The date of composition is unclear, but the address on the envelope that holds the score reads,

Miss Florence B. Price
647 East 50th Street
Chicago, Illinois

The year is probably around 1939.[64] More important, though, is what the envelope contains: the handwritten manuscripts of a four-movement orchestral suite that Price simply titles *Chicago*. The score is incomplete, but the names of each movement—"I. Skyline," "II. The Loop," "III. Forty-Seventh Street," and "IV. Buckingham Fountain"—are a window into the sites and landmarks to which Price attributes cultural and personal significance. She recognizes the influence of her Bronzeville neighborhood (as portrayed in "Forty-Seventh Street"), not as an isolated or exotic Black colony but as an integral part of the city (as mirrored by the way this movement is embedded in the suite's macrostructure rather than situated on the outskirts). She prizes Forty-Seventh Street in the same way that she prizes the architecture, avenues, and monuments that contribute to the cachet of the north.

The question of whom Price might be writing for remains unanswered. Is it the Chicago Symphony Orchestra, the Woman's Symphony Orchestra of Chicago, or the Michigan WPA (Works Progress Administration) Orchestra? Is this part of a WPA commission, like the Symphony No. 3 in C minor that she also writes around this time?[65] If so, why does *Chicago* remain incomplete? Does the symphony, among several other WPA commissions, pull her away from its completion? There are many unanswered questions that arise from the score. But what is certain is that *Chicago* is her claim to the city—an homage to its artistic and industrial progress, a celebration of its social dynamism. She writes the markers of modernity into her score as she explores the geography of public spaces and the geometry of urban structures.

"Skyline" contains the most notation of all the movements. Sweeping strokes and rippling gestures characterize its 137 measures, painting a panoramic impression of the city's skyscrapers (fig. 19). Broad blocks of sound, instead of intricately detailed motifs, affirm the wide angle from which Price writes. In a way that is representative of the whole movement, the opening eight measures feature swelling dynamics and gradually ascending contours. Major-minor juxtapositions and chromatic and whole-tone colorings abound in this excerpt and throughout (ex. 1). The

Figure 19. The Chicago skyline with Buckingham Fountain in view. Keystone View Company, The city of Chicago skyline, Chicago, Illinois, 1933 (Meadville, PA: Keystone View Company, Manufacturers and Publishers) Photograph. https://www.loc.gov/item/2018648952/.

music begins brass heavy, as if using the deep metallic timbre of the horns, trumpets, trombones, bass trombones, and tuba to establish the ground view of this urban vista. A cluster of woodwinds respond, with their airier timbre conveying a sense of greater height—of shifting the gaze upward, or of grand structures rising out of the ground, or of both. The music continues to move into the higher woodwind voices, with snare drum rolls and a punctuating bass drum and cymbal building anticipation and suspense in these introductory measures. The harp is also used to dramatic effect; with arpeggiated and scalic figures constructed on whole-tone scales, pentatonic scales, and dominant-seventh chords, Price employs the dreamy connotations of the instrument to portray the dizzying heights of the big city. She leans into the sonic effects of film music. Her use of long pedal points and sustained harmonies, alongside reedy and brassy timbres, even suggest the influence of her work as a movie theater organist.[66] "Skyline" is a cinematic conjuring of Chicago's modernist architecture, told from Price's perspective. And to take it all in, one must step back. That Price, an Arkansas native, begins her musical narrative on the outside is perhaps a subtle nod to her migration story and that of so many Chicagoans. With each movement, Price journeys through this urban landscape, finding herself at home in the various facets of her adopted city.

CHICAGO

I. SKYLINE

Example 1. Florence B. Price, "Skyline," *Chicago*, mm. 1–8.

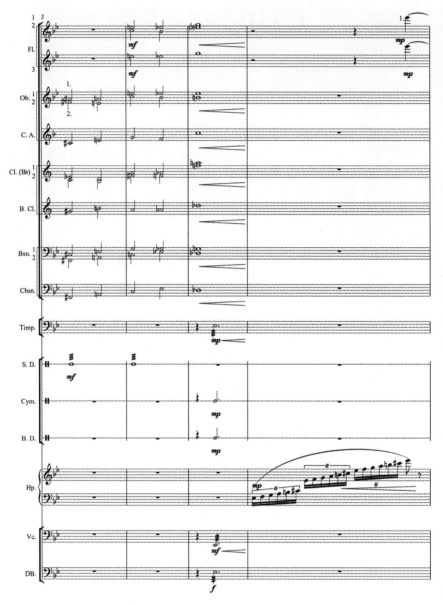

Example 1. Continued.

Figure 20. Russell Lee, photographer. *Movie Theater, Southside, Chicago, Illinois*. United States, Cook County, Illinois, Chicago, 1941, April. Photograph. https://www.loc.gov/item/2017788750/.

A page titled "The Loop" reveals only its name atop a series of blank staves. Nothing can be gleaned from the score and there are no further versions that illuminate Price's musical intention. However, its name suggests a transition from the sweeping vista of Chicago's iconic skyscrapers to a ground view of the Magnificent Mile tucked within. She is likely drawing us into the activity of the central business district. And as the home of her symphonic debut, among other performances and events, this movement also hints at her own personal connection to this geography.

"Forty-Seventh Street" moves the suite into Bronzeville, less than a mile northwest of where Price is living. As "the commercial and social heart" of the South Side, Forty-Seventh Street is home to an "intellectual and political heat [that radiates] far beyond the borders of Chicago and the United States."[67] This is "where the renowned Regal Theatre and Savoy Ballroom [are] located. There [are] fancy restaurants, exclusive stores" (figs. 20 and 21). It is also the home of the chic Madam C. J. Walker Beauty

Figure 21. Russell Lee, photographer, *Dress Shop which Caters to Negroes. 47th Street Chicago, Illinois.* Cook County United States Chicago Illinois, 1941, April. Photograph, https://www.loc.gov/pictures/item/2017788881.

Salon, located in the South Center Department Store—"the first Black salon in a department store in Chicago" (fig. 22). This is where Joyner gives Marian Anderson her first haircut and styles Billie Holiday when the gardenia-adorned star is in town.[68]

Price draws on Black musical idioms to capture the incandescence of this geography. Her approach recalls the third movements of her symphonies, which she titles "Juba" in direct reference to the Black antebellum dance traditions of the South. "Forty-Seventh Street" reveals stylistic similarities, from the syncopated motifs that lead the melodic content to the "oompah" rhythms of the percussion parts, which evoke the folksy foot-tap hand-clap accompaniments of the juba.[69] That Price cites this communally rendered Black antebellum art form in "Forty-Seventh Street" affirms the movement as a celebration of Black sociality and world-making, which would no doubt inspire the choreographies of Dunham had she the opportunity to hear this work.

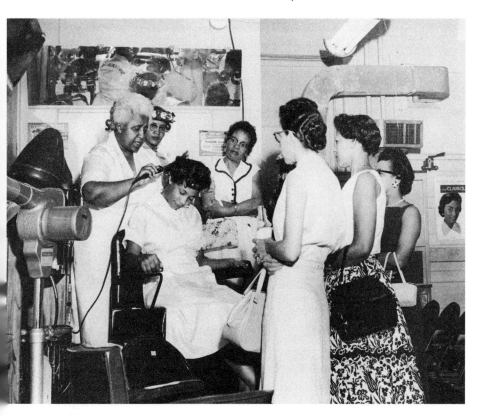

Figure 22. Joyner leads styling class, Madam C. J. Walker Beauty College in South Center Department Store building, Chicago, ca. 1945. Series 5: Madam C. J. Walker Beauty Colleges, 1922–1972, Box 47, Folder 383, Marjorie Stewart Joyner papers, Chicago Public Library, Woodson Regional Library, Vivian G. Harsh Research Collection of Afro-American History and Literature.

A syncopated and jovial motif, built on pentatonic intervals of African American folk influence, shapes the introduction. The motif journeys from the lower strings and woodwinds in measure 1 to the highest in measure 3. The dominant chord is sustained throughout and punctuated by all at the end of measure 4, with the bass drum, cymbal, and snare added for emphasis. Resolving to the tonic, what follows is a spirited passage that is neither blues nor jazz but is still steeped in shared vernaculars, such as the off-beat emphases of the percussion and pizzicato strings, call-and-response dialogue across parts, and melodies that dance around the pulse, playing with the expectations of metrical time (ex. 2). But this movement is not solely about pastiche: Price employs a vast orchestral palette, chromatic colorings, and dramatic twists and turns that give modern, cosmopolitan

III. FORTY-SEVENTH STREET

Example 2. Florence B. Price, "Forty-Seventh Street," *Chicago*, mm. 1–20.

24

Example 2. Continued.

Example 2. Continued.

flavor. She musicalizes the sociocultural dynamics of the Great Migration in which southern migrants southernize the North, just as Black northerners transform the politics and perspectives of the new arrivals, and "vestiges of southern black culture [are] transplanted and continuously renewed and reinforced" by Black women "in motion."[70] "Forty-Seventh Street" harbors a vestige (rather than pastiche) of Price's Black southernness, which she stirs into the cosmopolitan foundations of the score.

This movement portrays the cultural amalgam that typifies Price's Bronzeville. Her score even points to analogous use of musical medley as she quotes two hymns around the midpoint of the work: "Will There Be Any Stars in My Crown" and "No, Not One." With the first hymn, she places the melody in the ceremonial-sounding trumpet, which proceeds at a measured andantino tempo. Its stoic rendering, however, is disturbed by a clashing whole-tone figure in the clarinets, marked "blatant." Price is about to get playful. The second hymn follows immediately after with the instruction "Tempo moderato, flippantly with impertinence." That this next section opens with a short descending gesture in the trombone marked "Imitation of primitive laughter" shows that she is moving into Signifyin(g) territory.

Whether treated solemnly or parodically, these quotations imbue the movement with the musical signifiers of Price's religious life.[71] Her reference to these two gospel songs from a late nineteenth-century Anglo-American repertoire, rather than the newly emerging gospel sounds from Chicago's Black churches at this time, hints at her own experiences and preferences within the mostly light-complected, well-educated, middle-class congregations of her own churches.[72] Her choices evoke aspects of her autobiography; the musical signifiers that she amplifies in this movement are just as telling as those she negates.

Much like the gospel music of Chicago's Black churches, evident also is Price's avoidance of the South Side's vibrant blues, jazz, and other contemporary popular music scenes in her depiction of Forty-Seventh Street. Price is rarely vocal about her musical politics as they relate to popular music trends, but as a Black classical composer she learns to navigate the white expectation that her music must align to contemporary styles of Black music-making—an expectation to which she, at one point, takes great offense when it entails the Automatic Musical Instrument Company uninvitedly and sloppily reworking one of her compositions into what she describes as "jazz of an inferior sort . . . for the use of jazz orchestras."[73] Forming the broader context is a classist and covertly colorist framing of racial uplift in which classical music (as opposed to popular music) affirms genteel values, "mark[ing] out the practitioner, whether performer

Figure 23. John Buczak, Artist. Buckingham Fountain on Chicago's lake front, world's largest and most beautiful illuminated fountain . . . / Buczak. Chicago, Illinois, 1939. (Illinois: Federal Art Project). Photograph. https://www.loc.gov/item/97502889.

or listener, as a member of an elite group."[74] These tensions, in addition to the intraracial caste systems from which they stem, are implicit in the Black vernacular influences both present and absent in "Forty-Seventh Street."

This complexity defies any monolithic portrayal of the Black Belt, bringing varied timbre and texture to the cultural composition of the Black Metropolis. Price is writing about the Chicago she knows and in a way that parallels her conceptualization of the Symphony No. 3 in C minor, of which she will later say, "I tried to portray a cross section of Negro life and psychology as it is today, influenced by urban life north of the Mason and Dixon line. It is not 'program' music. I merely had in mind the life and music of the Negro today and for that reason treated my themes in a manner different from what I would have done if I had centered my attention upon the religious themes of antebellum days, or yet the rag-time and jazz which followed; rather a fusion of these, colored by present cultural influences."[75] Similarly, "Forty-Seventh Street" does not strive to tell an all-encompassing narrative of African American history; rather, it revels in the Race woman's modernity and migration journey, foregrounding Price's own perspective on the hustle and bustle of day-to-day life in the beating heart of the Black Metropolis.

There is no trace of the fourth movement beyond Price's jotted-down "Buckingham Ft" on the manuscript cover. Nonetheless, this movement directs us to the North Side and portrays one of Chicago's most imposing landmarks: a rococo-style fountain located in Grant Park near Lake Michigan (fig. 23). Where does Price direct her musical gaze? To the light red Georgia marble of its large shell-shaped basins? To the heroic bronze seahorse sculptures surrounding it? To the rush of 133 jets spouting 14,000 gallons of water per minute? Or to the nighttime illumination of the 133 streams in hues of red, amber, green, blue, and white?[76] The most that can be gleaned is that "Buckingham Fountain" intends to bring *Chicago* to a colorful and majestic close.

Although the entire suite is less than half complete, each movement sketches the cartography of the Race woman's realm. She is not limited to the Black Metropolis. In fact, it is because of what the Black Metropolis and its classical core of Race women affords her that she—yes, Price, but also Dunham, Joyner, and many more—dares to dream bigger.

INTERLUDE I

Race Woman's Guide
to the Realm of Music

Tucked somewhere in the first few pages of the *Chicago Defender* were Neota McCurdy Dyett's and Beulah Mitchell Hill's "In the Realm of Music" columns, keeping their readers abreast of various musical activities in the city of Chicago and beyond. The coverage of recitals, composer biographies, and club meetings signaled the realm of music's classical focus. Yet what unfolded in this domain was not simply an imitation of European culture-making; instead, what took shape, as Imani Perry articulates, was a "'black classical' . . . of the folk and voraciously and beautifully creolized."[1] Dyett's and Hill's columns chronicled, celebrated, and promoted Black concert culture in all its transnational glory. Building on the work of Nora Holt and Maude Roberts George, "In the Realm of Music" expanded the discourse in African American music criticism. Its authors spotlighted creative practices beyond solely popular music-making and ventured "beyond the blues," exemplifying the greater diversity of Black cultural production in the United States.[2] Like those before them, Dyett's and Hill's mission emanated from the conviction that its creators and their creations were worthy of such championing—which, in turn, stemmed from the belief that classical music was theirs for the taking, if they so chose.

The names and addresses given here reveal some of the people and places that constituted Black classical Chicago's realm of music. It features some predominantly white institutions, such as the Chicago Musical College, Auditorium Theatre, and Orchestra Hall. But many of those listed are historically Black, given the city's segregated makeup and the self-reliance of its Black populace. When mapped, downtown Chicago's cultural and geographical remoteness (or otherworldliness, as Michelle Obama describes it) becomes all the more apparent.

Styled after early twentieth-century directories for Black Americans wishing to know more of the city, this guide unfolds from the vantage point of the inquisitive musical Race woman. If printed like the Black social and civic manuals from this time, its preface would read (with adjustments to the gendered language in italics), "this little book does not pretend to be complete . . . but the information here gathered will prove invaluable alike to the stranger seeking a convenient guide, to the citizen desiring to post *herself*, and to the business and professional *woman* wishing to read a reference book of worth while [*sic*] Negroes in Chicago."[3] This guide, however, is more impressionistic than functional.

Not all the individuals listed were active at the same time, nor did they stay at the same abodes throughout their lives. Additionally, not all of the institutional spaces that these practitioners used remained where they were and as they were. After all, the realm of music was a living and breathing entity, a geography that responded to the call of its industrious and enterprising inhabitants. Still, traces of earlier lives led and legacies forged—such as that of Emma Azalia Hackley and her Normal Vocal Institute—were part of the cultural DNA of the Black classical metropolis. Therefore, superimposing the multiple temporalities housed in and around this interwar period of music-making achieves a means by which to convey the realm's genealogy and evolution. The result is not a full and final mapping. However, in drawing on the fragments of information available, what emerges is a multilayered collage of a history that is near symphonic in texture and ongoing in sociocultural resonance (figs. 24 and 25).[4]

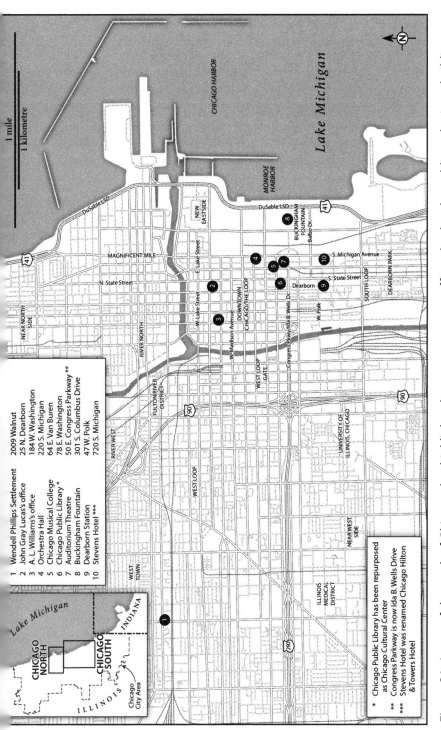

Figure 24. A map of the north of Chicago that highlights the concert venues, offices, landmarks, public and private buildings, transportation routes, and neighborhoods in this vicinity. The addresses used reflect a pre-1940, interwar time frame. Maps by Martin Lubikowski, ML Design, London, United Kingdom.

1	Wendell Phillips Settlement	2009 Walnut
2	John Gray Lucas's office	25 N. Dearborn
3	A.L. Williams's office	184 W. Washington
4	Orchestra Hall	220 S. Michigan
5	Chicago Musical College	64 E. Van Buren
6	Chicago Public Library *	78 E. Washington
7	Auditorium Theatre	50 E. Congress Parkway **
8	Buckingham Fountain	301 S. Columbus Drive
9	Dearborn Station	47 W. Polk
10	Stevens Hotel ***	720 S. Michigan

* Chicago Public Library has been repurposed as Chicago Cultural Center
** Congress Parkway is now Ida B. Wells Drive
*** Stevens Hotel was renamed Chicago Hilton & Towers Hotel

Figure 25. A map of the south of Chicago that highlights numerous homes as well as churches, schools, clubhouses, offices, public and private buildings, settlements, and neighborhoods in this vicinity. The addresses used reflect a pre-1940, interwar time frame. Maps by Martin Lubikowski, ML Design, London, United Kingdom.

INTERLUDE II

Fantasie Nègre

Upon Florence Price's 1927 Chicago arrival, the Black classical metropolis claimed the composer and musician as its own, and she claimed it right back. The magnitude of Price's output grew in tandem with the opportunities she encountered across the city. She was, as Helen Walker-Hill writes, "welcomed into a vital and nurturing community" on the South Side, and from there, a "constellation of events that could have taken place only in Chicago at that time gave impetus to her steadily growing fame." Walker-Hill cites Price's triumphs in the 1932 Rodman Wanamaker Contest and 1933 Chicago World's Fair as key components within this constellation (both of which chapter 5 discusses in more depth). Furthermore, Walker-Hill also considers the influence of Estella Bonds.[1] Estella was, as her obituary would later state, "one of the first local musicians to recognize and help launch the creative works of . . . Florence B. Price."[2] The Bonds matriarch likely saw in Price's musical Race womanhood a reflection of her own, which spurred her readiness to bring this southern newcomer into the fold.

Estella could see what Price was poised to offer as a composer, performer, and educator, so much so that she discerned that her daughter, Margaret, would benefit greatly from Price's musical instruction. Estella's foresight would result in situating Margaret as an inheritor of the Black Renaissance concert aesthetic. The younger Bonds immediately intuited the significance of these intergenerational exchanges: "I realized, very young, that I was the link, you see, between Negro composers of the past. You see, my mother was friends with all of them."[3] In fact, there is a piece in Price's catalog, written two years into her new Chicago life, that exteriorizes the social and creative dynamics that Margaret Bonds articulated and that Walker-Hill historicizes: *Fantasie Nègre* for solo piano, completed February 9–10, 1929, about a month shy of Margaret's sixteenth birthday.

Fantasie Nègre heralded the folk-inspired, nationalistically driven, and fantastically conceived orchestral works to come. Moreover, its inscription beneath the title, "To my talented little friend, Margaret A. Bonds," was emblematic of the South Side sisterhood undergirding Price's new compositional directions. This interlude therefore illuminates the many socially and musically significant threads that run through the work, beginning with an analysis of the music itself (informed more by my experiences as a performer of this work than from the perspective of a music theorist). This then leads to a discussion of the piece's own performance history and reception in Price's lifetime, encompassing the roles that Katherine Dunham and the Bonds family played in promoting and advancing the work, as well as the fantasie's Chicago-ness as a composition deeply rooted in its locale. This interlude reanimates the realm of music through Price's *Fantasie Nègre*. It positions the work as evidence of the exciting transformations that were taking place in Price's personal and professional world upon her entry into the Black classical metropolis.

• • •

Set in the key of E minor (a key that, for me as a pianist, feels earthy and sepia-hued, tinged with melancholy but full of resolve), this 1929 piece is the first in a series of four elaborate fantasies for solo piano that bear this title.[4] Before even approaching the notes, the title itself inspires a great deal of thought toward interpretation. To begin with, Price uses the German nomenclature, *Fantasie*, which describes a highly imaginative, florid, and free-form instrumental style that first emerged in the fifteenth century and journeyed through subsequent eras and wider geographies, filling the keyboard literature with a wealth of works bearing titles such as *Fantasia* (or *Phantasia*), *Fantaisie* (or *Phantaisie*), *Fantasie* (or *Phantasie*), and other variations. That Price embraces the German spelling is evidence of her affinity for nineteenth-century Romanticists of that region, such as Brahms and Schumann. For Price, just as it was for her European predecessors, the fantasies are not only vehicles for technical skill but also for an emotive expressivity, unbound by rules of form and convention. Her style imbibes the German patriarchs' characteristic harmonic warmth, dense chordal textures, cantabile lyricism, ornate passagework, brooding moods, and capricious moments.

Her citation of this past not only reflects the dominance of nineteenth-century German trends but also the pervasive understanding during her own time of German music as "universal music." Of course, German art music was as politically charged as any other, but under the guise of universalism, it held the promise of a blank slate on which Black practitioners could envision and enact new selves beyond the strictures of Jim Crow. In other words, it allowed African American artists to think and dream capaciously about their craft and, more profoundly, their place in the world.[5]

Undermining complete German influence, however, Price's use of "Nègre" introduces another cosmopolitan layer. The French orthography may lead listeners to draw connections with the French *fantaisies* of Chopin. Price's decorative musical gestures can certainly be heard in the context of Chopin's ornate style. Yet there is something about both the French spelling and German references that go beyond Eurocentric associations, evoking the heterogeneity of continental and diasporic Black cultures.

From this line of argument follows an interpretation that reads Black world-making into the text and therefore into the score. If the *Oxford English Dictionary* defines "fantasy" as "the faculty or activity of imagining impossible or improbable things," then *Fantasie Nègre* imagines a Black world, perceived beyond monolithic, primitivist, and anti-Black purviews. For Kevin Quashie, "'a black world' names an aesthetic imaginary that encompasses heterogeneity," a perspective that encourages us not to hear the classical voice in Price's *Fantasie Nègre* as a European import but as very much a part of that Black heterogeneity, for in such a world, "black being is capacious and right—not more-right-than, just right as-is. Life-as-is," Quashie explains. He further distinguishes, that "an antiblack world expects blackness from black people; in a black world, what we expect and get from black people is beingness." *Fantasie Nègre* dreams up alternative ways of being and becoming because "in a black world, every black being is of *being*, the verb that infers a process of becoming."[6] Yet with *Fantasie Nègre* marking the process of Price's own becoming (as well as, on a personal note, being the singular piece that fueled my ambition down the seemingly impossible and improbable path of a Black female musicologist and concert pianist), the work goes beyond fantasy, musically and materially conjuring up a beautifully tangible reality for Black classical lives.

With a melodic theme built on the Negro Spiritual "Sinner, Please Don't Let This Harvest Pass," *Fantasie Nègre* reimagines Black voices, Black vernaculars, and Black virtuosity. Of Price's four fantasies for solo piano, the first is the only one in which she directly quotes a Spiritual. Reflecting an *aaab* stanzaic form—whereby, in African American folk song, the melodic and rhythmic contours often varied across the first three phrases, even as the lyrics stayed the same—the Negro Spiritual behind the first fantasie begins,

> Sinner, please don't let this harvest pass,
> Sinner, please don't let this harvest pass,

Sinner, please don't let this harvest pass
And die and lose your soul at last.

The harvest signifies both physical and spiritual sustenance. To "let this harvest pass" is to go without the replenishments of faith and virtue, to perish as one would if starved of food. Its stern caution and sobering tone carry over into the solemnity of *Fantasie Nègre*.

A clarion call of a bold E minor chord across the piano's lower to middle registers announces the start of the piece. A shimmering cascade of notes that descends from the higher registers and dissolves into a fragment of the Spiritual's melody then answers. "Sinner, please," the piano whispers before taking off in an ascending flourish. "Don't let this harvest pass," the melody starts up again before drifting into a soft rippling figuration. These grandiloquent pianistic gestures build anticipation for the Spiritual to return—Margaret Bonds would have no doubt reveled in the dazzling display of technique and drama housed in the music's introductory page.

Toward the end of the introduction, the mood calms and melts into a full sounding of the melodic theme. *Fantasie Nègre* then unfolds as a set of variations on the theme. The Spiritual melody, where it appears, is always aurally identifiable, as is its harmonic underpinning, but the rhythmic, textural, countermelodic, and chromatic features of the accompanying material vary with each iteration, much like in the practice of folk song (exx. 3 and 5).

Price's approach cites folk Spiritual performance practice and its solely oral medium, for as Eileen Southern explains, "It was the performance that shaped the song into an entity" and as Sandra Jean Graham elaborates, "each performance was unique. With variable text and a loosely defined melody a folk spiritual was . . . 'a frame to be filled at the moment dictated.'"[7] Improvisation inhered within the performance practice; each verse could introduce extemporized timbral, textural, and temporal variations around the main melodic content. Although the limits of the piano do not allow Price to imitate this exactly, each iteration of the Spiritual melody hints at the improvisational foundations of the tradition.

As well as citing the singing practices that birthed Black folk idioms, Price also integrates plantation dance rhythms and kinetic evocations in her pianistic writing—to which the percussiveness of the instrument lends itself well—from the left-hand habanera-style syncopations (ex. 4), to stomp-like bass-clef octaves (ex. 5), and circling countermelodies that suggest impressions of the ring shout (ex. 5).[8] These features are rooted in West African performance cultures and were adapted in various forms of Black diasporic dance across the Americas.[9]

Example 3. Florence B. Price, *Fantasie Nègre*, mm. 17–31, with text added by the author. Copyright © 1932 (Renewed) by G. Schirmer, Inc., International Copyright Secured. All Rights Reserved.

Example 4. Florence B. Price, *Fantasie Nègre*, mm. 36–39. Copyright © 1932 (Renewed) by G. Schirmer, Inc., International Copyright Secured. All Rights Reserved.

Example 5. Florence B. Price, *Fantasie Nègre*, mm. 225–28, with text added by the author. Copyright © 1932 (Renewed) by G. Schirmer, Inc., International Copyright Secured. All Rights Reserved.

Ludmilla Speranzeva heard these dance connections when she saw Margaret Bonds play *Fantasie Nègre* in concert. This impelled her to arrange the work for Katherine Dunham's Modern Dancers (later known as the Negro Dance Group) for a December 23, 1932, premiere. Despite being a product of Russian training with evidently no background in American, let alone African American, dance, Speranzeva was "inspired by Miss Dunham's enthusiasm for a Negro ballet" and consequently "made the realization of this aim a definite part of her dance future."[10] As Speranzeva once cogitated, "Russians and Negroes both have—how do you say it?—soul."[11] It seems that *Fantasie Nègre* provided the ideal sonic landscape for the world Speranzeva sought to reinterpret through dance. And just as the choreographer Ruth Page did, Speranzeva also turned to the South Side in her mission to bring ballet into the avant-garde.[12]

The first ballet performance of *Fantasie Nègre* took place in the downtown location of the Stevens Hotel's Grand Ballroom—a place in which African Americans could perform but did not always feel at ease when staying as hotel guests for fear of the racist hostilities they anticipated at sites that largely catered to white clientele.[13] Transfiguring the space, Dunham starred as the "premier danseuse," while Price and Margaret Bonds accompanied, playing a two-piano arrangement of the work. The music portion of the performance must have been sonically and visually spectacular as Price and Bonds were joined by singer Gladys Hayden Sims for a performance that included the lyrics of "Sinner, Please Don't Let This Harvest Pass," making for a "thrilling climax" and one-of-a-kind rendering that departed from the original score for solo piano. Heightening the experience was the dance troupe's Afrocentric attire: "The costumes were directoire princess effect to the ankles with black braided wigs and bare feet." In the absence of a photograph, we might imagine echoes of African or, more specifically, Egyptian antiquity, captured in the regal drapes of the dancers' garments and the braided styles of their ebony locks.

An unnamed reviewer for the *Chicago Defender* identified the performance as the beginning of a new era in the history of African American dance, drawing parallels with the realms of literature and music: "As in the poetry and music of the Race, the dance has outgrown the elementary period of spontaneous expression which ignores the universal language of form and technique. Without the elementary period, the Race dance would lack richness and individuality; with form and technique, it will endure in a universal medium and become part of the inheritance of all posterity."[14] The word "universal" again recalled German ideals in a Black Renaissance aesthetic. On the one hand, the anonymous reviewer troublingly encoded notions of assimilation and white acceptance, subtly infantilizing and primitivizing African-derived traditions. On the other hand, their writing also evidenced the ways in which African American practitioners (including critics) internalized universalist ideals and, as Kira Thurman writes, "used them to articulate their politics of racial uplift and social advancement." These were the tools and tensions that arose in pursuit of Black cultural ascension in the Jim Crow era. But ultimately, Thurman shows, "Black musicians recomposed what musical universalism looked like or sounded like, anchoring it in the racial politics of the United States and beyond."[15] And what practitioners such as Price and Margaret Bonds achieved in music, Dunham embodied in movement.

Dunham's vision paralleled that of the Black Renaissance composers whose works affirmed uniquely African American traditions. Just as Price and her Black Renaissance peers did in the realm of music, so too did Dunham revolutionize the dance world with Afro-modernist flair. And much like Marian Anderson's future performances of Price's compositions, Dunham's own integration of Price's music (not to mention Bonds's as well) similarly made her (as Alisha Lola Jones writes of Anderson) "an impresario of black women's new works."[16]

Fantasie Nègre continued to shape Dunham's own explorations of rebirth and revitalization in Black American vernacular dance. As it had been with Ruth Page and other white and European collaborators, Dunham was not simply a passive figure in Speranzeva's vision. The ballet took on a life outside of the original 1932 collaboration. Dunham staged it on several occasions through the 1930s with the Negro Dance Group. One documented performance took place in October 1933 at the Punch and Judy Theater in the Loop.[17] Another, in December 1933, saw Dunham and her troupe return to the Punch and Judy Theater. Debussy's "Golliwog's Cakewalk" also featured on this program, during which dancers performed in "grotesque costume," a description that intimates a parody of the parody—a Signifyin(g) display à la Josephine Baker, to play with, subvert, and complicate the dehumanizing primitivist tropes that Europeans (and, of course, white Americans) used in their renderings of Blackness.[18] Dunham and her troupe performed a "black double-voicedness" that spoke over Debussy's distortions of African American culture, amplifying its ugliness not only through performance attire but through direct juxtaposition with Price's poignant musical portrait of Black pasts and futures.[19]

Price's music inspired a different kind of costume and choreography, which British photographer Bertram Dorien Basabé captured through the 1930s. A photograph of *Fantasie Nègre* in a 1936 performance shows five sepia-hued dancers, with Dunham in the center (fig. 26). Gone are the black braided wigs from the 1932 premiere; instead, the dancers' heads are

Figure 26. Dorien Basabé, Katherine Dunham and her company in the work, *Fantasie Nègre*. Katherine Dunham Photograph Collection, Special Collections Research Center, Southern Illinois University, Carbondale. Used with permission from Marie-Christine Dunham Pratt and Southern Illinois University, Carbondale.

wrapped in a turban style, with the scarf smoothed around their hairlines and the remaining material twisted into a halo around their crowns. Given that the original dresses were described as "directoire princess effect to the ankles," the 1936 performance suggests a more simplified design.[20] Basabé's photograph reveals unadorned long-sleeved dresses, with a high split to emphasize the shapes (and shadows) of the dancers' legs and bare feet. The dancers are portrayed with interlocked limbs composing multidirectional, triangular, and diamond-shaped lines. But theirs is not a harsh angularity, like the kind choregraphed in Stravinsky's (in)famous *Le sacre du printemps* (*The Rite of Spring*). Rather, Dunham and her troupe are captured as if moving in a single, gentle current—their contrapuntal lines in harmonious flow; they are deeply interconnected in their world-making. One can only imagine how video footage would animate their frozen motion. As Liesl Olson rightly states, "dance is notoriously difficult to archive" and there is little trace of the *Fantasie Nègre* choreography beyond a few local newspaper reviews across the Black and white presses and Basabé's photograph.[21] This image therefore provides a rare glimpse into the extent that Dunham and her troupe reembodied Price's fantasie through multiple interpretations, generating further scenes of Race women's world-making.

Price's *Fantasie Nègre* was distinctly Chicagoan for the ways that it was born of the Black classical metropolis, dedicated to one of the realm's most beloved musical daughters, and promoted by Dunham in citywide performances. The two-piano arrangement itself also alludes to the influence of Price's geography and network, for of note is the fact that Estella Bonds was not only "one of the first local musicians to recognize and help launch the creative works of . . . Florence B. Price," but she was also "one of the first music teachers to popularize two piano playing among her students" on the South Side.[22] The latter suggests that Estella not only built a generation of Black classical pianists with increased technical skill as ensemble players but may have also shaped the ways in which Price absorbed collaborative piano performance into her compositional directions. December 1932 is one of the earliest documented occasions of Price's two-piano performances, and it was certainly the case that in the Bonds salon, Price found the facilities and fellowship needed to advance her work. From the description of Estella's pedagogy, it seems likely that the Bonds family home housed more than one piano, allowing for Price and the mother-daughter duo to rehearse Price's scores in this intimate setting, rather than in the more detached space of the rented studio. There lay the subtle shades of Estella's impresarial advocacy, which were not defined by grand financial gestures but by her fostering of an interior climate of support that helped classical pianists develop into confident solo and ensemble musicians—as Margaret did upon her Chicago Symphony debut with John Alden Carpenter's Concertino for Piano and Orchestra and Woman's Symphony Orchestra of Chicago debut with Price's Piano Concerto in One Movement—and enabled composers to exercise the full extent of their ability—as Price did through the following years.

The *Chicago Defender*'s review of the original Price-Bonds-Dunham collaboration also included the observation that the two pianos "were ample as the number is written for orchestral use."[23] Whether the orchestral piece in question was Price's Concert Overture No. 1, based on "Sinner, Please Don't Let This Harvest Pass," or an entirely different, unarchived composition altogether, *Fantasie Nègre* was a pivotal work in Price's output, housing the deeper history of her artistic growth. It signaled the composer's emergence in a cohort of musical Race women world-makers and affirmed the Bondses' centrality to the process of her becoming.

In the subsequent years, Price embraced many more ambitious projects, all the while keeping up her steady staple of songs and not-too-demanding instrumental pieces. It seems Price rejected a sense of aesthetic linearity or hierarchical progress across the genres in which she composed. Instead, she moved from Spirituals to symphonies, and symphonies to Spirituals, ever stretching the breadth of her craft and bouncing back and forth between small-scale ideas, large-scale conceptions, and everything in between. Her deepening involvement in the Black classical metropolis drove her to push and prod at the social prescriptions and circumscriptions for those of her race and gender. Against such a backdrop, shaped by the expansive nature of Race women's world-making, she realized yet another "*fantasie nègre*": that of the first nationally recognized Black female symphonist.

PART II

Strategies to Symphonies

They have worked. They are now working harder than ever.

—Shirley Graham

4

Movements of a Symphonist

The US symphonic scene of the 1930s was a variegated but somewhat exiguous one. Casting its long shadow through the interwar period and beyond, the European classical tradition was an inescapable, dominating presence through which not all US composers could find their way. The hegemony of nineteenth-century German symphonists seeped into the New World and the next century, shaping the ways in which up-and-coming generations of American composers would go on to define and redefine a national school and its symphonic sound.[1] Yet even Europe's own post-tonal modernist backlash at the turn of the century to the Romantic and nationalist overtones of the earlier period further complicated ideas of where an American school might go from there. And deeply attuned to these unsettled currents was the acclaimed author-artist-activist Shirley Graham.[2]

"Among her millions of citizens, America can boast of but few symphonists. Delightful piano pieces, songs, marches—yes; but very, very few symphonies."[3] This was how Graham opened her 1936 article, "Spirituals to Symphonies," published in *Etude Magazine*. A survey of Black classical accomplishment unfolded across the several pages commissioned for the widely read journal, celebrating the path from Negro Spirituals to Afro-symphonies. Graham was one of the few Black female voices amid its mostly white male contributors; as such, she wrote to educate readers across the color line. Her piece spanned the 1871 founding of the pioneering Fisk Jubilee Singers through the stratospheric rise of Marian Anderson to the 1930s emergence of three African American symphonists: William Grant Still, William Levi Dawson, and Florence B. Price. Still's *Afro-American Symphony* (1930), Price's Symphony No. 1 in E minor, and Dawson's

Negro Folk Symphony (1934)—not to mention their respective world pre-
mieres with the Rochester Philharmonic Orchestra (1931), Chicago Symphony Orchestra, and Philadelphia Orchestra (1934)—marked historic
breakthroughs along this trajectory. These works sounded triumphant
finales to just over half a century of Black music-making in the United
States. But if Still, Dawson, and Price were but a few standout symphonists among the nation's "millions of citizens," then Graham's article was
also a subtle dig at the ways in which white American symphonists had
not entirely come into their own.

   While white American composers through the late nineteenth and early
twentieth centuries floundered about in the push of the cosmopolitan
school that deferred to the Bach-Beethoven-Brahms lineage of compositional technique and palette, and the pull of the provincial school that
resisted the influence of the Teutonic triumvirate, prizing instead indi-
vidualized, nonreferential, and nondeferential musical schemes, Black
classical practitioners claimed their craft, arriving at a point where, to
quote Graham, "for the first time the American Negro faced his own destiny and stopped apologizing for his music."[4] Standing in a light of their
own and defying the propaganda that white-maleness was the absolute
signifier of US citizenship and a prerequisite for the American symphonist
were Price, Dawson, Still, and others whose names and works are lost in
the annals of Western art music.

   Black symphonists evidenced their mastery of the genre, respecting
its fixed movements and set forms, but simultaneously pushing it to new
frontiers in which Black folkloric pasts coalesced with their visions for
Black liberatory futures. The path from Spirituals to symphonies was not
one of displacing that which came before but of upholding earlier legacies
in the making of new possibilities; theirs was a modernism that thematized
renaissance and reconnection over detachment and dissolution. This was
the essence of Graham's educative article, which exhibited her critical
finger on the pulse of American music and Black creative life, from cotton
plantations to concert halls.

   The only thing that was missing, observed Maude Roberts George on
reading the article, was mention of the behind-the-scenes support that
stemmed from organizations such as the National Association of Negro
Musicians (NANM). George was not interested in seeking the spotlight for
herself, but she felt that it was imperative for readers to know of the Black
institutions that helped shape these musical journeys. Speaking candidly
to her NANM colleagues in a meeting that took place on December 2,
1936, George expressed "that assistance rendered to [Marian] Anderson
by the NANM and to others to whom scholarships were awarded by the

NANM should have been included in Miss Graham's article." Still, giving Graham the benefit of the doubt, George added that Graham "never misses an opportunity to inform audiences to whom she speaks of these efforts to advance our own artists and students."[5] Graham unlikely intended any harm with this oversight, particularly as it was this concern—"to advance our own artists"—that brought her to nest and network in the Black classical metropolis, a few months before "Spirituals to Symphonies" was published.

As codirector of the Graham Artists' Bureau, Graham relocated to Chicago over the summer of 1936 to enact a more involved role in the agency that she and her brother, William B. Graham, had established in July 1936. Prior to Shirley's arrival, William set up offices in Bronzeville's South Center Building (417 East Forty-Seventh Street), which was a professional hub for many Black entrepreneurs. William aimed to expand their offices to the cultural capitals of New York and San Francisco and, across these three metropolitan bases, operate as a "foe" to the "exploitation of colored performers and musicians."[6] Chicago was a crucial starting point for the bureau due to the city being widely recognized as "the center of the Negro entertainment world." Upon the bureau's opening, and no doubt bolstered by the reputations of its sibling directors, "many of the top sepia bands and feature acts of the country [were already] negotiating to book out of [William's] office."[7] The Grahams were poised to bring marked change to an industry that routinely dimmed its sepia stars.

High hopes were held for their enterprise. The *Chicago Defender* anticipated "that with the wide and valuable contact these directors have and the fact they have always made a special effort to secure the right monetary award for those whom they seek to book, the Graham Artists' Bureau is destined to become one of the foremost booking agencies in America."[8] But to be one of the foremost booking agencies simply in Chicago, Shirley knew that the endorsement of the Black classical metropolis was paramount, which is why, on September 1, 1936, she attended a Chicago Music Association (CMA) meeting to rally greater support.

After a warm greeting from President Maude Roberts George and the assembled members, Graham briefly addressed those present. "Probably of chief importance," documented Recording Secretary George Howard Hutchison, "was the plea for assistance and cooperation from the CMA in making a proposed 'Artists' Booking Bureau' a living reality in Chicago." Graham affirmed that several prominent artists were on board.[9] She informed club members that the agency hoped to relocate to one of Bronzeville's most popular venues: the Regal Theatre Building, a sign of her investment in the geography of her enterprise. Where Graham would connect most deeply with her CMA audience, though, was in the moment that she "related the difficulties that Negro Artists have in the concert field, as well as the Negro Composers in disposing of their wares."[10] This was sure to resonate given the CMA's commitment to this area of African American artistry.

Only a year earlier, George was quoted in the Black press saying, "Although all musicians appreciate the merit of such composers as Mr. [Duke] Ellington, they cannot ignore the fact that they possess financial inducements that composers of symphonies like Dawson, Florence Price and William Grant Still lack."[11] George knew all too well of the myriad challenges and prejudices that dogged Black classical composers' access to the white classical mainstream, where greater resources abounded. She was therefore an empathetic ear to Graham's proposal.[12] Yet despite the air of optimism that flowed through the meeting, the Graham Artists' Bureau reportedly went broke less than three weeks later. The Grahams were not invulnerable to the barriers of access and opportunity that they aimed to navigate and negotiate for the artists in their care.[13]

And so, considering the unfavorable conditions that beset Black concert artists, classical composers, and promoters, the tone of entwined celebration and wonderment in Graham's article, published not too long after the demise of her own efforts, is palpable: "Spirituals to symphonies in less than fifty years! How could they even attempt it?" The emergence of three prominent Black symphonists in the space of four years, and in a climate so hostile to the nurturing of their success, was nothing short of extraordinary. "And one of these symphonists is a woman! Florence B. Price," Graham marveled.[14]

So how did Price arrive here?

This chapter examines how race, gender, and geography shaped the development of the African American female symphonist and anticipates the Black matriarchal influence of Price's eventual Chicago community. It sheds light on the amalgamation of histories, herstories, agendas, and ideologies that undergirded Price's own and subsequently aligned her with the South Side impresarios. In doing so, however, this chapter temporarily pivots away from Chicago, tracing Price's movements and migrations through her Little Rock upbringing, New England Conservatory schooling, and southern resettling amid the tightening grip of Jim Crow. The purpose here is not to reproduce Price's biography but to give a broader sense of where she came from, the wider historical forces at play, and the push and pull that drew her inevitably to Chicago.

With a goal to understand how Price arrived as the first Black female symphonist of her stature, I reject a reading of her path that fixates on her exceptionalism. I argue that this leads us to miss the earlier examples of Black women composers whom I refer to as *unfinished symphonists* in acknowledgment of the opportunities historically denied to them. The reading I pursue here actively listens for these earlier examples. Rather than dismissing their faint reverberations in the historical record as inaudible, I reframe them as ghost notes in the chapters of Price's trajectory and in the narrative of musical Race women's culture-making at large.

Listening between the Lines

The dearth of American symphonists may have evidenced a crisis of identity in the musical worlds of the white majority, but it also reflected the lack of opportunities available to those of African descent, especially women. As groundbreaking as Price's achievements were, it would be naive to think that she was the first African American woman in history capable of writing a symphony. Shirley Graham did not, for one moment, suggest this, but it is easy to miss the other examples of musical Race women that exhibited Price's symphonic promise and potential when preoccupied only with Price's exceptionalism. Viola Davis put it succinctly in relation to her own creative practice when in 2015 she became the first Black woman to win the Emmy Award for Outstanding Lead Actress in a Drama Series (the first since the Emmy's founding in 1949): "The only thing that separates women of color from anyone else is opportunity."[15] Although Davis became a historical first in that moment, she knew that she was by no means the only Black woman capable of earning such an accolade. How true this rang for Price, almost a century earlier, as she became the first Black female symphonist to be recognized by one of the nation's most elite orchestras.

Implicit in Price's symphonic triumphs are the herstories of the *unfinished* symphonists—that is, those who could not access such opportunities in the concert sphere and subsequently turned to other areas of activity that kept their creative flames alight, such as teaching, civic work, or even a musical shift to the popular genres of jazz and blues (which were comparatively more accepting of women despite their similarly patriarchal tilt).[16] For many Black women composers, Ora Williams observes, "there was no one to underwrite the considerable expense.... Black women were obliged to earn a living from other activities. Some had to teach in public schools or colleges in addition to giving private lessons, presenting concerts, or directing church choirs. Furthermore, they often sandwiched composing in between their working, caring for a family, and being involved in community activities." That the majority of works by historical Black women composers are vocal and choral compositions rather than instrumental is less a reflection of the extent of their abilities and more an indication of what was most pragmatic amid their busy lives. Furthermore, as Williams writes, "they were probably creating that which would most likely find an audience and be performed."[17] The centrality of the Black church in Race women's day-to-day, for example, instantly eased the task of finding soloists, choirs, accompanists, and a keen audience; these were the kinds of conditions that made composing such repertoire a significantly more feasible endeavor compared to the task of finding and funding a whole orchestra (of any race), as well as to financing the costs of a more mainstream venue and navigating the politics of a predominantly white and male sphere.

This pragmatism carried through long into Margaret Bonds's compositional career. When asked if she preferred writing for orchestra, voice, or dance, Bonds responded, "Most of the things I compose are because somebody asked me for something and so I don't really have any preference, it doesn't matter. If they ask me, I go on and do it and therefore I know that it's going to be performed."[18] While vocal works formed the bulk of Bonds's compositional output (which is hardly surprising given the deep network of Black classical vocalists that surrounded her, from Abbie Mitchell and Betty Allen to Adele Addison and Leontyne Price), Bonds also found that, more so than her art songs, her Spiritual arrangements, in particular, were the most popular among her singing colleagues—no doubt in part due to the growing tradition of African American concert singers ending their programs with Spirituals.

Evidencing the kinds of instrumental works that could emerge when the right platforms and opportunities were presented, however, are Helen Hagan's 1912 piano concerto (which Helen Walker-Hill identifies as "the earliest extant work in a large form by a Black woman composer") and Nora Holt's thesis composition from her master of music program at the Chicago Musical College—"a symphonic rhapsody of forty-two pages for an hundred-piece symphony orchestra," titled *Rhapsody on Negro Themes*, of which one of the melodies derived from the Negro Spiritual "You May Bury Me in the East."[19] Although neither are strictly symphonies, their overlaps with the symphonic genre suggest a much deeper history of Black women writing or at the very least being intellectually and artistically equipped to tackle large-scale orchestral works. However, that Price fulfilled her symphonic ambitions four times over with her additional Symphony No. 2 in G minor, Symphony No. 3 in C minor, and Symphony No. 4 in D minor says something of the ways in which Chicago Race women's networks, institutions, and geographically concentrated influence were key. While Hagan and Holt shaped the early makings of the Black classical metropolis, how different might their trajectories have been had they stayed to witness its communities mature and accessed the kinds of local connections and opportunities afforded to Price?

Their capabilities were never in question. Like Price, Hagan and Holt pursued composition in the most competitive of arenas. In 1912, Hagan became the first African American woman to graduate from the Yale School of Music, while on June 15, 1918, Holt became the first person of African descent (of any gender) in the United States to receive a master of music degree on completing her studies in piano performance, harmony, and composition (which included the submission of her thesis work, *Rhapsody on Negro Themes*) at the Chicago Musical College. Prior to this, Holt had studied operatic scores and orchestration in Chicago under Felix Borowski, who was recognized both locally and nationally as an "eminent composer and theorist" and was a professor of music history, composition, and orchestration at the Chicago Musical College. The *Chicago Defender* described Holt as "an earnest and sincere student and in striving for a place in the world of art is leaving no part neglected which tends toward making the finished artist."[20] Given Holt's drive and outlook, Europe seemed inevitable.

Whereas Price's music education never left American soil, Hagan and Holt went overseas—specifically Paris—preceding several Black women composers who studied there also, such as Chicago residents Irene Britton Smith and Carissa Hardy as well as postmodernists of the next generation, Julia Perry and Dorothy Rudd Moore.[21] As the winner of Yale's Samuel Simons Sanford Fellowship for foreign study—succeeding "in competition with white students much older than herself," as William Pickens of the *Baltimore Afro-American* emphasized—Hagan worked under composer and pedagogue Vincent d'Indy at the Schola Cantorum de Paris, receiving her diploma in 1914.[22] Just over a decade later, Holt left Chicago for Paris in 1926 to undertake a summer course in music theory, composition, and orchestration at the American Conservatory at Fontainebleau. She then returned in 1931 and studied under Nadia Boulanger.[23] Evidenced, then, is the reality that even in Europe, African American women composers were competing at the heart of contemporary musical developments (rather than operating on the periphery or not at all as their historiographical absences would suggest). But if Europe "appeared to offer African Americans a new cartography of hopes and dreams," as Kira Thurman describes it, then Black expatriates were in for a rude awakening upon their return to Jim Crow America.[24]

Upon repatriating, Hagan built her reputation as "a pianist of the highest stature," but "because Negroes were not booked by agents at that time, she turned to teaching as a career."[25] Even though the Black press thoroughly recognized Hagan's capabilities—Pickens hailed her a "true artist genius," Etta Augusta Deuce of the *Philadelphia Tribune* referred to Hagan's accomplishments as "beacon lights," exhibiting "a type of Negro Womanhood with the Negro's highest type of genius—the musician," and Holt in her *Chicago Defender* columns called Hagan a "master musician" in the making—the strictures imposed by the prevailing cultures of segregation and inequality compelled her to carve out the path of a pedagogue.[26] And she did so with aplomb. But what other opportunities might have grown out of a different set of social circumstances? Hagan's piano concerto gives us pause for thought, especially as performance was the main way in which Race women, with dual composer pianist identities, promoted their original works. If opportunities for Hagan to perform were limited, then so were the opportunities for her music to be heard. "Because the concerto is thought to be the only surviving work among Hagan's compositions," writes Lucy Caplan, "it takes on outsize importance as the primary evidence that remains of her dazzling creativity."[27] We are therefore reminded of the world of opportunities that could elude even a Race woman of Hagan's musical caliber, even one dubbed "one of the best piano artists of the world."[28]

As for Holt, the bulk of her catalog, comprising approximately two hundred unpublished manuscripts written for orchestra, chamber ensemble, voice, and instrumental solo, is presently missing. The storage site in which she kept her compositions during her travels was ransacked; the vast majority of her works are yet to be recovered. Only two compositions remain of her life's work: a short piano piece called *Negro Dance*, op. 25, no. 1 (1921) and an art song called "The Sand-Man," op. 30 (1921). These works were published in Holt's *Music and Poetry* journal, with the specific issue containing these two compositions now housed in the James Weldon Johnson Memorial Collection of African American Arts and Letters at Yale University.

Negro Dance is an intermediate-level piece—accessible but with a good number of fun, virtuosic flourishes thrown in. The music is written in ternary (ABA) form and begins in the key of G major with a hushed two-measure syncopated pattern in the bass clef. Its off-beat emphases recall the pattin' juba—a dance form that emanated from the performance cultures of the enslaved; it is a precursor to the cakewalk and ragtime and is famously referenced in R. Nathaniel Dett's 1913 "Juba (Dance)" (which is the fourth and final movement from his *In the Bottoms* suite for solo piano), as well as in the third movements of Price's symphonies and the closing section of her Piano Concerto in One Movement. After *Negro Dance*'s short

Example 6. Nora Holt, *Negro Dance*, mm. 78–88.

introduction, the main melody enters, twirling between folksy simplicity and chromatic colorings that add layers of whimsy and unpredictability to the melody's direction. The contrasting B section moves into the relative minor key of E and engages an increasingly chromatic palette. The dissonances are never harsh or startling; they merely add suspense and excitement to the music's ascending and descending contours. Following a series of decorative gestures, the quiet two-measure pattern in the bass clef returns, signaling the final A section. Toward the end, Holt reinvokes her earlier dramaticism: the tempo quickens, chordal textures thicken, and with a pause before the final measure—as if to play with the listener's anticipation—she draws the work to a humorous staccato close (ex. 6).

A significantly less animated work, "The Sand-Man" is built on two stanzas, practically identical in structure. Although Paul Laurence Dunbar wrote a poem of the same name, Holt's text differs from his and additionally does not cite his name in the score, suggesting that the poetry that she uses might be her own original work also. Set in the airy key of E major, a breezy piano accompaniment comprising gentle chords and uncomplicated rhythms begins the song. Holt writes "Playfully" just ahead of a vocal entry that unfolds with childlike simplicity. In this verse, the protagonist cheekily bemoans the Sandman's unwanted appearance and closes with the line "O, how I hate the Sandman." The second verse, however, begins "Wistfully" as the protagonist reflects, "You know when you jump and romp and play, / You get so tired at the close of the day," and in this case, the Sandman is a welcome visitor. The final few bars rise a tone to the

The Sand-Man

N. DOUGLAS HOLT
Op. 30

Example 7. Nora Holt, *The Sand-Man*, mm 1–14.

key of F-sharp major as the singer dreamily croons, "It's then I love the Sandman, / I'm sure I do love the Sandman too." The whole piece has the buoyant lilt of a nursery rhyme and, like Holt's *Negro Dance*, is hardly representative of a catalog that contains compositions for one-hundred-piece symphony orchestras and other large ensembles (ex. 7).

Gleaning more of who Holt was as a composer from what remains of her catalog is a challenge. But we know that *Negro Dance* barely scratches the surface regarding her solo piano works because its opus number hints at a larger body. We know that many more art songs flowed from her pen because she performed them, either as both the singer and accompanist or as the accompanist to her soprano colleagues.[29] And we know that she, like Price, was a symphonist because her thesis composition tells us so. Even though we may never hear how the influences of Holt's musical training took hold in her wider oeuvre, we can be sure that those who had the privilege of hearing it—from her Chicago Musical College peers and instructors to national and international audiences comprising Boulanger—certainly took notice.

Today, Hagan, Holt, and the many unknown Black women who, for various reasons, curtailed their compositional ambitions or were simply not survived by any of their manuscripts, represent an unheard canon. They are further muted in histories of women in classical music that prioritize white womanhoods and histories of African American composers that almost exclusively highlight Black male composers.[30] Yet, as Mia Bay reminds us, "silences are rarely complete," and this is where Price's narrative assumes greater signification.[31] Price's path is certainly not a stand-in for the narrational gaps that fragment the historiographies of her Black female peers, but it can serve as a window into the variety of historical Black women's lives and livelihoods in the United States during the first half of the twentieth century; it can offer a glimpse into the sorts of conditions that birthed a distinct generation of musical Race women and compelled them to find and fashion possibilities and consequentialities beyond that which their predecessors had known. And most pertinent, Price's path—from home-taught piano lessons that molded middle-class girlhoods, through the conservatory training that forged young womanhoods, to the mature music-making and networking that coalesced around Black institution-building—grants the possibility to hear the herstories of the unfinished symphonists as ghost notes between the lines of her movements. Although the wider compositional catalogs of Hagan and Holt, as well as Elnora Manson, Carissa Hardy, and Martha Bonner (the last two were well known in NANM circles), may never come to light, traces of their lives and legacies nest along Price's journey.[32]

And so, to chart the movements of a Race woman symphonist is to delve into the work that was required in the making of one, regardless of whether her journey found resolution in the craft of composition, patronage, performance, teaching, homemaking, or civic endeavors. For Shirley Graham, it was all about the work: "[They] have not depended on their 'natural talent,'" she wrote of Price, Still, and Dawson. "They have worked. They are now working harder than ever." Graham added, "Nor did they become 'symphonists' overnight."[33] Price's success was not instant, nor was it guaranteed; moreover, there were many like her who similarly "worked" but fell into the cracks of historiographical invisibility—not for a lack of ability but for a lack of opportunity in their lifetimes. However, a closer listen to the pattern of Price's own movements through the developmental phases of her girlhood, teen womanhood, and adulthood not only reveals the contours of her own work but contributes also to the greater project of recovering the quiet, undisputed canon of Race women actively shaping the realm of music—symphonically and otherwise.

The Birth of the Black Piano Girl

Music-making and community-building converged in Price's childhood home in Little Rock, Arkansas. Hailed as "the Great Negro State of the country" during Reconstruction, Arkansas had proved hugely appealing to families like Price's—that is, families where fathers were dentists, doctors, and lawyers, and mothers were accomplished classical musicians, educators, and society women.[34] As Black migrants of the professional class drawn to the prospects of a state in which they could exercise greater autonomy, this was how Price's father, Dr. James H. Smith; mother, Florence Irene Smith (née Gulliver); aunt, Olive Gulliver Lucas; and uncle-in-law, John Gray Lucas, found their way to Arkansas.[35] In Little Rock, Dr. Smith established a "large and lucrative" dental practice, popular "among the white wealthy class" to the extent that even the governor of Arkansas was a client.[36] But it was in the Smith family home, which served as a hub for impassioned Race men and intrepid Race women (years before the Bonds matriarchs fashioned their South Side salon), that Price absorbed the meanings and makings of Black musical excellence.

Born in 1888 and known as "Bea" to avoid confusion with Florence Irene, a three-year-old Price began piano lessons with her mother.[37] Mrs. Smith was a "talented soprano and concert pianist," and with Dr. Smith's passion for the arts and sciences, Price wondered in later life, "Perhaps his love of originality was passed on to me and given expression through that medium with which my mother was gifted."[38] In any case, Price affirmed, "Both parents favored my choice of music." Had Dr. and Mrs. Smith favored her musical path but not had the resources to support it, Price's childhood might have been one of working alongside her parents for long hours, finding pinches of time in which to study her craft, seeking funds for music lessons from the communities and churches to which she belonged, as was the story for countless talented rural girls from the lower classes. Instead, Bea's girlhood differed vastly; she was afforded the time and space to learn, play, practice, create, and refine. Out of this context, the Black piano girl was born.

The work of Judith Tick shows that the Victorian image of the flaxen-haired piano girl, who played for pleasure and social currency, became an outdated archetype in American musical culture by the turn of the century. As women's political activity increased through the Progressive era, so too did the possibilities for them to lead professional lives beyond the domestic sphere. Tick shows how American women sustained careers that displaced the passive piano girl stereotype, ushering in a new era of activity that included women writing concertos and symphonies.[39] But for Tick, as well as other foundational authors whose much needed interventions boldly advanced a new, feminist musicology, *women* equates to *white women*.[40] Absent are the narratives of the piano girls with textured hair, smoothed into fashionable pin curls or updos, for whom playing for one's own pleasure and social currency was a defiant act. Well documented by Black feminist scholars is the reality that chattel slavery and its afterlife had marked the bodies of Black girls and women sites of pleasure and modes of currency to be used by everyone but themselves. The Black piano girl's practice was, therefore, an act of self-reclamation. And what was the relationship between the Black piano girl and the Race woman impresario? Well, I argue that the practice, play, and performances of the former allowed young girls to explore their own self-making and navigations of Black social utility, preparing them, if they so chose, for the vocation of the latter. Furthermore, that several Race women impresarios entered the realm of music by way of the piano (such as Holt, Estella Bonds, Gertrude Smith Jackson, and Neota McCurdy Dyett) suggests something of the way that the instrument served as a conduit for Black sociality and a purposeful life led at the heart of public culture. In the period that Tick's research highlights, from 1870 to 1900, Black women's classical music–making fed into broader reconfigurations of African American life in the post-Reconstruction era, intersecting with the formation of Black upper and middle classes and the rise of the intellectual Race woman.[41] That Black piano girls grew up to use their music for community-building—particularly in the capacity of performers, pedagogues, and patrons—reflects the ways in which their craft consciously and self-directedly intersected with their sense of social responsibility. In her book *Unbinding Gentility: Women Making Music in the Nineteenth-Century South*, Candace Bailey restores the agency of the piano girl more broadly, considering the role of women's music-making beyond the lens of a white patriarchy and delving not only into the professional and artistic aspects of women's musical experiences but the amateur and social dimensions too. She compellingly dismantles these dichotomies to reveal a more fluid dynamic.[42] Although Bailey's attention to Black women is wanting compared to her manifold narratives around white womanhood, the frameworks that guide both Bailey's and Tick's scholarship encourage thought around their applicability to Race women's music-making, with Price's own girlhood bearing the potential to give voice and visibility to the underexamined history of Black piano girls and the early impetuses behind their multifaceted, musical Race womanhoods.[43]

With the Smiths' home serving as a dependable space for traveling musicians whose race prohibited them from staying in the hotels of the white establishment, there were many opportunities for Price to meet esteemed Black practitioners and further develop her skills as a pianist and composer. Price recalled her parents hosting the virtuosic pianist and composer John William "Blind" Boone along with the impresario John Lange Jr. and Mr. Lange's wife (and secretary to the Blind Boone Concert Company), Ruth Lange. Boone's performances engaged popular genres like ragtime, as well as Negro Spirituals and canonic classical repertoire, modeling the kinds of syncretism that would distinguish Price's own compositional voice. In later life, Price described a memory of her, at three years old, "composing little tunes for Blind Boone, who with his [manager] Mr. Lange and Mrs. Lange always stopped with us when giving a concert in Little Rock."[44] This portrait of the Black piano girl's prodigious talents being displayed for esteemed visitors could similarly be drawn for Hagan in New Haven, Connecticut, where she was "the pride and wonder of the Hagan family." William Pickens recalled from his time with the Hagans,

> She was the one whom they [her parents, John A. Hagan and Mary Estella Neal] "showed off" when a guest or friend was to be entertained. Taking her seat upon the piano stool, and being hardly tall enough to reach the pedals with her toe, she would astonish the visitor—for visitors do not expect much from children whom proud parents put forward as "wonders." But when little Helen waked the lyre, it was something out of the ordinary in the line of piano music from a mere child.[45]

Like Price's, it seems that Hagan's home played host to a variety of Black professionals that Hagan must have engaged with, even as a child. This would certainly have been the case for Holt in Kansas City, Kansas, given the deep civic engagements of her parents, Rev. Calvin N. Douglas, a presiding elder of the African Methodist Episcopal Church, and Gracie Brown, the first matron of the girls' dormitory at Western University at Quindaro, Kansas (where Rev. Douglas was also a trustee and Holt was a student ca. 1914).[46]

Records confirm that the Smiths accommodated notable Black leaders of the time in addition to musicians like Boone. Price was only a few months shy of two years of age when Frederick Douglass stopped with the Smiths during his 1889 visit to Arkansas. Judge Mifflin Wister Gibbs (also of Little Rock and the first Black judge in the United States) joined Dr. Smith and a host of other local Race men to assist Douglass with his stay. Around this time, Gibbs's daughter, Miss Hattie A. Gibbs, later known as Harriet Gibbs Marshall, was enrolled at the Oberlin Conservatory of Music. Two decades Price's senior, Marshall would later become the first person of African descent to earn a diploma from the institution. The collegiality and geographical closeness of the Smith and Gibbs patriarchs lends credibility to the idea that the dynamics of exchange and nurturing that unfolded with a three-year-old Bea and Boone may have similarly transpired with Hattie. That Price wrote to Marshall in adulthood, "I have long regarded you as a pioneer whose efforts will not have been spent in vain," suggests a deeper history of their interaction and collaboration— more than the public record shows.[47]

Better documented, however, is the fact that the Smiths counted Carrie Fambro Shepperson, the mother of William Grant Still, as a family friend. "Yes," Still confirmed, "Florence Price was from Arkansas, and was a good friend of our family . . . and they belonged to our social set—which as you already know, consisted of people who were interested in intellectual matters."[48] And in Still's recollection of his Arkansas boyhood, certain parallels with Price's Arkansas girlhood and the girlhoods of other musical Race women may be drawn, specifically regarding access to the arts. Such access would have engendered opportunities to read, listen, and imbibe, to create and experiment with musical sound, and to learn the language of its organization. Still's description inspires further thought around how the Smiths' even more advanced social standing may have generated greater formative experiences for Price:

I knew neither wealth nor poverty, for I lived in a comfortable middle-class home with luxuries such as books, musical instruments and phonograph records in quantities found in few other homes of this sort. All of this was the result of my having had the good fortune to have been born to intelligent, forward-looking parents, as well as to the fact that Little Rock, where I grew up was considered by many of us to be an enlightened community in the South. It is true that there was segrega-tion in Little Rock during my boyhood, but my family lived in a mixed neighborhood and our friends were both white and colored.

The words "intelligent," "forward-looking," and "enlightened" overlook the constructs of class, colorism, and caste that rendered the light-com-plected Shepperson-Stills assimilable in Little Rock. Still even remarked, "My parents were far removed from the sort of colored people we now term the 'stereotypes,' and their circle of friends matched them in fine upbringing." Evidently, their interracial neighborhood demanded social conformity and congruity—albeit more so from its Black residents—to function as it did. Yet another one of Still's reflections, regarding how his "association with people of both racial groups gave me the ability to conduct myself as a person among people instead of an inferior among superiors," certainly lends insight into the esteem-building environment in which Price was raised and her own ability to navigate predominantly white spaces, such as the New England Conservatory.[49]

Although the inner unfoldings of the Smith family home are elusive, it remains that nested in this progressive enclave were culturally educative domestic realms where Black bourgeois sociality shaped childhood homes. Similar dynamics unfolded in Helen Hagan's New Haven, Nora Holt's Kansas City, Estella Bonds's Chicago, and countless other geographies where the Black professional classes took root. In the intimate settings of their homes and around their pianos, music and politics entwined. There, Black piano girls developed the intellectual, creative, and communal tools they would need in future years to build expansive womanhoods—both in the impresarial, curatorial, practical, compositional, and pedagogical realms of music, and in defiance of the color line and gender bar.

Race Womanhoods in White Music Schools

The history of African American women pursuing greater musical oppor-tunities, previously unavailable to those of their race and sex, was, by the time of Price's enrollment at the New England Conservatory in 1903, almost half a century old. Black women had been in and out of conservato-ries since the years of the American Civil War. Josephine Wright explains that prior to 1860, "emigrant musicians (generally Italian, French, and

German masters) provided the mainstay of musical instruction" for African Americans. But the "decade of the 1860s," Wright continues, "brought the first real opportunity for some Afro-American women to receive first-rate conservatory training at home when a few Anglo-American institutions began to accept them." Wright names the Oberlin Conservatory of Music (Harriet Gibbs Marshall's alma mater), the Boston Conservatory, the New England Conservatory, and New York's short-lived National Conservatory of Music of America as some examples. Alongside these white music schools, however, were also "Negro land grant colleges" such as Fisk University and the Hampton Institute, which, Wright reveals, not only provided women with a "strong musical education" but also "produced a generation of highly motivated, gifted women, such as Ella Sheppard and Julia Jackson of the Fisk Jubilee Singers, who became cultural leaders around the turn of the century."[50] In academic spaces across the color line, dating as far back as the mid-nineteenth century, evidently existed a tacit curriculum of musical Race womanhood, designed by Black women themselves who melded musical training with a sense of social responsibility and civic purpose.

Attesting to the notion of the musical Race woman's self-directed but community-inspired sociomusical curriculum were the careers of Price's Race woman predecessors at the New England Conservatory—for example, Rachel M. Washington, Nellie Brown Mitchell, Maud Cuney Hare, Fannie Barrier Williams, Sissieretta Jones, Georgina Smith, and Georgina Glover. All studied there during the late nineteenth century, with careers thereafter that spanned performance, composition, pedagogy, music history, and entrepreneurship.[51] Who might have been the other Black women in their midst, similarly excelling across these fields? How many were written off the record like Effie Ella Grant, Hagan's predecessor at Yale, who despite completing the requirements of her bachelor of music program never had her degree conferred?[52]

Like Yale and other "Anglo-American institutions," the New England Conservatory proved similarly precarious terrain for the ambitious Black woman. The conservatory prided itself on offering a safe and intellectually stimulating space for women, but such protections and promises were only conceived of with white women in mind. An 1889 feature on the conservatory read, "Nowhere is a young woman safer than here, and nowhere would she enjoy the best things in social life away from home more than in Boston, with the conservatory as a social and literary centre," but such safety and joy were not the entitlements of Black women, as the experiences of Maud Cuney Hare and Fannie Barrier Williams showed.[53]

As a student in 1891, Hare faced and resisted protest from white students who did not wish for her to remain in their shared dormitory, which was known as the "Home of the Institution" or the "Home," for short. Hare's parents received a letter from the conservatory, explicitly stating that Hare would not be protected from the entangled racism and sexism of her white peers:

> Despite our best effort, we realize that we cannot save the colored ladies in the Home, from the possibility of disagreeable experiences, and while all the educational advantages of the Institution are open to them, it seems advisable for their own comfort, for the stability and welfare of the Institution whose advantages they covet and enjoy, and for the advantage of all concerned, that they make their home with friends outside.

Cautioning the Hares not to overstep the mark—particularly with that subtle reminder of the "advantages" that their daughter already had access to and should therefore be grateful for and satisfied with—the conservatory prioritized its self-image over the task of fulfilling its promise as a haven for all women. The Hares fought back and won, but their victory was not without a price. "I refused to leave the dormitory," Hare recalled, "and because of this, was subjected to many petty indignities." Although the directors later relegated the incident to a "misunderstanding," followed by the declaration that "there was no color bar in the institution," the experiences of Fannie Barrier Williams, only three years on, showed just how prevalent systemic racism and sexism remained at the New England Conservatory.[54]

Williams was forced out of the institution when then-director of the conservatory Carl Faelton argued, as Williams recalled, that "it would imperil the interests of the school if I remained, as all of his Southern pupils would leave."[55] Her race rendered her womanhood unworthy of protection; just as it was for Hare, the New England Conservatory's self-image was paramount and inextricably tied to white supremacy. Notably, Margaret Bonds, as a music student at Northwestern University, would later encounter a similar dynamic to Williams regarding the hostility stirred up by white southern migrants. For Bonds, Northwestern proved a "prejudiced university, terribly prejudiced," made so by the fact that the suburb in which it is located (Evanston) was, as Bonds put it, "controlled by southerners." Bonds would recall her chance discovery of Langston Hughes's poem "The Negro Speaks of Rivers" in the basement of Evanston Public Library "help[ing] my feelings of security, you see, because in that poem he tells how great the Black man is." In addition to finding comfort in the words of her future collaborator and friend, studying relatively close to home and having the fortification of the wider Black classical metropolis likely eased the violent discomforts of her Jim Crowed institution.[56] Williams, contrastingly, never found such solace.

Williams wrote, "I never quite recovered from the shock and pain of my first bitter realization that to be a colored woman is to be discredited, mistrusted and often meanly hated." That inimical experience at the New England Conservatory stuck with her throughout her life as an example the innumerable ways "in which an ambitious colored young woman is prevented from being all that she might be in the higher directions of life in this country," as she worded it.[57] In one stroke, Williams succinctly underscored the ways in which white institutions—even the ones in the seemingly more progressive North—actively disrupted and discouraged Black women's creative and intellectual strivings.

The names of Race women known and unknown, the accolades earned but ungiven, and the protections ostensibly promised but ultimately denied, reinforce the reality that female practitioners of African descent continued to navigate incredible challenges in their musical training and professional prospects. Price's entry into conservatory life therefore both confirms and complicates the narrative of Black women's mitigated progress in the classical music sphere at the turn of the century.

"Mother took me to Boston in 1903," wrote Price in later life in a brief summary of her educational and musical path. "[She] entered me in [the] New England Conservatory from which I graduated with honors from two full courses simultaneously in 1906," the two courses referring to her double major in organ performance and piano pedagogy. Price recalled being "selected to play [the] organ solo on [the] Senior Class Program" on June 14, 1906, having emerged as one of the most artistically advanced organists of her cohort. Her selected work was none other than her organ professor Henry M. Dunham's Sonata in G minor, evidencing the high esteem in which her instructors held her. Another crowning moment soon followed when Price "appeared on [the] front page of [the] *Boston Daily Herald*," no doubt in recognition of her innumerable successes at the conservatory.[58]

But how exactly did Price appear in that first-page spread? How readable was her Race womanhood?

Price's daughter, Florence Louise Robinson, revealed many years later in conversation with Price biographer Mary Dengler Hudgins, "My grandmother didn't want my mother to be a Negro, so when she took her to Boston she rented an expensive apartment with a maid and forced my mother to say her birthplace was not Little Rock but Mexico."[59] French, Native American, and Spanish were how Mrs. Smith identified (tactfully

omitting any traces of African American ancestry given her strong inclination toward racial passing), and it was into the Spanish side that Price
leaned. This was a side in which Price's phenotypical traits could be recon-
textualized and reinterpreted given the ethnic and cultural heterogeneity
of her new nationality. Under Mrs. Smith's instruction, Price changed her
place of birth mid-study, shielding her racial identity from her institution
and using the presence of her presumably Black and darker-complected
maid to further augment herself and therefore pronounce a non-Black,
near-white femininity to those who did not know the truth of her heritage.

In a photograph of the Class of 1906, Price stands on the right-hand side
(circled in fig. 27); a young Black man stands in the farthest corner on the
left. Sullen white faces (with perhaps clandestine white-passing ones in
the mix) fill the gulf between them. Unknown is the extent to which the
gap between Price and the Black male student from her cohort remained
in the context of social interactions or how her relationships with Black
students across the conservatory transpired. That Price engaged in racial
passing at all, however, alludes to what must have been complex social
navigations for the teenaged student in this environment. That Price lived
separately to her peers suggests that she may have had to contend with
the themes of "loss, alienation, and isolation" that racial passing so often
generated, as Allyson Hobbs meticulously explores in relation to what she
calls "a chosen exile." Yet significant is the fact that Price herself did not
choose this exile; her mother did. In fact, beneath the surface of her passing, Price found ways to assume Blackness, not just as a racial identification
but as the vista through which to articulate and enact her intellectual and
creative self. In this sense, she was very much her father's daughter.

And so, as Price graced the cover of the *Boston Herald*, her appearance
as a Black woman may have only been perceptible to those who knew her,
such was the interiority and surreptitiousness of racial passing.[60] However, that Price continued to embrace the identity that her mother had
directed her to conceal (and chose to never again cede to the world of
racial passing), ultimately aligned her to a history of Black women in white
conservatories, from Maud Cuney Hare to Fannie Barrier Williams, who
sounded proud Race womanhoods amid the cacophony of a vagarious
racial climate.

In addition to negotiating the complex gendered, interracial, and intraracial dynamics of the New England Conservatory, Price also navigated a
broad and demanding curriculum. On top of her piano and organ training
(which included performance, instrumental tuning, sight-reading, and
ensemble playing), she took classes in harmony, theory, analysis, counterpoint, composition, choir training, music history, concert deportment,

Figure 27. New England Conservatory Class of 1906. MC 988, Series I, Folder 12, Box 1, Florence Beatrice Smith Price Collection, Special Collections Department, University of Arkansas Libraries, Fayetteville.

hand culture (for pianists), and normal classes (in music pedagogy).[61] She competed against her peers, winning exciting opportunities to showcase her talent in prestigious venues that included "fashionable and historical" churches and, of course, the conservatory's own Jordan Hall.[62] "[I was] selected to play many times in Jordan Hall during [my] school career at NEC," Price recounted. "Upon one occasion, I played Guilmant's D-minor Sonata for organ. The composer, in America on a concert tour[,] was in the audience. He came forward to shake hands and congratulate me before the audience."[63]

Price's reputation preceded her because present, too, was Clarence Cameron White—the pride of Black classical Boston.[64] White was a preeminent violinist who had recently left the Oberlin Conservatory to pursue a professional life in performance and composition. Later, he would become the president of NANM (1922–24). But at the time of Price's recital, he was the freshly appointed head of the string department at the Washington Conservatory of Music in D.C., newly founded by Harriet Gibbs Marshall for the purpose of bringing nascent Black practitioners to a level that would allow them to compete in the classical mainstream, all the while uplifting Black institutional life. White sat in Jordan Hall "with a host of other friends"—all of whom "thrilled with pride when the French master stepped forward at the conclusion of the number and publicly congratulated [Price] upon the execution and interpretation of the difficult number." Price's racial passing must have been an open secret among Black society (just as her mother's would be), for it would appear that decades before her Chicago arrival, she was already gaining recognition in the Black concert scene.

Boston seemed full of antecedents to Price's eventual life in Chicago, for it was during her studies that she began work on her first symphony. We do not know if this was a direct forerunner of the Symphony No. 1 in E minor, but we do know that it immediately grabbed the attention of its viewer (much like her later one). As reported in the *Chicago Defender* many years after the fact, "George Chadwick, then director of the conservatory upon seeing the score of Mrs. Price's first symphony based upon Negro folk themes, offered her a scholarship in composition in his own private class."[65] The Smith salon, broader culturati of her Little Rock, and formal styles of African- and European-descended Romantic and nationalist composers would have had a formative impact on her approach, but so too did the rurality of her Arkansas and the Black folk traditions of the enslaved that grew from a violent plantation economy. Price wrote in later life, "Having been born in the South and having spent most of my childhood there, I believe I can truthfully say that I understand the real Negro Music."[66] The teenaged Price drew on all that shaped her, presenting Chadwick with an impressively developed symphonic voice.

Significant is that in an environment shaped by the Second New England School or the "Boston Six" to which Chadwick belonged (alongside Amy Beach, Arthur Foote, Edward MacDowell, John Knowles Paine, and Horatio Parker), Price cultivated an American music that resisted the school's full influence. The Second New England School, though mostly trained by European pedagogues, sought to establish an indigenous American sound. Rejecting the cosmopolitan stance of employing models that owed heavily to European traditions, the Boston Six leaned toward a more provincial outlook for the future of American music. While Irish and Scottish folk songs wove their way into their national vision, many agreed that the Black musical idiom (and ironically even Native American influences) had no part in it.

"We have here in America been offered a pattern for an 'American' national musical costume by the Bohemian Dvořák," wrote MacDowell, "though what the Negro melodies have to do with Americanism in art still remains a mystery."[67] "It is not a question of nationality, but individuality, and individuality of style is not the result of imitation—whether of folk songs, negro melodies, the tunes of the heathen Chinese or Digger Indians, but of personal character and inborn originality," proclaimed Paine.[68] "The African population of the United States is far too small for its songs to be considered 'American,'" asserted Beach. And after conceding, "I am not sufficiently familiar with the real negro melodies to be able to offer any opinion of the subject," Chadwick then went on to say, "Such negro melodies I have heard, however, I should be sorry to see become the basis of an American school of composition."[69]

Given Horatio Parker's association with this circle and his presence at Yale, it becomes more understandable as to why Hagan, having not been born in the South, did not experiment with Black musical idioms during her time there but, three years after graduating, committed to "making a tour of the South . . . to study the folk songs of the American Negro" (just as Maud Cuney Hare and Camille Nickerson did with the Creole cultures of the South and Caribbean a few years after).[70] It would seem that Hagan was seeking to recover an aspect of her education that she felt had been missing along her path so far. And so, what did it therefore mean to write one's Blackness into the whitened curricula of American music education, as Holt was similarly inspired to do during her own studies at the Chicago Musical College? Certainly for Price and Holt, to express themselves in such spaces with symphonic works that brimmed with Black folkloric color were bold acts. In Price's case, it was also an assertion of a cultural identity that her mother sought to conceal.

By the end of her studies, Price had made significant impressions across the color lines of the musical elite. But like so many Black women before her, she would have to adapt to the limited opportunities that lay ahead outside of the conservatory setting. Still, the tacit curriculum of musical Race womanhood had prepared her. As she returned to the South and settled into a career of service to Black communities, she carried with her the mission of earlier Race women who similarly ventured to make their privately acquired musical training available to the masses. The symphonies would have to wait as she matured into a new Race womanhood and the community consciousness that came with it.

Shifting Terrain in the Jim Crow South— Chicago Beckons

Price returned to Little Rock in 1906 and, in the wake of her parents' separation, lived with her father. Her inner symphonist lay dormant for the time being for, as Tammy L. Kernodle asks rhetorically, "where in Arkansas was the possibility to really compose at that level?"[71] Instead, what came next for Price very much reflected the maximum opportunities available to a well-educated, middle- to upper-class southern Black woman in the era of Jim Crow. As she immersed herself in the professional world of education, her postconservatory career anticipated Hagan's future direction.[72] As it would be for Hagan in the classrooms of Tennessee State College, New Jersey's Bordentown School, Texas's Bishop College, as well as in her own private studios in Chicago, New York, and elsewhere, teaching grounded Price in the immediate needs of her race and locale.[73] De jure segregation meant that she, like Hagan, taught in institutions that served a Black demographic. Education did not wholly level the playing field, but it did allow Race women to push at the boundaries of access, possibility, and opportunity for the wider Black populace. Teaching was a way in which to put one's social privilege and individual circumstance to civic use and communal benefit. Price therefore followed in the footsteps of numerous Race women educators before her (such as Harriet Gibbs Marshall, Emma Azalia Hackley, and Elnora Manson), diffusing her talents and expertise into her community.

Price first taught at Cotton Plant–Arkadelphia Academy. Then, after less than a year there, she joined the music faculty at Shorter College, which still exists today as a two-year historically Black liberal arts institution. However, Price's employment there came to an end soon after the passing of her father in 1910. She subsequently moved to Atlanta, Georgia, where she became the head of the music department at Clark University (now Clark Atlanta University).[74]

Clark University was "a Christian school, founded in the year 1870 by the Freedman's Aid Society of the Methodist Episcopal Church . . . open to students of all classes, and both sexes, the sole conditions of admission being a desire to learn, good moral character, and obedience to lawfully constituted authority." The institution, redolent of Talented Tenth ideology, admitted students from the age of six and up and permitted boarding for those above the age of fourteen. For older students pursuing higher education, the university offered two main courses of study: the classical course, which led to a bachelor of arts, and the normal course, which trained the next generation of educators and led to a diploma. Students on either the preparatory track of the classical course or the normal course received one period of music a week (the full classical course did not include music at all). The school offered a more specialist track for music students that enabled them to enroll under the condition that "they devote at least four hours per day to music, and that they take at least one other

Figure 28. Clark University, 1910–12. (Price, second row, first on the left.) MC 988a Box 2 Folder 1, Florence Beatrice Smith Price Papers Addendum, Special Collections Department, University of Arkansas Libraries, Fayetteville.

subject prescribed by the head of the department of music," which was Price's role (fig. 28).

Being the head of music cemented Price's place among the many Race women actors shaping musical futures for girls and young women of African descent. Records show that in the 1911–12 academic year, the number of students studying music via the preparatory classical course was 65 (55 male and 10 female), the number of students studying music via the normal course was 137 (all female), and the number of music specialists was 40 (1 male and 39 female). The notably heavier presence of music in the academic lives of Clark University's female students aligned with national data that showed women's increased professional activity in music across the United States.[75] As an educator in Black community settings, Price extended these possibilities to women of African descent.

But as Price became increasingly involved in the music-making and instructional dimensions of Black institutional life, her mother began to strategize her exit. In 1911, the year before Price returned to Little Rock, Florence Irene relocated to Indianapolis, employing the services of the young lawyer (and future son-in-law) Thomas Jewell Price to help her settle the estate of her estranged and now deceased husband. Florence Irene sold every item that had belonged to her and Dr. Smith and, in doing so, erased all traces of her life as a woman of color in Little Rock. As her granddaughter recounted, "My grandmother destroyed many pictures because she didn't want to be connected with her life in Little Rock after my grandfather died. . . . She did decide to go back to the other side"—that is, the white side.[76] However, Florence Irene's racial passing as a white woman was likely an open secret among Black society. In the same year that Florence Irene left for Indianapolis, she surfaced in the society updates of the *Chicago Defender*. Mistaken for her sister, Olive (who had gone with her husband John Gray Lucas to attend a show at the popular Pekin Theatre), the purported sighting of Florence Irene caused "quite a little excitement" and made page-one news. In the commotion documented,

> several ladies were heard to say, why, Mr. Lucas is showing his wife's sister our theatre. Several thought it was another visitor of the east and two ladies in the middle aisle, were heard to say: 'Tis! 'taint! 'tis! 'taint! Why do you say it 'taint, then. Why she was never that stout and she hardly ever wore black.

The argument was settled when "a reporter for the Defender assured the ladies it was the attorney and wife," to which the two arguing women in the middle aisle said nonchalantly, "I knew it was she," in an abrupt shift from the earlier drama.[77] It is a humorous story that would have entertained its readers. However, it also reveals that John Gray Lucas, Olive, and Florence Irene were well-known protagonists in Chicago's Black society and, seemingly, to the wider readers of the *Chicago Defender*—why else would a sighting of Florence Irene have been newsworthy? Even though there was little in the public record of who Florence Irene was or what she became in the aftermath of her Indianapolis return and veritable rebirth into the dominant culture, her impression on Black Chicago was clearly a lasting one.

As expected, Florence Irene's influence also extended to how Price went on to fulfill the marital expectations of her gender, class, and caste. When Price returned to Little Rock in 1912, she soon married Thomas, an ardent Bookerite and similarly racially ambiguous Race man. Thomas Price actively endorsed Booker T. Washington's strategies toward racial uplift, which foregrounded the importance of industrial development, racial self-help, and a more conciliatory (often framed as accommodationist) approach to assimilation among the white masses.[78] Much like Dr. Smith, John Gray Lucas, and Scipio Africanus Jones (another eminent Little Rock lawyer), Thomas, formerly of New Haven, had also seen Little Rock as a city full of prospects for professionals of color, so much so that he encouraged his peers to follow suit.[79] But the proficient and erudite ways of the privileged few were not a panacea for the social ills that befell the underprivileged majority. Making this abundantly clear was the Red Summer of 1919.

Four years on from publicly espousing the South as a forward-looking haven, Thomas and Scipio Africanus Jones took on one of the most well-known cases in Arkansas history.[80] The Elaine race riot of 1919 (also known as the Elaine massacre) reportedly saw five white men murdered and eleven Black men slain.[81] The number of Black casualties was higher than what was officially reported and may have reached into the high hundreds, as the investigative journalism of Ida B. Wells revealed.[82] In the violent aftermath, Phillips County grand jury charged 122 Black men with the crime of inciting the race riots.[83] Jones and Thomas Price represented the first twelve Black men convicted by the court, working to secure their freedom.

Anti-Black violence was not a uniquely southern phenomenon, but those of Florence Price's generation were attuned to the fact that through the next decade, Arkansas moved further and further away from the Black paradise of their younger years. If, for Thomas Price, the initial pull of Little Rock had been its professional and economic prospects, then, by the 1920s, this was now the draw of Chicago. In many ways, his impetus to move on from the South was tied to his gendered role as the head of the household, but it may also have been tied to the well-warranted fear of lynchings—a particular violence used by the dominant culture to curb Black male behavior irrespective of social background. That Thomas had come to the defense of the Elaine massacre's Black victims, for instance, certainly represented the kind of out-of-line behavior that racist southern vigilantes were inclined to violently correct. (Ida B. Wells assiduously documented these kinds of terror in her reports.)

The specter of southern violence would have been a major push factor for Florence Price, as it was for all those who joined the Great Migration. But where she differed from her husband was in the fact that the call of Chicago was not only tied to economic opportunities. Her motives were far more personal; they were familial, social, musical, and deep rooted. For example, Price's father had been "an early Chicago settler" who, "as a very young man[,] opened dental offices in the loop at the corner of

State and Madison" and even served as superintendent of Quinn Chapel Sunday school.[84] He might very well have stayed in the city had his dental practice not perished in the Great Chicago Fire of 1871, prompting his move to Arkansas. And so, there was the Chicago that Price knew through her father, but in addition to this, some sources even suggest that Price actually lived in Chicago for a short spell as a child, attending Forrestville Elementary School before "return[ing] with her family for high school" in Little Rock.[85] If true, it was also around this time, toward the end of the nineteenth century, that Price's maternal aunt, Olive, and uncle-in-law, John Gray Lucas, emigrated to the Black Metropolis, no doubt encouraging periodic visits through the decades that followed from a prepassing Florence Irene (likely with a young Bea in tow). In any case, it seems that Price had known Chicago all her life.

With deep family ties to the city and a vocation that placed her beyond the types of labor typically available to Black women in the Midwest, it becomes necessary to consider, as Darlene Clark Hine points out, "the non-economic motives propelling black female migration" to this region, particularly as they related to a Race woman such as Price. During World War I, Hine explains, "a great number of black women found work in midwestern hotels as cooks, waitresses, and maids, as ironers in the new steam laundries, as labelers and stampers in Sears Roebuck and Montgomery Ward mail order houses, as common laborers in garment and lampshade factories, and workers in food processing and meat packing plants."[86] Price's social circumstances, however, prepared her for no such reality; for her, the call of Chicago came from higher echelons.

Price landed in Chicago's circle of esteemed Race women and men not by chance but by the design of Black society. As a light-complected, racially ambiguous woman of color born into the moneyed and propertied class of post-Reconstruction Arkansas and later bolstered by her conservatory education, respectable teaching career, and marriage to a lawyer, Price's background conduced her to the necessary connections for an active life in the city's Black concert scene. This is not to interpret hers as a life of ease, nepotism, and romance (especially as she experienced many forms of challenge, precarity, discrimination, and violence—both in her marriage and as a witness to white terrorism in the South).[87] Rather, this is to develop a perspective that is less fixated on her assimilation from the margins to the center of white acceptance and more attentive to her journey through Black society, Race women's community-building, and her ability to avail herself of all that the South Side impresarios could offer.

Unlike so many southern visitors and migrants whose accents, dialects, fashions, religions, complexions, and castes set them apart from

Chicago's Old Settler, upper-class urbanites—consequently compelling Race women and men to invest in the intraracial acculturation of these seemingly unworldly, unlettered southerners and mold them into paragons of respectability—Price better assimilated. The bourgeois mores and uplift ideologies that framed the sociocultural dimensions of her childhood, adolescence, and early adulthood aligned with those of the South Side's Black culturati. Like those who awaited her visits—the Lucases, the Holts, the Georges, the Bondses, and others—Price embodied a cosmopolitan air that, alongside her class, complexion, and comportment, situated her within a distinct social network. In turn, she too became familiar to the city and its people to the extent that her visits were even deemed newsworthy.

"Mrs. Price Returns Home," read the headline of a short feature printed on September 7, 1918, in the *Chicago Defender*'s "All around the Town" segment.[88] The brief paragraph of society news read:

> Mrs. Thomas J. Price, nee Florence Beatrice Smith, wife of Atty. Thomas J. Price, Little Rock, Ark., left for home this week after a visit of more than a month with her aunt, Mrs. J. Gray Lucas, 503 E. 36th Street.[89]

Florence Price's and her aunt's marital affiliations were the points of interest here, evidencing the extent to which women (regardless of their social standing) were often written into the shadows of their husbands' lives. Of greater significance were Thomas, known to Black Chicago society as a prominent Arkansas lawyer, and John Gray Lucas, who ran his thriving law practice on 25 North Dearborn Street in the Loop.[90] Had the name Florence B. Price been deemed newsworthy in its own right, the article might have granted more insight into what actually happened during her stay. But as it did not, let us speculate.

Was this the moment in which John Gray Lucas—a Race man whose bureaucratic skills and singing talents situated him squarely in the matriarchal structures of music-making on the South Side—began to orient Price in the burgeoning Black classical metropolis? There is little reason to imagine Lucas as anything but a progressive and empathetic champion of Price and her potential and as a useful guide through the city's dynamic Black concert scene. Might regular Chicago visitor Clarence Cameron White have been another point of connection to the South Side classical community that awaited her? Might the late summer of 1918 have been the moment in which Price met the indefatigable Holt?

If an avid reader of the *Chicago Defender* and a keen follower of the "Woman's Page," then Price would have known of Holt ahead of her summer visit. The Woman's Page was typically vast and incisive in its purview even as it perpetuated traditional attitudes about gendered difference.

On the one hand, some of its articles revolved around the "four F's" of "food, family, fashion and furnishings," but on the other hand, there were columns that captured Race women beyond these associations, shining a light on their radical, revolutionary, and racially uplifting paths.[91] As Price turned to the Woman's Page of the June 29, 1918, edition, a photograph of a poised and pensive-looking Race woman, captioned "Lena James Holt, M.M.," would have caught her attention.[92] Price would have read the story of how Holt earned "the honor of being the only artist of the Race holding the degree of M.M." and "won her degree and highest honors" with her *Rhapsody on Negro Themes* for orchestra.[93]

If Price already had a particular eye and ear for the goings-on in the Black classical metropolis, then she would have known that Holt's pursuits in the Black classical music scene predated her academic honor. Price would have read Holt's reviews of the operatic and orchestral programs of the Chicago Symphony Orchestra and classical recitals of Black artists, with a certain Mrs. Estella C. Majors (née Bonds) often receiving praise for her performances.[94] And of course, there were the reviews of the Second Annual All Colored Composers Concert, which featured Holt as both composer and performer.[95] Holt may therefore have been a familiar character to Price in print, if not (yet) in person.

As Holt's 1918 celebratory feature in the Woman's Page drew to a close, Price would have noted the open invitation from Holt's South Side abode to the Black classical metropolis and beyond: "The Holts extend a hearty welcome to their many friends, and Mrs. Holt particularly offers the hand of fellowship to members of the art world."[96] Did Price accept this invitation in the summer of 1918?

In any case, Price was starting to respond to the call of Chicago. Extended trips, such as the aforementioned, provided her with the opportunity to connect with the growing networks and infrastructures of the Black classical metropolis. In addition to building her social world, Helen Walker-Hill demonstrates how Price "took every advantage to grow musically, attending Chicago Musical College, Chicago Teacher's College, the University of Chicago, Central YMCA College, and the American Conservatory of Music."[97] With each visit, engagement, and music class, Price inched further out of her husband's shadow, moving into a light that marked the dawn of a new symphonic and Black sisterly chapter.

Coda

In NANM's second year, the home of its highly anticipated convention moves from Chicago's Black Metropolis to New York's Black Mecca. On

July 27–29, 1920, NANM convenes at Harlem's Bethel African Methodist Episcopal Church (West 132nd Street).[98] A variety of programs, set to foster "fellowship [and] pride in Race achievement" and to engage "renowned artists, both white and Colored," unfold over the three-day affair; its interracial purview speaks to the association's growing influence and recognition in wider music circles. Robert Nathaniel Dett (future NANM president, from 1924 to 1926) holds a conference on "the folk songs of the Negro," invoking the contentious issues of authenticity and (mis)appropriation as he argues "how this music must be regarded as sacred" and kept "above the level of the minstrel stage." But he is just as wary of modernism's more experimental and destructive strains, as he speaks cautiously, even critically, of the attempts "on the part of some composers to give this music new settings."[99] Overlapping with Dett's themes of preservation and posterity are the views of New York's H. Lawrence Freeman; in his talk, "Negro Music as a Basis for Symphonic and Operatic Development," Freeman deliberates the topic of presenting Black folk songs and Negro Spirituals in a contemporary Black concert aesthetic.

The scholars and critics also say their piece—or, at least, intend to in the case of the *New York Tribune*'s Henry Edward Krehbiel. Krehbiel is scheduled to speak on "The Relation of Folk Music to Masterpieces" but is unable to attend, explaining, "I am ill and work is out of the question; if any of my friends make inquiry of me, please say that they are in my kind remembrance, especially Mr. Dett and Harry Burleigh." Although absent, Krehbiel's note attests to the expansion of NANM's networks and endorsements. Present, however, is NANM vice president Nora Holt, who delivers "a most interesting paper on 'Musicianship'" in which she "[exhausts] . . . in a most scholarly manner" the importance of music theory and reiterates its benefits for the concert performer.

Another highlight of the convention is Harriet Gibbs Marshall's talk on "The Pioneer's Task" in which she illuminates "her struggles in starting the Washington Conservatory of Music." During Marshall's segment, other pioneers are credited, ensuring that those influential names baked into NANM's own foundations are not forgotten. Among those mentioned are the original Fisk Jubilee Singers, coloratura soprano Madame Marie Selika Williams (who is in attendance), musical director John Turner Layton of Washington, D.C. (whose son of the same name and musical leaning will later achieve great success in Europe), and Emma Azalia Hackley. In fact, Hackley is due to deliver a report called "The Results of My Itinerant Community Work" but cannot attend the convention as the invitation, in her words, "came too late, besides there is too much to tell in a report."[100] What is more likely, though, is that Hackley's ailing health, which she strives to shield from public view, precludes her from journeying to Harlem at this time.[101]

Nevertheless, Hackley is right: there is a great deal to discuss all around (ranging from Black music preservation to pedagogy to patronage to performance) and only a few days in which to cover it all before the two hundred or so delegates—comprising "teachers and supervisors in Negro schools and colleges, conductors of private schools, heads of Negro conservatories of music, well known concert artists, as well as promising young Negro students of music"—return to their respective hometowns. Morning and afternoon sessions brim with conferences, open conversations, roundtable discussions, and paper presentations. Evening sessions comprise recitals of burgeoning and finished Black concert artists; they feature pianists Hazel Harrison and Helen Hagan and singers Florence Cole Talbert and "that muchly praised and widely heralded Philadelphia girl, Marian Anderson."[102] But NANM's greatest commitment remains to its composers.

NANM's Committee on Composition, chaired by Carl Rossini Diton (who will later preside over NANM from 1926 to 1928), exists in direct response to the association's firmly held belief that "no phase of great work that our National will and must do could be of more importance than that of encouraging the Negro composer, by giving his composition publicity whenever possible." The pronoun "his" functions customarily in the gender-neutral sense, for a small handful of Race women appear on NANM's radar. "By no means have we exhausted the number of composers," Diton explains, "but we will mention the list thus far obtained":

> Helen [Hagan], Henry L. Grant, Phaon Martin, Roy Tibbs, [Major] N. Clark Smith, Gerald Tyler, Harry Burleigh, Melville Charlton, Will Marion Cook, F. Hall Johnson, Rosamond Johnson, Harry Williams, Martha Bonner, Shelton Pollen, Clarence [Cameron] White, Carissa Hardy, Harvey Hebron, [Edward] Hill Jr., [Edward] Hill Sr., Alfred Johnson, Randolph Smith, Carl Diton, Nathaniel Dett. Among the styles of composition are piano concertos, songs, orchestral numbers, chorus with orchestral accompaniment, chamber music, violin and piano, piano sonatas, string quartets, organ fugues, etc.

Diton provides an invaluable window into the wider canon of Black Renaissance composition and the range of instrumental and vocal genres within it. Like Harriet Gibbs Marshall, Emma Azalia Hackley, and the Fisk Jubilee Singers, many of these composers will have faced the pioneer's task of shifting the frontiers of Black classical accomplishment so that those who follow—it is hoped—will not have so far to travel. Unfortunately, most of these names will disappear from the public record in the decades that extend beyond the years of each composer's activity. Awaiting future recovery will be the music of Grant, Phaon-Martin, Tibbs, Tyler, Williams, Bonner, Pollen, Hardy, Hebron, Hill Sr. and Jr., Alfred Johnson, and Randolph Smith. However, due to the cumulative nature of Black institution-building, their work will remain deeply embedded in the fabric of Black concert culture and in the canon to which Price will soon belong upon proving her mastery in multiple genres and arriving in a new generation of Black symphonists alongside William Grant Still and William Levi Dawson.

In August 1940, NANM, under President Mary Cardwell Dawson (no relation to William Dawson), will return to Chicago for its annual convention. There, Price will be celebrated in the midst of Maude Roberts George, Abbie Mitchell, Anita Patti Brown, Camille Nickerson, Robert Nathaniel Dett, and William Dawson as Clara Hutchison gifts the thoroughly established Chicago composer with a token of appreciation on behalf of the city's musicians (figs. 29 and 30). Housed in this gesture will be the clear acknowledgment not just of how far Price has come but of the legacies she has uplifted along the way.

For the 1920 NANM convention, however, the only place where Price is visible is under the "Members" section of the minutes, next to her home state of Arkansas. Still, her membership marks an important beginning, one that signals the growth of her musical world. Among those listed as members under her future home state of Illinois are Nora Holt, Irene Berenice Hudlin, Pauline J. Lee, Martha B. Anderson, Clara E. Hutchison, James A. Mundy, T. Theodore Taylor, J. Wesley Jones, Walter E. Gossette, Estella "Stella" Bonds, and fellow New England Conservatory alumna and future director of music at Wendell Phillips High School Mildred Bryant Jones.[103] Her soon-to-be South Side neighbors are also listed, like Nannie Mae Strayhorn of Maryland and Florence Cole Talbert of Michigan by way of Tennessee. When Price eventually moves to Chicago, her connections to the lives of these musicians (and numerous others) will become all the more tangible. Her work will take root alongside theirs in the physical and psychic composition of her new urban landscape and in a history of Race women who actively restructured Chicago's associational and institutional foundations, long before her arrival. But as her movements culminate in the Black classical metropolis and as her musical Race womanhood finds new symphonic expression in this realm, her work will also continue to hold the herstories of the unfinished symphonists—that is, the earlier examples of musical Race women who exhibited similar promise and potential, examples otherwise unheard and unseen in the discourse of Price's singular exceptionalism.

Figure 29. Photograph no. 2. Persons famous in the music history of the race gathered for Honors Night. Left to right: Maude Roberts George, publicity chairman; Florence B. Price, Chicago composer; Abbie Mitchell, actress and concert artist; Mary Cardwell Dawson, association president; Anita Patti Brown, pioneer singer; William L. Dawson, Tuskegee, composer; and Camille Nickerson, Howard University. MC 988a Box 1 Folder 5 Item 1, Florence Beatrice Smith Price Papers Addendum, Special Collections Department, University of Arkansas Libraries, Fayetteville.

Photograph no. 5. Chicago musicians present token of appreciation to Mrs. Florence B. Price. Clara Hutchinson [*sic*], historian, makes the presentation. MC 988a Box 1 Folder 5 Item 1, Florence Beatrice Smith Price Papers Addendum, Special Collections Department, University of Arkansas Libraries, Fayetteville.

gure 30. Party given by Club of Graduate Musicians. Martha Mitchell-Parks, orga-
zer. Monday Aug. 26, 1940 "Chicago Night," after program. Left to right, Nathaniel
ett, Mary Cardwell Dawson, Florence B. Price. Photo by Alwyn Adams. 4642 Win-
rop Chicago, Sunnyside 7270. MC 988a Box 2 Folder 4, Florence Beatrice Smith
ice Papers Addendum, Special Collections Department, University of Arkansas
braries, Fayetteville.

5

Seizing the World Stage

As preparations for the 1933 Chicago World's Fair Century of Progress Exposition gathered pace, some Black Chicagoans feared history would repeat itself. They wondered to what extent (if at all) their communities would be represented in the city's celebrations. Although those of Maude Roberts George's and Estella Bonds's generation would have been of childhood age when the World's Fair reached Chicago in 1893 with the World's Columbian Exposition, Black underrepresentation was part of this fair's legacy and therefore of the lore learned by younger generations of Black Chicagoans. Those of John Gray Lucas's and Florence Price's father's generation would have seen the hypocrisy firsthand as the white press characterized the city as highly "cosmopolitan"—"the new Babel" even—and praised the fair's ethnic and nationalistic diversity.[1] Populated with white neoclassical buildings that earned the site the appellation of the "White City," the 1893 World's Fair spotlighted the Swiss demographic; the Scotchmen, "thousands strong, with hundreds of pipes"; the Bohemians, featuring a concert with "six of their best composers—Dvorak, Smetana, Napravnik, Hlavac, Bendl, and Fibich"; "our Irish Brethren"; and "the queer people of the universe from China to the top and round again."[2] But there was a glaring absence: neither optimistically as "brethren" nor pejoratively as "the queer people of the universe" were African Americans granted visibility at the fair. They simply did not exist.

In response, a cohort of civic leaders and activists comprising Frederick Douglass (the World's Fair representative for Haiti), Ida B. Wells, Irvine Garland Penn, and Ferdinand Lee Barnett eked out space in the Haitian building and, from there, distributed their coauthored pamphlet, *The Reason Why the Colored American Is Not in the World's Columbian Exposition*.[3]

The document cited the long-lasting impact of slavery and in Barnett's closing chapter, titled "The Reason Why," he concluded that "theoretically open to all Americans, the Exposition is, literally and figuratively, a 'White City,' in the building of which the Colored American was allowed no helping hand, and in its glorious success he has no share."[4] The 1933 World's Fair seemed, to some, doomed to repeat the past.

Rumors flowed far and wide: "'The Race will not take part,' said some of them. 'The Race will be barred from everything within the gates of the exposition grounds,' said others. 'The Race will not be represented in the official set-up at the fair,' said still others. To all these rumors there seemed to be no answers," reported the *Chicago Defender*'s Dewey R. Jones.[5] But the Chicago Music Association (CMA) were at work and had been for the past year or so, pushing to provide answers in the form of music.

Estella Bonds was the CMA's representative for the Century of Progress World's Fair Committee, and in a CMA meeting that took place on May 17, 1932, Bonds "brought back a request" from the committee that the CMA "join hands with other Negro organizations, civic and otherwise[,] to help gain Negro representation in the fair of 1933." Moving in quick response, a "committee consisting of Mrs. George, Mrs. Bonds, and Mrs. [Anita] Patti Brown were chosen to represent and act for the [CMA] in whatever steps were taken to gain this recognition."[6] From there, the Negro in Music emerged, not out of the perceived silence interpreted by the unknowing majority but out of a small underground chorus, diligently strategizing how to seize their representation at the World's Fair.

This chapter builds on a question posed at the start of this book: how might progress be told along the Race woman's timeline to reveal the ways in which she, like her white counterparts, took her place in the Century of Progress, rather than waiting for it to be given? Journeying through the key events of the Rodman Wanamaker Awards, the transformative role of the Bonds salon, and the realization of the Negro in Music, I delve into the incisive strategies and intimate settings that Race women utilized to affect and bolster the current of Black concert culture. I demonstrate how their efforts culminated in the Black classical metropolis's arrival on the world stage.

Of course, conceptualizing arrival in the dynamic sphere of public culture—a realm that is always in motion—necessitates embracing the figurative. When and where an individual or collective exhibits a deep presence in, and connectivity with, a particular moment or event indexes that a symbolic destination or pinnacle has been reached. Historicizing this therefore means identifying the perceived stillness and timelessness around certain phenomena. Naturally, the stillness and timelessness do not actually exist, but their impression does, which is what creates the perception of arrival. In turn, these impressions mark the milestones along the path of social progress.[7] For the Black classical metropolis, the 1932 Wanamaker Awards and the Negro in Music embodied such cultural capstones. That is not to say that these events existed on a smooth plane of linear progress. Far from it. They were fraught with the regressive and transgressive obstacles of a white hegemony. Nevertheless, they signaled arrival for the ways in which Race women and men, not only in the Black classical metropolis, took stock of the historical moments in question and beheld the gravity of those phenomena with a profound sense of the here and now.

Price returns to the fore as I examine how the Black classical metropolis claimed their representation in the Negro in Music via her award-winning symphony. Yet rather than emphasizing a solo biography, I seek the aspects of Price's narrative that evince Race women's contrapuntal lives and the paradoxes that permeated their collective progress. Like Alisha Lola Jones who states, "I am inclined to move away from proving Price's proximity to Great White Male Composers as her life's goal and career highlight," I also aim to dissociate Price's journey from this line of interpretation. Instead, I build on Jones's work, offering an interpretation that amplifies "the sound of Black sisterhood" along Price's trajectory.[8] With this framing, as Jones argues, Price's accomplishments are less a pinnacle for their adjacency to white classical accomplishment and more a pinnacle for the story they tell of Race women's prototypical Black feminist activism and their push for self-representation in all facets, from civic spheres to the world stage.

Race Women Taking Their Part

What did it mean for the Black woman to "take her part in the Century of Progress," as Elizabeth Lindsay Davis put it, rather than to merely *take part*? In her foreword to the monumental *Lifting as They Climb* tome of Race women's social, cultural, political, and economic milestones (published by the National Association of Colored Women's Clubs), Davis chose her language carefully, employing what Cheryl R. Ganz describes as "political and exposition rhetoric to write that a new day and a new deal had arrived for American women."[9] However, in emphasizing Black women's roles in particular—stating, "It is fitting at this time that the Negro woman should take her part in the Century of Progress and prove to the world that she, too, is finding her place in the sun"—Davis brought a more intersectional dimension to the framing of American womanhood.[10] The possessive pronoun marked the Race woman's intentionality; it asserted her right, responsibility, and relevance to the project of progress in the United States. To "take her part" was no passive move. Rather, it was an active stance that proudly pronounced the Blackness of her womanhood and the womanness of her racialized existence. To "take her part" was therefore to claim the Century of Progress in the project of Race women's world-making.

That said, you would never know the extent of Black women's part-taking and world-making from the way that the official guidebook of the 1933 World's Fair was written. Its tone typified that putatively objective voice, disguised as neutrality when in fact cloaking the politics, perspectives, and propaganda of white patriarchal supremacy. The guidebook depicted progress as a graduated scale from a demonized indigeneity to a lauded imperialism. Under a subtitle that read "A City Lifted from Mud" flowed the romanticized history of how early nineteenth-century Chicago "was a huddle of huts, hewn of logs, clinging to the shadows of Fort Dearborn for safety from the Indians." The program then boasted of the city's increased population and industrialization: "Today it is nearly 4,000,000—3,376,438 for the sake of accuracy, by the census of 1930—and growing at a rate of 70,000 a year. Chicago in a century has climbed to her place as second largest city in America, fourth in the world." In sum, the guidebook purported, Chicago—this once "youngster of the New World"—"had fought the wilderness and won, and had welcomed peoples of many bloods who came and helped build."[11] The guidebook painted Native Americans as the aggressors (note the impression created of settlers *clinging to safety*); it portrayed Indigenous ways of life as anti-progress (as encoded in the word "wilderness"), while the white settlers were shown as the underdogs—that is, the ones to root for in this story, the ones for whom victory was most deserving. There was, of course, no mention of the human trafficking, slavery, and indentured servitude in the state of Illinois that brought as much blood as it spilled.

Unsurprisingly, a century on, Black women still found themselves writing counternarratives to the nation's whitewashed history. In addition to contending with the dominant voice of the 1933 Chicago World's Fair, they also had to navigate the segregationist outlooks of white women organizers and the male-dominated community leadership of African Americans. Ganz's exploration of women's spaces at the fair shows how white women spearheaded efforts toward female representation, all the while deliberately writing women of color out of decision-making processes and an overall purview of what (and who) constituted gendered progress. However, where white women were unsuccessful in their campaign to erect an official "woman's building," Black clubwomen, Ganz observes, "created their own space even amid tremendous obstacles." Under the banner of the National De Saible Memorial Society, founded by Race woman Annie E. Oliver in 1928 and named after the African-descended Jean Baptiste Point du Sable, who was Chicago's first settler and therefore complicated the white lens of Chicago's origin story, Oliver and her band of Black clubwomen "achieved at the fair what black male community leaders could not: a pavilion of self-representation."[12] Although Ganz makes no mention of the musical spaces that African American women additionally seized, her discussion of the racial and gendered dynamics that shaped broader representation at the fair provides invaluable insight into the kinds of contentious dynamics that Chicago's musical Race women would have encountered.

Estella Bonds, Maude Roberts George, and Anita Patti Brown were deeply attentive to the need for Black women's representation at the Chicago World's Fair. And through their efforts, the Negro in Music came to achieve exactly that, with the Black classical metropolis asserting their representation through Florence Price and Margaret Bonds. The visual of an all-white and all-male American orchestra rendering the work of a Black female composer, as well as playing behind a Black female instrumentalist, had likely not been seen in the United States since Helen Hagan's years at Yale, where she not only performed her piano concerto with the student orchestra but also with the New Haven Symphony under conductor Horatio Parker. Of course, the Negro in Music was on an entirely different scale—not that the arena or occasion particularly mattered though, because as the work of the South Side impresarios showed, there was no area in which they did not take the matter of Black women's representation seriously.

It would be remiss, however, not to flag and interrogate a notable controversy in the Negro in Music program. Strikingly, the evening opened with the overture "In Old Virginia" by the avowed segregationist and Virginian composer John Powell. Although stylistically not out of place with its Romantic orchestral palette and evocative Americana soundscape, the composer's politics were the antithesis of everything that the program stood for. Only a few months prior to the Negro in Music, Powell's declaration, "There is no real American Negro music," had resurfaced in the public sphere. According to Clarence Cameron White, Powell's statement was part of "an old press copy that Mr. Powell's press agent has sent out from time to time since 1911." White believed that the purpose of "sending out this nonsense to the press," as he put it, was to help promote Powell's upcoming concerts. In other words, it was a publicity stunt.

And it succeeded in attracting attention, drawing several prominent Black Renaissance artists and activists, including Robert Nathaniel Dett, Lillian LeMon, and Alain Locke into debate with Powell's virulent claims.[13] So, several months on, how did Powell's work become the overture for the whole Negro in Music program? Given what Stephanie DeLane Doktor recognizes as the "fierce response" from Black concert practitioners and intellectuals, who, then, was responsible for Powell's presence here? If the early music criticism of Nora Holt is anything to go by, Powell had long been an antagonist of the Black classical metropolis.

In 1921, Holt attended the premiere of Powell's *Rhapsodie nègre* for piano and orchestra (originally completed in 1918 and deliberately ascribed a lowercase *n* for *nègre* as a reflection of Powell's belief in Black inferiority). That Holt's own *Rhapsody on Negro Themes* (which emerged in the same year as Powell's *Rhapsodie nègre*) disappeared (both figuratively and literally) from the record, while Powell's rhapsody became one of "the top ten works performed most frequently by American orchestras," evidences white audiences' proclivity for advancing white supremacy even as it related to their consumption of Black (or perceived-to-be-Black) artistry. It backs Doktor's assertion that "white supremacy was part and parcel of US modernist culture."[14] Furthermore, it unveils the purposefully institutionalized racist and sexist structural devices at play that would allow the interpretation of African American life through the hateful gaze of a white supremacist to be touted over the perspicacious lens of a Race woman such as Holt.

The Chicago Symphony Orchestra gave *Rhapsodie nègre* its first performances on March 4 and 5, 1921, with Powell at the piano and Frederick Stock conducting. Richard Brockwell—who, unbeknownst to Holt, was Powell's alias—penned the program notes. His profuse and overly prescriptive writing style "out-rhapsodied his rhapsody," as Holt satirically put it in her *Chicago Defender* review. Noting the jarring disparity between the music, which to Holt's ears was nothing extraordinary (though finely rendered), and the hyperbole housed in Brockwell's commentary, she reported that "the rhapsody in itself was sane, bright, forceful, understandable and brilliantly interpreted." Nevertheless, it unfolded contrarily to the inflammatory notes that Brockwell used to index the African Americanness of the rhapsody. Phrases, aligning with the primitivist vogue of the age, like "uncouth harmonies," "tragic wail," "fanatic frenzy," and "voodoo orgy" dotted his descriptions. Yet the reality of Holt's listening experience was rather bland—predictable, even. "Instead," she explained, the work "faithfully followed the now patented procedure with our music: a downward intonation on a minor third, giggling figures, syncopated rhythms in various choirs, one good old tune that every one [*sic*] has heard stated in unison or with simple harmonic treatment, the shuffling of a second bar, clap-clap of a paddle, a boom and a crash, and there you are—an imitation, but not a faithful reproduction of Negro Music." The rhapsody, Holt declared, was nothing special.

Grabbing her attention with greater force, however, was Brockwell's outright racism: "The most astounding statement of Mr. Brockwell in his note," wrote Holt, "was his indictment, 'For the Negro, with all the lovable and simple heart of the child, has also the mentality of the child.'" Although Holt was not aware of the fact that she was dealing with the same racist figure across both the composition and its commentary, she astutely recognized the ill-intent behind the work and that even the most anti-Black composers could not resist the bandwagon of Black cultural (mis)appropriation. Her review continued, "Since Mr. Powell permitted the writer to use that phrase one doubts the sincerity of both—the writer blatantly assists the composer to 'put over' his rhapsody and Mr. Powell, following the lead of many Americans when they are void of public notice, grasps the last straw—the Negro. Their pretended regard and interest in us is also doubted by the use of a small 'n' for Negro." Holt's criticism not only assessed the music (per her duty), but it also set Powell-Brockwell in the context of his racist politics and fearlessly called out his attention-seeking motives and wholly unoriginal artistry.

In light of Holt's influence, both in the institution- and community-building of the Black classical metropolis and as a music critic who, as Lucy Caplan argues, "used atmospheric details" in her commentary to "advance an alternative model of embodied listening" and invite her readership to become "vicarious concert goers," there is little reason to think that over a decade later, the South Side impresarios behind the Negro in Music would have touted a figure such as Powell.[15] Holt was a maker of taste and culture; her philosophical presence lingered long after her physical departure from Chicago. On top of that, Powell's politics reentered public discussion in early 1933. The Black classical metropolis would not have been so quick to forget. So, might Powell's admission into the Negro in Music program have been a choice of the white establishment? After all, Powell was not only a comfortable presence in the programs of the Chicago Symphony Orchestra, but *Rhapsodie nègre* had made him one of the most-performed American composers in the national orchestral scene of the 1920s and early '30s.

That the Black press made no mention of Powell's presence on the Negro in Music program strongly suggests that he was not endorsed in the realm of African American concert culture. So, was Powell's inclusion an involuntary concession or compromise for the South Side impresarios in a program that otherwise may have been deemed too proudly Black to white audiences' "Jim Crow ears"? Critic Claudia Cassidy had positioned the programming of John Alden Carpenter's Concertino for Piano and Orchestra (performed by Margaret Bonds) as taking up the white man's burden. But if that was how Cassidy could frame Carpenter, who contrastingly had a far more collegial relationship with Black practitioners than Powell, then what did it mean for the program to open with an all-white, all-male orchestra performing the music of a man whose politics encompassed "enforced segregation and eugenical sterilization" of the Black populace and the advocacy of "a white ethnostate"?[16]

Powell's overture had (much like the official Century of Progress guidebook) the veneer of that putative neutrality, so easily afforded to the white male voice. But in reality, the piece sat as a prelude of white patriarchal supremacy in a program of Spirituals to symphonies and therefore as a microcosm of wider tensions embroiled in Race women's pursuit of visibility and audibility at the World's Fair. The Negro in Music program was not unique in this regard; racism was baked into the varying levels of African American representation across the exposition despite the fair touting "a policy of inclusiveness." For example, Black visitors were refused service at on-site restaurants, while "Negro" attractions portrayed stereotypes of happily acquiescent slaves.[17] This was the ongoing dynamic in which Black women took their part, a dynamic rife with contradiction, violence, and hypocrisy. But per the nature of their activity, Race women worked *against* and *toward*, *in spite of* and *because of*, *in contrast to* and *in concert with*.

They countered a white establishment fixture like Powell with strategic silence in the Black press's commentary and criticisms of the Negro in Music, *working against* the notion of the white man's burden and *working toward* the narrative of African Americans' autonomy. They pooled their own resources (in the form of finances, labor, knowledge, networks, and institutions) *in spite of* the uphill battle that often awaited those of their race and gender, and *because of* the paramount importance that Chicago should know, hear, and see the talents of the nation's Black concert artists. Finally, they chose a woman composer—a symphonist, no less—to represent the Black classical metropolis *in contrast* to perpetuating yet another all-male-composer program and *in concert* with Race women's proclivity for lifting as they climbed.

Whereas the voice of a white supremacist opened the program, in all that followed, the South Side impresarios, alongside a multigenerational display of Black concert artists and artistry, sounded the final word. For Race women, taking their part meant pushing through the paradoxes and using the Century of Progress as a platform to show the world exactly what they were capable of as well as what they could become with access to the right opportunities—opportunities like the Rodman Wanamaker Awards.

The Inner Workings of the Wanamakers

When the 1932 Rodman Wanamaker Music Contest announced its call for compositions, the Black classical metropolis responded, as if in unison, to an opportunity that was poised, in the words of the *Chicago Defender*, to "undoubtedly show the remarkable progress made in musical composition by this Race."[18] On the one hand, the Wanamaker prizes would prove the advancement of Black classical composers in the quality of their training and growth of their craft, but on the other hand, they would affirm new cultural heights in African American concert life writ large, as well as validating deep networks of support that bolstered the Black classical landscape. Unsurprisingly, Race women's response to the Wanamakers' call engaged the wide range of sites that constituted their creative and intellectual work. Incisive strategies fostered in the intimate settings of the Bonds salon and club meetings were enacted in the public-facing forums of Maude Roberts George's "News of the Music World" columns and the Black church. Building on a multidecade-long history of Black impresarial organizing, the South Side's classical community coalesced around a mission to advance the possibilities for their composers; a triumph for one of their own was a triumph for all, and the magnitude of victories claimed would publicly pronounce arrival of the Black classical metropolis.

Established in 1927 by Philadelphia philanthropist and storeowner Lewis Rodman Wanamaker, the contests were born out of its founder's sympathetic disposition toward African Americans and his desire to create a platform that exclusively elevated Black composers. As Rodman Wanamaker did not live to witness the development of the contest beyond its first year, his son, Captain John Wanamaker Jr., continued the contests in honor of his father's legacy. However, the death of Wanamaker Jr. brought an end to the contests all together. When this era came to a close, Maude Roberts George lamented, "The NANM misses the encouragement of the Wanamaker Awards in music. During the period of the Wanamaker contests, musicians who thought they might win a prize were persuaded to devote more time than they ordinarily could to serious work. Composition flourished at that time."[19] The absence of the awards thereafter made the dearth of financial opportunities for African American classical composers all the more palpable.

The *Atlanta Daily World* printed George's words under the title "Sepia Composers in Need of Funds," while a reprint in the *Pittsburgh Courier* carried the banner "'Musicians Need New Angel' Says Mrs. Maude George." In both cases, the tone of each title reinforced the necessity of financial backing while George's specific reference to the Wanamaker Awards in the article evidenced the ways in which the contests had come to represent more than just a music competition: they were a history-making cultural event on a national scale. The Wanamaker contests had sustained the musical activity of those first marginalized by race (and other intersecting factors) and further marginalized by their compositional pursuits in the classical sphere. They held a tremendous significance, leaving a void that was poignantly felt in their absence. But ultimately, the precarious nature of white patronage and philanthropy was why systems of self-help were (and continue to be) so prevalent in Black communities. And glossed over in George's lamentations were the significant roles that she, along with the other impresarial angels of the South Side, played in manifesting the miraculous.

The first Wanamaker Awards were announced at NANM's eighth annual convention, which took place in Philadelphia on July 25–31, 1926. George, a NANM board member at this time, recalled the brilliant reaction of attendees in her "News of the Music World" column: "The great thrill which went to the souls of the musicians brought forth one of the greatest spontaneous outbursts of applause and cheering ever heard from that artistic group."[20] George fully understood the cause for celebration; she was all too aware that if African American composers were to develop major works, then they (much like their counterparts in popular music) required the financial means to make this both a feasible and rewarding endeavor.

As much as Black communities could provide realms of institutions and ideas, networks of support and sisterhood, and channels of communion and communication, the financial resources of the white majority, by design, far outweighed the monetary contributions that Black institutions could offer. For all the precarity, not to mention the conditionality, of white patronage, George, her NANM colleagues, and her even closer-knit CMA network recognized the necessity of the Wanamakers. Reassuring, however, was that the contests impaneled Black Renaissance practitioners (amid an integrated cast) such as Harry T. Burleigh, Carl Diton, and Clarence Cameron White of the inaugural 1927 awards and later J. Rosamond Johnson and Melville Charlton of the 1932 awards, therefore evidencing how Black agency could be exercised under white sponsorship.[21]

Applicants for the 1927 contest were guided by a set of ten rules, most of which pertained to matters of presentation, legibility, submission processes, copyright, and performance permissions. The fifth rule, however, stressed an idiomatic preference:

> 5—The employment of the Negro musical idiom melodically, rhythmically and harmonically will largely influence the judges in determining the winning compositions although quality of musical thought and workmanship will be the first consideration. The Negro idiom is preferable, but not necessary.[22]

Despite the qualifying statement of the idiom being "preferable, but not necessary," adjudicators were no doubt listening for what might best be described as a Black nationalist voice. Samuel A. Floyd Jr. notes that many African American composers, especially all "whom Coleridge-Taylor influenced," were already operating in a Black nationalist compositional framework, as evidenced by their predilection for interweaving African, European, and New World musical narratives. By "Black nationalism," Floyd means cultural movements and schools of thought where Black intellectuals and creatives took "pride in their African heritage and desire to control their own destiny and communities," as opposed to seeking "separatist movements and thinking."[23] For those engaging in such Black national and transnational modernist trends, the fifth rule would not necessarily have limited their agency as composers. Nevertheless, the specter of white patronage certainly complicates the intention behind the rule.[24] Was it merely suggestive or covertly instructional? Was it designed to boost contemporary trends in African American concert culture or confine practitioners to a certain aesthetic?

A great number must have had faith in the former because the inaugural 1927 contest approximately received an impressive 260 submissions countrywide. Prizes totaled $1,000. In each category (listed below), five prizes were available: first place won $100, second won $50, third won $25, fourth won $15, and fifth won $10.[25]

> 1—A Hymn of Freedom. This number to be a four or more part chorus either a capella, that is, without accompaniment or with accompaniment for orchestra or piano.
>
> 2—A Love Song. This may be a song for any voice, soprano, tenor, contralto, baritone or bass (but only for solo voice). The accompaniment may be for piano or orchestra. Or the composition may be a purely instrumental one for orchestra or solo instrument.
>
> 3—A Lullabye [sic]. This number may be in the form of a spiritual, either an old tune with a new harmonization or an original

composition. But the form and character of a lullabye [*sic*] must be maintained. It may be, as in No. 2, vocal or instrumental.

4—A rhythmical step to be entitled "Prestidigitation." A jig, dance or scherzo in any form for piano, band or orchestra.

5—Melodies and Motifs of Synchronous Effects, that is, two or more melodies, either old ones or original, or both, worked together at the same time in the composition; a theme or melody with variations or elaborations in free form.[26]

Black nationalist overtones reverberated in the call for hymns of freedom; one might imagine submissions of rousing anthems evoking the sentiments of the Johnson brothers' "Lift Every Voice and Sing." Also bearing Black nationalist connections are the references to Spirituals and "old" melodies from which we might infer as meaning folk inspired. The fourth category invokes the Black vernacular trope of Signifyin(g) and therefore may have entailed composers humorously and rhythmically reinterpreting and revising the classical and Black folk-infused aspects of their style.[27] Across the five categories, however, vocal compositions seemed to be the priority, and it was no coincidence that these were the primary outputs of African American composers. Applicants could submit purely instrumental works as well as write for larger ensembles (i.e., band and orchestra), but the option of pared-down accompaniments, or even none at all, foregrounded a criterion of practicality—a criterion that Black composers applied to their craft out of necessity.

Significant, then, is that by 1932, the weighting of vocal versus instrumental works shifted drastically. The five categories were reduced to three, with the prize money divided in a way that acknowledged the demands of large-scale composition: applicants could be awarded $250 for Class I, a song with words; $250 for Class II, a piano composition; and $500 for Class IV, a symphonic work of no fewer than three movements. Class IV had been carried over from the 1931 categories to the July 15 deadline for the 1932 contest, a detail that was widely publicized in the Black press. Although the reasons for the carryover were not explained, a composer might have read this as an indication that stronger submissions were required. Alternatively, considering NANM's insider status and the South Side impresarios' influence, were the Wanamakers waiting for Price and her finished symphony?

Price started writing her Symphony No. 1 in January 1931, coinciding with her divorce from Thomas Price. Having also broken her foot at this time, the recovery period gave her the time, space, and resolve to pursue this large-scale composition. She wrote of the great irony to a friend: "I found it possible to snatch a few precious days in the month of January in which to write undisturbed. But oh, dear me, when shall I ever be so fortunate again as to break a foot."[28] However, as Price's mobility increased, the symphony seemed to come to a standstill as she returned to the various demands of life as an educator, community figure, active musician, and now-single mother in the wake of her divorce from Thomas.

The composer found herself in a new, unwelcome economic situation that stood in contrast to the life she had known. "At one point Miss Price was in such bad financial shape that my mother moved her into our house with her two children in order to relieve her mind of material considerations," wrote Margaret Bonds in her self-penned 1967 essay, "A Reminiscence." In addition to granting financial relief, Price's temporary living situation with the Bonds family proved conducive to her work as a composer. She returned to her symphony with the support and assistance of an invested, tight-knit, faith-driven community and with the two pianos of the Bonds salon at her disposal. So striking is the visual that Bonds paints of these intimate settings:

> During the cold winter nights in Chicago, we used to sit around a large table in our kitchen—manuscript paper strewn around, Florence and I extracting parts for some contest deadline. We were a God-loving people, and, when we were pushed for time, every brown-skinned musician in Chicago who could write a note, would "jump-to" and help Florence meet her deadline.[29]

One of these deadlines was July 15, 1932, the date on which submissions for that year's Rodman Wanamaker Music Contest were due. Price, aged forty-six years by the time she entered the 1932 contest, was not a nascent composer. However, due to her "retiring" disposition, as Maude Roberts George put it, as well as being, by the composer's own admission, "woefully lacking in the hardihood of [aggression]" and in constant "battle" with a "hounding timidity" around promoting her own works, much of Price's accomplishments prior to her Wanamaker successes were largely unknown beyond her immediate network.[30] Greatly needed, then, was not only the Wanamakers' exposure but the esteem-building advocacy of the South Side impresarios.

Price's stay with the Bonds family appeared to slow the pace of mounting pressures, granting Price again the time and space to delve into her craft, but this time, she also had the communal encouragement around her to fuel her resolve. Notably, Price's temporary residence with the Bonds family and its transformative impact on her work was not public knowledge at the time; it did not surface in the Black contemporary press or other kinds of commentary from this period. The story of Price's stay instead came from Margaret retrospectively, rather than from Price herself. Price was reserved by nature and may well have regarded her stay with the family as a personal matter, not to be publicly disclosed. Nevertheless, Margaret's account—more than three decades after the fact—is of wide significance and helps historicize Price's compositional path. Her recollection reveals the hand of Black women's fellowship, working behind the scenes, entwining uplift and spirituality.

"We all prayed," Margaret recalled of that period, "and Florence won $500 for a symphony (awarded by the Wanamaker Foundation). Our prayers were powerful because Florence also won $250 for a piano sonata, and I won $250 for an art song," called "Sea Ghosts."[31] These triumphs had a transformative effect on Price's finances and subsequent trajectory. Up until that point, it had not been financially viable for Price to invest time in composing large-scale works and depend on their publication for a steady source of income.[32] Sandra T. Dougherty notes that "due, in part, to 1930's publishers seeking shorter pieces," many of Price's large-scale compositions, notably the orchestral and chamber works, "remain[ed] in manuscript" and were, as a result, "unavailable for performance" for many decades after Price's death.[33] Another factor beyond the whims and preferences of publishers was that Price's work unfolded in "the highly politicized arena of classical music"—a climate where historical "misconceptions about the intelligence of (white) women and African Americans created a virtually insurmountable barrier for any black woman aspiring toward 'serious' composition." As Teresa L. Reed observes, "This barrier would succumb to Florence Price, the first black female composer of distinction."[34] However, this would be the result of strategies that emanated from the interior, sisterly support systems of the Black classical metropolis.

Price's time with the Bonds family provided her with a kind of cocoon within which she could leave behind the identity of Mrs. Thomas J. Price and work through the various stages of her metamorphosis. From the spiritual fellowship of Estella and Margaret to the musical fellowship of Black Chicago's best creative practitioners, Price's invitation into the Bonds family home both relieved her mind of material considerations and granted her the supportive environment needed to fully devote herself to composition. Decades of expertise informed her craft, but it was not until her individual expertise converged with the collective support of an uplifting community that Chicago's most-celebrated Black female symphonist would emerge.

To better understand the conditions that birthed such productivity amid an era of great uncertainty, however, let us spend more time with Bonds's accounts and the ways in which she captured this conflicting period of personal strain and professional transformation in Price's life. If the written words of Bonds's 1967 reminiscences evoke the visual of how Price navigated the time preceding the 1932 Wanamaker deadline, then Bonds's spoken words from a recorded interview that she gave in December 1971 (four months before her sudden passing) conjure up the visceral of how it felt to be with Price in those moments.

"Florence B. Price, did you ever hear of her?" Bonds quizzes her interviewer, James V. Hatch.[35] Compared to the cosmopolitan Nora Holt, one of the few other Chicago-affiliated musical Race women from this era whose speaking voice still exists on record, Bonds has a much more localized accent. The nasal undertones and pinching of her vowels in certain places contrast the crisp and heavily cultivated contours of Holt's fashionable transatlantic accent.[36]

Hatch does not verbalize a response to Bonds's question. Maybe something in his facial expression or a gesture, such as shaking his head, prompts the composer to see if she can trigger his memory. "She has one very, very famous spiritual arrangement called 'My Soul's Been Anchored in the Lord.'" She interrogates Hatch again: "Haven't you heard that?" There is a slight pause, perhaps as Hatch attempts to recall. She tells him, "You *must* hear—Leontyne sings it," in reference to Leontyne Price who, like Marian Anderson, made the work a staple of her repertoire. Bonds then proceeds with her story.

"Mother took her into our house," she begins, echoing the narrational structure of her 1967 essay. But this time, she gives even more insight into Price's psychological state, particularly in the aftermath of a second failed marriage, this time to Pusey Dell Arnett.[37] Bonds reveals, with a bleakness of tone, "She had two children and she had trouble with the second marriage. She was very, very down and out and Mother moved her into our house." The mood then starts to lift as she animates scenes of the Bonds salon: " We had, in Chicago, a tremendous kitchen. And you know the weather in Chicago was so cold . . . and we didn't have the kind of heating then that we have now—and Florence and I would sit in that kitchen"—she gives a raspy chuckle, then picks up—"and I was trying to help her with extractions of orchestration parts and whatnot, you know. And then sometimes when she would get pushed"—her giggles ripple through once again—"almost every Black musician in Chicago would be farmed out to help Florence get her work done." The last four words are lost in a cloud of smoky, cough-infused laughter. "I'm not kidding you!" she says once the smoke clears.

Bonds, perhaps not sure of how to best put it, then gifts the listener with revelatory insight into Price's personality: "She would, um—she had a—she seemed to procrastinate." Bonds's words break into full-bodied waves of rhythmic laughter, the kind that makes the upper torso bob to the cadence of one's amusement. But her smoky cough rears its head again, with more force this time. While Bonds tries to compose herself, Hatch chimes in, "She knew she'd get help!" Still recovering, Bonds expels a deep phlegm-filled rumble. She is not well but resumes the story as soon as she can.

Affirming Hatch's quip, she continues, "When Florence had something that she had to do"—she giggles once more—"every musician in Chicago—Black, who could write"—her words are again submerged in waves of laughter—"was either scratching mistakes or copying, or extracting, or doing something to get Florence's work done."

"Isn't that the craziest thing?"[38]

This interview grants deeper perspective on what this period in Price's life meant to the composer, to Margaret Bonds, to Bonds's mother, and to the wider Black classical metropolis. Bonds's written words paint a rather solemn picture of their collegiality. They communicate the urgency and flurry of brown hands wading through stacks of manuscript paper; looming deadlines convey the seriousness of the task at hand. And yet Bonds's oral account invites the listener to feel the comedy of it all and laugh with her. Of course, she does not downplay the seriousness of Price's personal circumstances—the gravity is palpable in Bonds's tone. Yet she encourages the listener to look back on this time with her and see it in a different light. Revealed are the warmth and levity of the Black classical metropolis, which brought great relief to the personal plight of one of its own against the backdrop of large-scale economic decline and the city's harsh winters.

Bonds's anecdotes illuminate the power of interpersonal forces, largely hidden from the public record but decisively bringing events such as Price's Wanamaker triumphs and World's Fair debut into specific alignment. Bonds breathes life, laughter, and complexity into the Price narrative, piercing through any fixed impressions we might have today of what Depression-era Chicago meant to those who lived through it. Bonds does not negate the gloom or struggle of that time, but in foregrounding Race women's capacity for lightheartedness and optimism amid a historical moment characterized so antithetically, Bonds's stories attest to just how revolutionary it was for the Black classical metropolis to push through with care and concern for Price's compositional aspirations. Around the Bondses' large kitchen table, Chicago's brown-skinned musicians, whether they knew it or not, were writing a new era of Black classical arrival in the stars.

News of the Music World

Upon winning first place with her Symphony No. 1 in E minor, Price's Arkansas roots seemed even further behind her as Black news outlets affirmed her arrival as one of the city's own and a symphonist of the highest caliber. The responses of the Black press to Price's as well as Bonds's Wanamaker triumphs reflected the collective understanding of what it meant in that particular moment for two of Chicago's musical Race women to be recognized in such a way. "Chi Takes All Wanamaker Prizes," announced the *Baltimore Afro-American*.[39] "Chicago Women Capture Wanamaker Music Prizes," read the *Norfolk Journal and Guide*.[40] "$750 Prizes Result of Injury: 2 Chicago Women Get All the Cash Given in Music Contest," sensationalized the *Atlanta Daily World*, referencing Price's foot injury.[41] "Chicago Women Win Prizes for Negro Composers," reported the *Washington Tribune*.[42] "Chicago Women Win $1,000 Prizes in Rodman Wanamaker Memorial Contest," published the *New York Age*.[43] Predictably, the South Side stood proud: Price's and Bonds's victories were felt all through the Black classical metropolis and the *Chicago Defender* enthusiastically emphasized these local ties.

Maude Roberts George used her pen as music critic and power as the current CMA president and incoming NANM president to show wider Chicagoland what the Black classical metropolis had accomplished. She reported on how thrilled local musicians were to learn of two fellow Chicagoans winning Wanamaker prizes and detailed the awards ceremony that took place on September 25, 1932.[44] "Metropolitan Community church was filled to overflowing for the festival program and the announcement of the Rodman Wanamaker awards in composition. Special reservations were made by groups from the North Shore and many teachers from Loop schools were in the audience," she wrote using the latter piece of information to show that it was not only South Side residents who were present but also practitioners from across the city's segregated geography who joined the Black classical metropolis in their celebrations.[45]

That the accomplishments of Price and Bonds resonated with, and stood for, Chicago's Black community writ large strongly suggests that there was a deep investment on the part of the Black classical metropolis to direct Price's and Bonds's Wanamaker triumphs into something even greater. In light of what came next, George's network likely leveraged the Wanamaker Awards as a launch pad for further opportunities. Maneuvering from Black Chicago's representation in the Wanamakers to the Negro in Music seemed highly strategic on the part of the South Side impresarios, particularly given the way that George's coverage in the lead-up to the Negro in Music hinted at the connectivity of these threads. "Chicago musicians will be represented by the symphony of Mrs. Florence B. Price, 1932 Wanamaker prize winner in composition," George reported, capturing the communal symbolism of Price's composition in the Negro in Music program.[46] Behind the public record was evidently a deeper narrative of musical Race women's method, mission, and foresight in feeding the Wanamaker Awards into the World's Fair.

Using her "News of the Music World" columns as amplification, George reviewed one of Bonds's student recitals at Northwestern, which took place in early May 1933, the month before the Negro in Music. Like Holt before her, George wrote to affect the cultural tastes of the Black classical metropolis and beyond and put Black artistry in the spotlight. George began with a clear picture of Bonds's artistry and accolades: "Miss Bonds is a brilliant pianist, splendid technique and plays not only with intelligence but real musical feeling. A charming stage presence is coupled with genuine love of her art, which thrills her audience as she seems to completely lose herself in the interpretation of her music." George then detailed Bonds's program, which "throughout was played with an accuracy which brought her many personal compliments from teachers and musicians present" and featured canonical favorites such as Franck, Debussy, and Villa-Lobos. Bonds closed with a two-piano arrangement of Carpenter's Concertino for Piano and Orchestra, which she performed with her Northwestern piano instructor. In her comments on the final work, George's review became an open invitation for Carpenter to witness Bonds's brilliance firsthand. She wrote the following, knowing of Bonds's imminent debut:

> Mr. Carpenter is a composer of international reputation and is a Chicagoan. It is hoped that he will have the opportunity of hearing Miss Bonds play his Concertino, for she displayed such rare understanding and fine musicianship that we feel sure the composer would have been as thrilled as was the audience.[47]

Bonds's programming of Carpenter's Concertino was no coincidence. In preparation for any piano concerto performance, it helps a great deal for the pianist to gain experience with the work on the stage, even with the composition's two-piano arrangement. And with Estella Bonds's proclivity for two-piano playing and pedagogy, the Bonds salon would have provided a vital training ground for this performance, alongside the instruction Margaret received at Northwestern. The May performance of Carpenter's Concertino, which might be thought of as a preview, alludes to the depths of preparation that involved not only Margaret as an individual but her intimate network of support. George's review of Bonds's student recital was not only a strong endorsement of the young pianist's musician-ship, it was also an overt advertisement—even targeting Carpenter—for the immense skill that Margaret would display in her Chicago Symphony debut a month later.

The Negro in Music unfolded under the auspices of the Chicago Friends of Music, Inc., which comprised 22,500 members. Senior officers included president Frederick Stock and several vice presidents, including Carpenter and Charles B. Goodspeed. The wives of Carpenter and Goodspeed joined their respective husbands on the executive committee as well as the board of directors where the name of Rudolf Ganz—well known in the city's music and society circles—could also be found. But beyond the promi-nent names of white Chicago's classical music establishment were realms of institutions that were firmly located in the Black Metropolis. Listed beneath the declaration that "the Board of Directors of Chicago Friends of Music, Inc. wish to acknowledge with gratitude the cooperation of their membership" were the following Black-led organizations: the Apollo Music Club of Chicago (which was cofounded by Pedro Tinsley and Mat-tie Johnson Young at the turn of the century and made their appearance in the Chicago World's Fair of 1893); Chicago Colored Women's Band of which cornetist Irene H. Harrison was the director; Chicago Music Asso-ciation; and Mundy Choristers, under founder and conductor James A. Mundy. The earlier goals of George, Estella Bonds, and Anita Patti Brown to "represent and act for the [CMA]" in the Century of Progress World's Fair Committee and "join hands with other Negro organizations" had resulted in greater representation of Black classical musicians, both on and (just as important) off the stage.[48]

Placed in the program after Roland Hayes's rendering of Berlioz was Price's Symphony in E minor, beginning with the pentatonically patterned "Allegro ma non troppo," set to evoke the sound world of Black folk song; followed by the solemn "Largo, maestoso" second movement, with hym-nal overtones, organ-like colorings, and pendular third contours; then complemented by a playful "Juba Dance," steeped in the kinetic rhythms that accompanied the musical sounds of plantation life; and rounded out with a "Finale" that returns to the modal, folkloric atmosphere of the first movement but proceeds with a more vigorous energy, propelled by its compound duple meter. In an era where white American and Euro-pean male composers of the mainstream were inclining more toward the melodically abstract, harmonically rootless, and rhythmically complex, the impetus for Price to not only lean heavily into the conventions of late nineteenth-century orchestral writing but to also cite sonic evoca-tions of African American folk traditions in her craft derived from her embodied and studied knowledge of Black concert aesthetics. Her symphony sounded the deep, transatlantic history of Black classical life; and with Bonds placed after the intermission, both symphonist and soloist, in their intergenerational dialogue, affirmed Race women's own advancement in and of the realm of music.

As the final sounds of Bonds's concerto debut died down in the Auditorium Theatre, the audience burst into applause and Bonds, "who was literally covered with flowers," recalled Herman Devries in his review, "might have counted at least six recalls to the platform." Glenn Dillard Gunn praised her "vivid style and able technique," adding the racist note that her "rhythmic instinct which may be racial or musicianly, and doubtless is both, made the graceful work glow with a fire more experienced pianists well might envy." Focusing more on the fruits of her technical training rather than veering toward scientific racism as Gunn so often did, Edward Moore emphasized Bonds's "brilliant, well developed technic," observing that "she played with much composure and good sense of lines of construction in the work." Eugene Stinson described it as "an admirable performance" from a "brilliant and dependable pianist." Kathryn Irwin of the *Chicago Bee* acknowledged that Bonds "made a lasting impression by her excellent technique and her charming stage presence." Resituating Bonds's performance in its symbolic representation for the Race, George of the *Chicago Defender* enthused that the young Bonds had "reached the heights expected of her in her rendition."[49] In George's estimation, Bonds's and Price's contributions held and fulfilled the collective expectations of Black Chicago.

"No one could have sat through that program sponsored by the Chicago Friends of Music . . . and not felt, with a sense of deep satisfaction, that the Race is making progress in music," wrote the *Chicago Defender*'s Robert Abbott. "First," he noted, foregrounding the racial dynamics and cultural stakes, "there was a feeling of awe as the Chicago Symphony orchestra, an aggregation of master musicians of the white race, . . . swung into the beautiful, harmonious strains of a composition by a Race woman." In Rae Linda Brown's assessment of this remark, however, she notes how "curious" it is that Abbott "fails to mention Price by name preferring to accentuate the cultural significance of the experience." Brown recognizes, "Of course, the *Defender*'s black readers knew to whom Abbott was referring; he was invoking a kind of common familiarity that bonds the black community." But unmentioned were the details that, as Brown puts it, "this concert marked the first time that a major orchestra had performed a work by a black woman composer" and that the concert itself was born out of the South Side's Black musical sisterhood.[50]

Through a patriarchal lens, Abbott opined, "you could not have heard this concert without realizing that your people not only are coming ahead in music, but that, in the higher arts, our white brother is growing less and less fractious. As we listened to that concert we took hope again that there may yet be real brotherhood in this land of ours."[51] The focus on white and Black fraternity not only negated the deeper dynamics of gender but, with regard to Abbott's own geography, minimized the specific role of Chicago's musical Race women.

Nahum Daniel Brascher's vivid *Chicago Defender* review took a similar approach to Abbott's, accentuating the wider significance over the specifics of Price's historic breakthrough and the roles of impresarial Race women:

> Picture the famous Chicago Symphony orchestra, conducted by Frederick A. Stock; Roland Hayes, international tenor; Margaret Bonds, piano solist [*sic*]; Florence Price, composer of a symphony; John Alden Carpenter, composer, representing Chicago's highlight socially, as well as musically; George Gershwin, a guest in Mr. Carpenter's box; the famous Auditorium diamond horseshoe, occupied by those whose names have given Chicago A Century of Progress; other boxes, the balcony and numerous galleries filled with our own music lovers and musicians; glorified appreciation of every number on the program; unstinted and unending applause, all under the direction of Chicago Friends of Music, official music expression of the World's Fair A Century of Progress.[52]

Brascher's evocations are vivid, visceral, and suspended in time; they are a still frame, bearing a panoramic view of the concert hall and its attendees. Brascher paints an unambiguous portrait of Black classical arrival. Notably, however, he subsumes the credit for the Negro in Music under the broader Chicago Friends of Music, rather than locating it in the specific influence of the South Side impresarios. Although the program was sponsored by the Chicago Friends of Music, one specific organization, from the outset, had taken charge in shaping the event. Catalyzed by Estella Bonds's work as the CMA's representative for the Century of Progress World's Fair Committee, followed by the formation of another committee comprising George, Bonds, and Anita Patti Brown, the CMA had a significant hand in bringing the program to fruition. Entirely passed over in the white and Black press at the time was the fact that in addition to Race women's various forms of committee work, CMA president George underwrote the Negro in Music at a cost of $250.[53]

Building on Rae Linda Brown's assessment of Abbott's commentary, Black readers of Brascher's review, particularly those who were attentive to the goings-on in the realm of music, likely connected the dots between the concert, the Chicago Friends of Music, and the Black classical metropolis. However, the omission of this deeper narrative in the immediate coverage of the event skewed an understanding of just how thoroughly involved Black women were in the making of the Negro in Music. The details of their inner workings were inadvertently erased. While the unspoken dimensions of Race women's behind-the-scenes work were evidence of a common understanding across their networks, the tacit, interior nature of this understanding generally eluded critics engaging with the legacy of the Black classical metropolis from the outside. The effect subtly perpetuated a narrative of white saviorism, giving disproportionate credit to the white benevolence of the Wanamakers and senior board of the Friends of Music for their championing of Black classical practitioners.

It might be argued, however, that George was also complicit in her own erasure. In the aftermath of the Wanamaker Awards, George wrote, "Since the death of Mr. Wanamaker the association [i.e., NANM] has sought in vain for a fund to set up as inducement to classical composition. The establishment of such a fund would mean much to the Negro and the musical literature of the United States."[54] This framing overstates the value of white philanthropy and underplays the ability of Race women to translate the 1932 awards into something even greater—that is, the Negro in Music. Running as a consistent thread, however, none of George's music columns spoke self-referentially about her role in the 1933 Chicago World's Fair. Compared to Holt's earlier pieces for the *Chicago Defender*, which never shied away from self-advocacy, George kept a more critical distance, emphasizing the activity of others over her own. She utilized a self-determined invisibility to ensure that others were better seen. In this regard, the motives for her erasure differed from Abbott's and Brascher's, whose writings flowed from a Black patriarchal frame. George's discourse was symptomatic of the typically quiet coordinating of Race women's work, which influenced numerous trajectories in the art world but unfolded in a way whereby all that would be visible and audible to the music-loving public was the talent housed in the artistry of their people.

George was intentional about how she positioned herself in the discourse of Black classical arrival, as revealed in the minutes of a CMA meeting that took place on July 20, 1937. CMA secretary Josephine Inniss documented that as topics turned to the transition from outgoing president George to president-elect Estella Bonds, the latter expressed gratitude for the service of the former. George's response noted, "the only thanks that she desired was that those whom she had recommended for important engagements measured up to her classification of them," to which CMA members applauded. George then further contextualized her impresarial role in the project of collective uplift over her own self-promotion, recalling how "in 1933, she was interested to the extent that she made it possible for the Negro Program, June 15, in a Century of Progress Music Series at the Auditorium Theater by underwriting the contract with Dr. Frederick Stock, Conductor of the Chicago Symphony Orchestra." The final portion of her minuted speech brought her altruism to the fore and was met with another round of applause:

> The support and active effort that she has given to International Artist Recitals and Loop affairs here never meant one cent to her in compensation over the period of years because she had always been anxious that the sponsor of artist performance in Chicago should realize the talent and hear the rendition of our people.[55]

And there lies the key to how we might articulate progress along the musical Race woman's timeline. The performances of Price, Margaret Bonds, Roland Hayes, Marian Anderson, and so many more contained a deeper canon of Black classical life—comprising the impresarial figures of George, Estella Bonds, Anita Patti Brown, and the countless brown-skinned musicians of the CMA, NANM, and Bonds's kitchen table sessions. This deeper canon existed in a time of in-betweenness and epoch-making, economic depression and cultural renaissance, and fraught advancement and clear pinnacles. Paradoxes abounded, extending to the ways in which George co-fashioned with her sisterhood a mode of impresarial advocacy that seemed to sound all but its own name. In these contradictions, however, we come closer to hearing this history as it was and, as a result, to hearing the profundity of Black classical arrival on the world stage amid the cacophonous nature of social progress.

Finale

The year is 1939. Fascism is on the rise. A Great War tail ends the Great Depression and nations, if not already embroiled, are on the cusp of deadly conflict. Even closer to home, "the Daughters of the American Revolution [declare] war on the Declaration of Independence by denying Constitution Hall to Marian Anderson."[56] Black America, once again, holds a mirror to the hypocrisy of a United States that touts ideals of freedom and democracy while a relentless white supremacy prevails in all sectors of society—as much wielded by white women as it is by white men. Under a Black patriarchy, it remains the perennial hope that "there may yet be real brotherhood in this land of ours."[57] But as unknown and unacknowledged factors in both the woman question and race problem, Black women do not hold their breath as they await this ever-elusive brotherhood or resolution in the similarly volatile dynamics of interracial sisterhood.[58] Rather, Black women persist within frameworks of racial self-help and intimate sisterly bonds; from there they transform these hostile terrains, and as Anderson's involuntary battle with the Daughters of the American Revolution shows, music remains one of Black women's key strategies in the fight against racist and sexist assaults.

Anderson will later recall how "it was only a few weeks before the scheduled date for Washington that I discovered the full truth—that the Daughters of the American Revolution, owners of the hall [i.e., Constitution Hall], had decreed that it could not be used by one of my race. I was saddened, but as it is my belief that right will win I assumed that a way would be found."[59] Anderson anticipates correctly as her performance venue moves to the steps of the Lincoln Memorial. A colossal stone sculpture of President Abraham Lincoln, the "Great Emancipator," recapitulates the ideals of freedom and democracy as she takes center stage.

The date is Easter Sunday, April 9, 1939, coinciding with Florence Price's fifty-first birthday. On this day, Anderson sings before an audience approximately 75,000 strong and a radio listenership in the millions. In his dedication address, United States secretary of the interior Harold L. Ickes (whom Maude Roberts George called on just over a decade earlier to support the musical program of the 1927 Negro in Art Week) proclaims that "Marian Anderson's voice and personality have come to be a symbol of American unity."[60] For those who first heard Anderson's contralto tones at NANM's inaugural convention amid the city's deadly race riots of 1919, there is likely a hint of déjà vu as Anderson's voice soars above the violent disharmonies of American life and the global conflict that makes imminent a second world war. The sociopolitical and spiritual significance of Anderson's performance is not lost on Daniel "Dan" Gardner Burley, an active musician and reporter for the *New York Amsterdam News* and also a former student of Wendell Phillips High School who worked during his schooling as a newspaper boy and burgeoning columnist for the *Chicago Defender* at the time of the city's race riots.[61]

Capturing the stillness, timelessness, and gravity of Anderson's performance, Burley writes,

> Nothing could make me believe war was near, or that hunger and want faced the populace while listening to Marian Anderson's superb contralto Sunday. All thought of discord slipped away while the great singer weaved a spell over countless hearers both in Washington and elsewhere. Her open air concert climaxed a glorious Easter, and peculiarly

Figure 31. Carol M. Highsmith, photographer. Mural "An Incident in Contemporary American Life," by Mitchell Jamieson at the Department of Interior, Washington, D.C. Washington, DC, United States, 2011, September. Photograph. https://www.loc.gov/item/2013634359/.

the idea occurs that it was a master stroke to present her to millions of Americans as a living sacrifice on the altar of racial discrimination at a time when this country is all worked up over discriminatory racial [practices] abroad. Standing, with the towering memorial of the Great Emancipator casting its shadow over the dais from which she sang, Marian Anderson's voice, cast to the four winds, probably carried the point home with more telling force than anything that has taken place lately in our fight for racial equality and economic freedom. The event will remain significant in the annals of the Negro.

The metaphors housed in Charles Dawson's "O, Sing a New Song" iconography resurface as Anderson, like the Race woman chanteuse in his artwork, stands on the edges of a deeply complex, transatlantic history. Dawson's artwork will later be met by a poignant counterpart in the commemorative mural of the white American artist Mitchell Jamieson. The latter will capture Anderson, flanked by the statue of Lincoln behind her. The former president's partial visibility between the great, symbolic columns of the exterior will hint at the incomplete fulfillment of the nation's democratic vision. However, signaling the possibilities for a racially harmonious future will be the living, breathing, integrated masses of Anderson's audience. Unlike Dawson's detailed Race woman, Jamieson's Anderson will be portrayed as a silhouette in the distance, elevated above the masses, embodying both a peak along the mountain of social progress and Burley's conjuring of "a living sacrifice on the altar of racial discrimination."[62] If Dawson's perspective digs deep into the Race woman's ancient African past, then Jamieson's mural will serve to depict her under a global spotlight as the hope for the nation's redemption (fig. 31).

Anderson closes the concert with Price's 1937 arrangement of the Negro Spiritual, "My Soul's Been Anchored in the Lord." With this musical selection, Anderson nests her finale in the vivid legacy of Chicago's Black musical matriarchy; she embodies and "envoices" the sounds, scenes, and sites of Race women's community-building and culture-making in the Black classical metropolis.[63] "I'm going to pray and never stop / My soul's been anchored in the Lord / Until I've reached the mountain top / My soul's been anchored in the Lord," sings Anderson in the closing verse above a piano accompaniment that uses Price's signature minor-key solemnity and folk-inflected Romanticism. As the last musical sounds die down and the rush of applause fills the air, the Race woman's proverb, "Lifting as We Climb," is enacted on the world stage. The mountaintop becomes a metaphor for the uphill battle against inequality. And "in the quiet, undisputed dignity" of Anderson's womanhood (as well as the womanhoods of Price, Holt, George, and innumerable others who helped compose this very moment), then and there, the Race enters with her, toward the mountaintop.

CONCLUSION

In Honor of
Mrs. Maude Roberts George

Your abrupt demise by no means unmakes the history you wrought, nor does it dim the power of your legacy. You were certainly not the only one of your cohort to have the magnitude of your life's work seemingly disappear from the public record, particularly in the press. Florence Price, though continually programmed by Black concert singers (such as Marian Anderson and later Leontyne Price), suffered a similar fate with regard to the press; her name, as Rae Linda Brown observes, appeared "less frequently in the *Chicago Defender* as a composer and almost never as a performer" by the late 1940s.[1] In fact, I have little doubt of the direct correlation between the end of your tenure as the *Defender*'s chief music critic and Price's decreased presence in the columns of the Black periodicals through this period. This never struck me as a coincidence but, rather, proof of the symbiosis that constituted the particular ecosystem of Chicago's Black concert scene during the interwar period. Neither you nor Price were forgotten by your communities, but it would not be until the recovery work of Black Power–era musicologists like Eileen Southern—who Guthrie P. Ramsey Jr. argues "should certainly be considered a 'race woman'"—for this history to be relaunched into the wider public consciousness.[2] In sum, your sudden retirement from public life (which included your withdrawal from the *Defender*) in the aftermath of a tragic near-death incident on October 21, 1940, closed a critical chapter in the curation and communication of life in the Black classical metropolis. The realm of music subsequently lost a crucial voice and stalwart champion of Black women's creative and intellectual ambition.

Reopening the conversation, then, I reflect on the last decade of your life and posthumous resonance before expanding to a broader consideration of the South Side impresarios' impact and afterglow. Encompassing how you moved in the aftermath of the Century of Progress, how Margaret Bonds found her voice in the civil rights era, and how Price's music reemerged with widespread acclaim in the twenty-first century, I affirm your network's covert influence at the heart of it all.

Collectively, you lived and breathed the reality that Race women, in your own words, "have had a large part in the development of young musicians and are some of the outstanding artists of the world."[3] As an individual, though, you were as much elusive as you were ever present regarding the part that you played within these dynamics. Yet this duality proved an essential, deliberate strategy as you sought to revolutionize the classical world but away from the spotlight so as to redirect all attention to the artist. I therefore meditate on your agency and legacy as a proverbial hidden figure. I further assert your place within both a Black feminist project and Western art music historiography.

Although I accept the slight peculiarity of framing my closing thoughts as an open letter to the one person who certainly will not see it, the directness and immediacy of this approach allows me to situate all that you achieved in urgent dialogue with the present historical moment. I invoke the discursive practices of the *Chicago Defender* that served to ground readers in *the now*, from the world-making strategies of published letters and open invitations, through the educative profiles of Black women's public lives, to the immersive vividness of Race women's music columns. Here, I continue to build on Black feminist interventions in the ways our stories are often told at arm's length, if at all.

· · ·

You were a bastion of musical Race womanhood, unshakably committed to the uplift of your locale and, more important, the people within it. What began as a time of transition upon your marriage to Judge Albert B. George and the birth of your son, Albert George Jr., turned into a clearly defined epoch of community-building and culture-making. You modulated seamlessly from active musician to musical activist. Ideas and institutions flourished under your leadership. Artistic careers (and even political trajectories) bloomed from your sponsorship. On the surface, you embodied the respectable: you checked the boxes of marriage and motherhood and never set out to court public scandal. But respectability was only one part of a much bigger picture. For you to envision space and dream new vistas for "our people" (as you put it) amid the realities of an anti-Black world was as much an act of rebellion against the status quo as it was an act of deep care for the future of the Race.[4] You perfected the balance of the respectable veneer and radical core, using the resources afforded to you via the path of the former to enact the sociocultural transformations that fueled the fire of the latter. Your generation of musical Race women was unmatched in the art of this dance, and there was something of this era that died with you.

Inevitably, the climate was shifting anyway, with your generation being supplanted by one collectively more impatient with the pace of progress.[5] World War II spurred the "Double V" rhetoric of victory at home and victory abroad as new generations of African Americans challenged the disturbing hypocrisy of fighting a fascism on foreign shores that was all too familiar at home. A tangible anger ripped through respectability discourse, fomenting a new civil rights era. Had you lived to see it, would the class and caste constructs born out of Talented Tenth ideologies and the intellectual work of nineteenth-century Black women have retained their hold on your political outlook? Or would this new era have brought even more of your revolutionary spirit to the fore and burst open the model of the seemingly composed Race woman? Perhaps the latter disposition was more for the next generation, as this was the direction in which Margaret Bonds moved.

Bonds's "Musical Mission" to develop "Racial Harmony" undoubtedly echoed the documented efforts of your colleague Nora Holt, who, in 1918, espoused the view that "the open sesame to music appreciation is music understanding" and that such appreciation and understanding would lead to the realization of racial harmony.[6] However, Bonds was speaking in 1964; the context, an interview with the *Washington Post*'s Christina Demaitre, which carried a direct message for white America. This was a different era, galvanized by an uncompromising urgency for freedom now. The Civil Rights Act of 1964 had recently passed, prohibiting discrimination on the basis of race, color, sex, and national origin and therefore outlawing the tyranny of Jim Crow. A crop of charismatic Black male leaders, such as Dr. Martin Luther King Jr., Malcolm X, and Stokely Carmichael (Kwame Ture), to name a few, had taken charge. But as ever, Black women from across the social spectrum also claimed their political callings, from Bonds to Mahalia Jackson, from Fannie Lou Hamer to Nina Simone. Freedom songs born out of Black folk origins and present-day protest underscored a variety of issues, including Black solidarity across class constructs and the geographies of the urban north and rural south, as well as the power of grassroots resistance.[7] This was now Bonds's social, political, cultural, and musical milieu, and she readily aligned her compositional craft to the cause, which by this time stood at approximately two hundred works, ranging "from spirituals to jazz to symphonies and musical shows."[8]

On the topic of her musical mission, Bonds emphasized "determinedly" in her interview with the *Washington Post*, "I want to project my own people to blot out the negative image. I want to show that the Negro is not a rapist, or ugly or stupid." Stemming from a mix of her characteristic outspokenness and the tenor of the times, Bonds publicly vocalized that which you and your generation of Race women knew to be true but seldom said in public—likely for fear of the white supremacist backlash, patriarchal pressure, and intraracial opprobrium that earlier iconoclasts such as Ida B. Wells faced when speaking bluntly.[9] Bonds additionally followed up with the gendered component to her craft: "People don't think that a woman can really compete in this field."[10] Again, this point would not have been a revelation to you and your peers. This had been your daily battlefield. Yet Bonds's arguments captured the assaults largely unspoken in the public realm by your generation of Black female classical practitioners—assaults that not only pertained to dismissive attitudes but the abject dehumanization of Black women.

There seemed to be a generational divide in how (and to whom) these issues were communicated. After all, you or Price would not have spoken so unreservedly, even in the safer spaces of the Black press, let alone in the white presses of the *Washington Post, Chicago Tribune,* or *New York Times.* Even the public prose of the typically forthright Nora Holt was never this direct. But the strongest connection across the generations lies in the absence of defeat in Bonds's tone.

"Heritage Motivates Composing Career," stated the article, noting that Bonds felt uninhibited by her Blackness and that "being a Negro has helped rather than harmed Margaret Bonds in her career as a composer."[11] This commentary reflects the self-esteem-raising ethos of the Black classical metropolis that she grew up in, of the politically attuned musical world that Estella fostered in the salon and sanctuary that was their South Side abode, and of the organizing work that you and numerous other local impresarios enacted during her most formative years. Four decades, World War II, and a new civil rights era may have passed between Holt's interwar philosophies and Bonds's postwar reflections on the analogy between social and musical harmony. Race women's class-stratified civic work may have given way to what we might think of today as more intersectional Black feminist visions. Freedom songs may have taken the place of Negro Spirituals as modes of protest and resistance. But the interior drive for change never faltered, and Bonds's connection to you and the nested herstories of interwar Chicago's other musical Race women remained unsevered.

Had you lived to see this new dawn, you likely would have attended "An All-Margaret Bonds Concert" of her compositions for which this daughter of the Black classical metropolis returned from her adopted city of New York. The concert took place on January 31, 1967. Bonds performed at the piano, joined by sopranos Olivia Sheppherd and Rita Carrington-Todd, contralto Prudence Wilson, and baritone Wendell Turner. The Alpha Omega Choral Club, with their conductor Maurice Collins and accompanist Archie Brown, also featured. Sponsored by the Chicago Music Association (CMA), under your successor, incumbent president Theodore Charles Stone, and held at Berean Baptist Church, the decades-long religious base of Estella, the concert took place "in observance of National Negro History"—a forerunner of what we now have as Black History Month.[12]

The program comprised concert Spirituals, such as "He's Got the Whole World in His Hands," "Ezekiel Saw de Wheel," "You Can Tell the World," "Dem Bones," and "Sing Aho." There were also her settings of Langston Hughes's poems in the duet "African Dance," the solo-voice works of "Dream Variation" and "I, Too," and the excerpts performed from her Christmas cantata, "The Ballad of the Brown King." The cantata premiered just over a decade earlier on December 12, 1954, in New York, but Bonds subsequently stored it away until she "became enraptured by the Montgomery, Alabama passive resistance movement of Dr. Martin Luther King, Jr." and evidently found the work to hold new significance in the current climate.

Bonds also rendered her three-part *Spiritual Suite* for solo piano—one of my personal favorites.[13] I find that the last movement, "Group Dance" (later renamed "Troubled Water"), unfolds as if in dialogue with Price's first *Fantasie Nègre* (the one dedicated to Margaret and championed by Katherine Dunham). From its direct Spiritual quotation (i.e., "Wade in the Water") and the E minor melancholy of its declamation to its Black diasporic dance rhythms, virtuosic flashes, and powerful resolve, "Group Dance/Troubled Water" is a work in which I hear the classical strand of the Black Chicago Renaissance and the contrapuntal lives of its musical Race women—you, Estella, Price, Dunham, Holt, Shirley Graham—skillfully interwoven. Only a few years earlier, Dunham's student, choreographer Talley Beatty, commissioned "Troubled Water" for his 1964 ballet titled *The Migration* (which portrayed the journey of the enslaved African from their home continent to the New World). Then, in the summer of 1966, Bonds not only recorded the complete suite in New York's Steinway Hall under the supervision of Nigerian composer Féla Sowande for a series called "Operation Music One" that was "to be used in all Nigerian Educational Centers" (fig. 32), but also a symphony orchestra performed "Troubled Water" at the Watergate Amphitheatre in Washington, D.C.[14]

Figure 32. Margaret Bonds, June 1966—Steinway Hall, New York City, during taping of "Spiritual Suite for Piano" for Operation Music One to be used in all Nigerian Educational Centers. Taped under supervision of Mr. Féla Sowande, Nigerian Composer ([Northwestern University] Anthropology—1964–65 now Prof. at the University of Ibadan). Margaret Bonds, Box 71, Folder 1280, Series 4: Photographs Others (A–B), Center for Black Music Research at Columbia College Chicago.

From the interdisciplinary duet between dancers and musicians, through the transatlantic dialogue of African-descended practitioners, to the compositional movements from Spirituals to symphonies, Bonds's artistry carried the imprint of the Black classical metropolis.

Bonds therefore becomes to this era what you and your peers had been to the interwar period: a seasoned and highly accomplished matriarch of the art world, an example for younger generations, a conduit to African American folk traditions, and a paragon of Black women's artistic excellence and activism.[15] As organizers of the Bonds concert who had once worked so closely alongside you during the interwar years, CMA president Stone and board members such as Walter Dyett, James A. Mundy, Ruth P.

Henderson, and Grace W. Tompkins must have surely felt the strength of your influence and the weight of your absence in the present celebratory moment. In fact, this likely applied to numerous others who had, by this time, either moved elsewhere (like Holt) or passed on (like Price, Estella, Neota McCurdy Dyett, Beulah Mitchell Hill, and Anita Patti Brown).

In the early hours of Monday, October 21, 1940, you survived the bullet that tore through the corner of your mouth and lodged itself "at the base" of your brain.[16] The story made front-page news in the widely read Black presses of the *Chicago Defender*, *New York Amsterdam News*, and *Pittsburgh Courier*, sending shock waves through Black society at large, given your national repute. In his statement to the police, your son said that "at an early hour in the morning he heard a noise" in the home that you shared. The noise, he claimed, emanated from somewhere near his bedroom and yours—both of which were on the second floor. Albert Jr. recounted calling you twice "when he heard a noise in the house and when there was no response he rushed downstairs with the pistol and from a distance he saw a form in the half darkened kitchen and fired." Your neighbor, Irving Miller of 3233 Vernon Avenue, "first informed [the police] of the shooting," while your other neighbor, James Bell of 3227 Vernon Avenue, rushed you to Provident Hospital.[17] This was where the police found your son before taking him into custody. Your condition was critical, but you would live. Although you would not be well enough to attend any of the court sessions, you would, in your own statement, corroborate your son's story, confirming that Albert Jr. had shot you, mistaking you for a burglar. To your relief, the charges against him were dropped. But there were rumors around the incident, stirred by "alleged friends and relatives." One theory was that you, "despondent of the loss" of your husband earlier that year and the "resultant financial reverses and family troubles, had attempted suicide." The police probed this angle further, weighing "the possibility that after the victim survived this attempt on her life the son sought to conceal his mother's act by advancing the accidental shooting version."[18] Your story prevailed, but this tragedy marked the beginning of the end, for you were only in your fifties when a bout of illness claimed your life in 1943.

Do I dare broach the possibility of suicide, traversing not only issues of spiritual and religious taboo but potentially legitimizing a gossip-driven narrative? Or do I accept the incident as told, all the while cognizant of how it perpetuates the stereotype of Chicago's violent, criminal underside?[19] Torn, I opt for a middle ground in which your demise ultimately reminds us of the historical precarity and unprotectedness of Black female life in the United States and that—for all its touted rhetoric of universalism and transcendence—"classical music cannot save anyone."[20]

The death of your husband left you more exposed than ever to the harsh elements of a white supremacist patriarchy. You may have retained your social status within the Black professional class, but your financial circumstances took a turn for the worse, exemplifying the ways in which the perception of material wealth could differ from the reality in Race women's worlds.[21] In other words, you were vulnerable, and as a Black woman further bound by your intraracial social caste, you were not expected to outwardly show it, per the "culture of dissemblance" that saw respectable Race women shield their inner lives from public view.[22]

This aspect of your lived experience remains impermeable. Yet other aspects of your inner life gift us with an immensely optimistic portrait. Your quiet acts behind Chicago's classical music scene (in addition to your public-facing endeavors at the fore) generated paths and possibilities beyond those that were generally available to Black women, men, and children at this time. The achievements of Black classical composers, performers, educators, and more were not products of the fallacy that is classical music's inherent saviorism but evidence of how the "liminal space" of Black classical world-making and the agents working within it can, as Kira Thurman writes, "[encourage] us to consider the full range of experiences that should be available to people of color."[23] And it is in this capacity that you were remembered—that is, as an architect of vast experiences, outlets, platforms, and opportunities, coconstructed with your network for a wide range of African-descended classical practitioners, from burgeoning artists to the most seasoned stars.

Your obituary in the *Chicago Defender* highlighted your "civic work and music promotion." Citing your contributions as a clubwoman, the tribute noted your role as the National Association of Negro Musicians (NANM) president and your fervent activity across numerous other civic clubs and organizations. It also acknowledged your impresarial range "as an early patron of Marian Anderson" and as a promoter who "presented Roland Hayes . . . many times in Chicago." You were behind some of the biggest names and events in Black classical history, in the city and beyond.

With a more local focus, another passage read,

> She was in charge of the music for the Negro in Art week, given by a committee of prominent Chicago citizens in 1927, and underwrote a concert in the "Friends of Music" series in connection with the World's Fair in 1933: at this concert Margaret Bonds, young Chicago pianist, appeared with the Chicago Symphony orchestra under Dr. Frederick Stock.[24]

Price's name is notably absent from the closing accolade, which I imagine was not as you would have wanted it but very much in keeping with

Rae Linda Brown's observations of the drop-off around Price's name in the media during the 1940s. Your own columns were so often a catalog of Race men and *women's* (emphasis on the plural) musical achievement. Soon after the Negro in Music at the 1933 Chicago World's Fair, your enduring commitment to Race women in the realm of music was documented in one of the most comprehensive historical records of Black women's multifaceted activity across the country: *Lifting as They Climb*. Amid pages upon pages of reports and essays sat your article, "Women in Music." There, you listed the contributions of several nationally and internationally renowned performers, composers, and music educators. In the tradition of intellectual Race women's "listing" (whereby "Black women name the names of other Black women that are doing the work as a way to resist historiographical silencing"), brief paragraphs of biography and praise followed the names printed.[25] From "some of the outstanding artists of the world" to the "many heads of music departments" and "supervisors of music in the public schools . . . who deserve mention" (but whose numbers were too large to include), you sounded a polyvocal survey of Race women's accomplishment in the realm of music, subtly signaling the ghost notes of their institution-building and sociocultural influence amid the grander displays of their performance, compositional, and scholarly lives. In the essay's preface, you acknowledged that "space will not permit a lengthy analysis of the achievements of each, but it is the purpose to definitely establish some whose contributions are nationally known." Your resolve to uplift the Race was unfaltering, and your dedication to women's rights made you deeply attentive to the ways in which you could explicitly advocate for the most unknown and unacknowledged factor at the intersection of the two: Black womanhood.[26]

Your essay celebrated itinerant singers who charted new frontiers in the concert halls of Old World Europe, proving the fallacy of what Jennifer Lynn Stoever calls the "sonic color line" with their mastery of German, French, and Italian diction, and subsequently reimagining—as well as challenging their European audiences to reimagine—what Thurman articulates as "the ties that bound together race, culture, and nation."[27] You wrote of Mme. M. Calloway Byron's "time abroad, in Russia, where she was successfully heard in concert for fourteen years and was a renowned beauty."[28] The reference to how audiences viewed Brown's physical appearance was no extraneous, superficial detail. For centuries, the European gaze held Black women's bodies not just as "erotic objects" but as symbols of "the most extreme sexuality imaginable: wild, insatiable, and deviant."[29] And so, that Russian audiences received Byron's physical presentation beyond these dehumanizing tropes was as much cause for celebration as the fact that, musically speaking, "all of the principal cities of Europe were scenes of her triumphs."

Mentioned, too, were Lillian Evanti's successful appearances "in opera in Italy and France" and her German debut, "which was given a great ovation," as were Mme. Florence Cole Talbert's performance "in the title role of Aida in Italy a few years ago" and of course the groundbreaking accomplishments of Marian Anderson, whom you described as "a young artist, who occupies the foremost place of achievement of any of the present day international artists."[30] Such segments exhibited great pride in the internationalism of these Race women, who not only conquered Europe but brought their craft to the Caribbean and Canada (i.e., Mme. Anita Patti Brown), as well as Australia (i.e., Mme. Neal Hawkins Buckner, one of Chicago's old-timers who had been a soloist at the 1893 World's Columbian Exposition).[31] You additionally used your platform to give an impresarial boost to the "internationally renowned soprano and dramatic artist" Abbie Mitchell, noting, "It has been said by many that [she] should be heard in opera, because she has the dramatic training to make her ideal." Readers familiar with your work would have known to trust your judgment.

Black women's breakthroughs in the international concert scene meant a great deal, but so too did their more local activities. Mentioned was your Indianapolis counterpart Lillian LeMon, noting her current position as NANM president and the recognition of her Cosmopolitan School of Music by the school systems of her city and the state of Indiana. Even closer to home were Pauline James Lee and her Chicago University of Music and Dr. Mildred Bryant Jones and her music department at Wendell Phillips High School. Feeding into these educational threads, you also highlighted both Florence Cole Talbert and Antoinette Garnes ("a soprano of merit, a violinist and pianist") as past recipients of the Alexander Revell Diamond Medal of the Chicago Musical College. And then there were the hallmark events of Black classical Chicago, including the solo performances of Lillian Evanti and Hazel Harrison (yet another itinerant Race woman) in the 1927 Negro in Art Week, and Florence Price's Wanamaker Prize for her first symphony and her subsequent debut with the Chicago Symphony Orchestra. Predictably, your own impresarial hand in shaping the Wanamaker awards and Price's premiere went uncited, just as it did for your entries about Evanti's and Harrison's contributions to the Negro in Art Week. You used this essay to amplify others rather than as a project of self-promotion.

Also drawn into this rich record of Black women's classical music achievement were Emma Azalia Hackley's countrywide tours of Black folk and concert repertoire, Shirley Graham's *Tom Tom,* and Camille

Nickerson's and Maud Cuney Hare's scholarly and compositional work on Creole music. Of Hare, you also underscored her academic contributions in the form of "a book, to be known as 'A History of Afro-American Music and Musicians.'" (The book would later be published in 1936 after Hare's premature death and titled *Negro Musicians and Their Music*.[32]) "Women in Music" captured the highly cosmopolitan yet deeply grounded nature of Race women's work. However, what made each and every one of these Black women extraordinary was neither their womanness nor their Blackness but the fact that they—as women of African descent—accomplished what they did amid the Jim Crowism of the United States, the imperial and fascist terrains of Europe, and the global landscape of white supremacy and patriarchy. In other words, the astonishment lies in the systemic racism and sexism that they endured, not in the magnitude of their ambition.

In 1938, the *Chicago Defender* reprinted your essay under the title "Women Contributors to the World of Music: Short Sketches of Women in Music," alerting even wider audiences to these revelatory herstories.[33] Even if readers did not know about your work behind the scenes to facilitate the careers of those mentioned and events such as the 1927 Negro in Art Week or the 1933 Negro in Music, your drawing together of these women and their accomplishments in such a monumental anthology of Black women's history (and later for the *Chicago Defender*) at the very least hinted at your significant standing within this sphere.

Yet privy to the inner depths and breadths of your impact were those operating in the Black classical metropolis. On October 6, 1933, the Chicago and Northern District Association of Colored (CND) Women's Club music committee, under music chair Martha B. Mitchell (your presidential predecessor at the CMA), "entertained with an afternoon of music, in honor of Mrs. Maude R. George, newly elected president of the National Association of Negro Musicians." Gathered at the organization's clubhouse were guests such as Price, Elsie Breeding, Margaret Bonds, Antoinette Tompkins, Clara E. Hutchison, Anita Patti Brown, Irene Howard Harrison, and Gertrude Smith Jackson. Present, too, were prominent clubwomen Carrie B. Horton and Helen Brascher, the CND Women's Club district president and vice president, respectively.

Your entwined patronage and philanthropy were foregrounded in the *Chicago Defender*'s report of the event:

> This lovely affair . . . was in appreciation for the wonderful aid Mrs. George has been to all clubs and organizations in arranging programs and carrying them out successfully. She has also sponsored some of the

most successful young musicians of the city and is keen to appreciate the future of the youth in the music world. Her sole ambition and aim is always to be of assistance to them.[34]

Your generosity toward others no doubt inspired another party, held in your honor on September 8, 1934, and hosted by CMA board member James W. Benson. You were, by this point, president of both the CMA and NANM—a huge organizational feat and testament to your leadership.

Standing in the second row of a photo that captures you and your CMA colleagues (of whom nearly all pictured were board members) are your host, James Benson, who became chair of the Social Committee under your presidency; Clarence Lee, who had been the publicity chair under your predecessor, Martha B. Mitchell; Iceler Petty Tittle, an active soprano and future parliamentarian under the succeeding presidency of Estella Bonds; soprano Fannie Carter Woods and future membership chair under Bonds; and J. Marcus McCown, who became parliamentarian under your presidency. Pianist and musical director Grace W. Tompkins, J. Wesley Jones, George Hutchison, and Herman Billingsly complete the second row.[35]

In the first row sits a line of the city's most celebrated musical Race women: Anita Patti Brown, Clara Hutchison, Price, Estella Bonds, and Nannie Strayhorn Reid, as well as special guests Lillian Evanti and star of the stage and screen Etta Moten-Barnett (who had recently married Chicago's Claude A. Barnett, founder and director of the Associated Negro Press).[36] I cannot help but notice how you are in the center of the photograph and yet also not. There you are, seated on the sofa in the middle. You share the seating with the stars of the movie screen and concert stage—Moten-Barnett, Price, and Evanti. However, you are positioned to the side, simultaneously in and out of the spotlight (fig. 33). And it is this subtle maneuverability that I have tried to convey in telling what I can of your story and of those stories nested in the larger composition of your influence.

• • •

In redrawing the canon of Western art music around the contours of your and other Race women's lived experiences, what emerges is a more expansive paradigm that accounts for the multifaceted dynamism of Black women's classical cultural production. To consider how musical Race women found their place in the sun is to reconfigure the typically Euro- and androcentric framing of the classical music landscape—a framing that persists regardless of the geography in question. Such a reconfiguration makes visible the nested narratives of the South Side impresarios as

Figure 33. Party in honor of Maude R. George, 1934, MC 988A, Box 2 Folder 1 Item 1, Florence Beatrice Smith Price Papers, University of Arkansas Libraries Special Collections, Fayetteville, with names provided by the personal archives of Anthony E. Philpott.

Back, left to right: Clarence Lee, J. Wesley Jones, George Hutchison, Iceler Petty Tittle, James Benson, Grace W. Tompkins, Fannie Carter Woods, Herman Billingsly, and J. Marcus McCown.

Front, left to right: Anita Patti Brown, Clara E. Hutchison, Etta Moten-Barnett, Florence Price, Lillian Evanti, Maude Roberts George, Estella Bonds, and Nannie Strayhorn Reid.

well as those of local and nonlocal African-descended concert artists and practitioners whose trajectories intersected with the female-led inner workings of the Black classical metropolis.

Through this storytelling, I have aimed to challenge the notion that the specific geography—and specifically *Black* geography—of your cohort renders this a microhistory in classical music's more sweeping periodizations. After all, how often are whole epochs in the Western classical tradition defined by the activity of a select few white male composers operating in limited spaces? Rather, redrawing the canon's contours around the activity and locale of your immediate network not only affirms the existence of a female-led classical Black Renaissance but reveals musical Race women's craft as a microcosm of the macrohistories that are African American intellectual traditions, Afro-diasporic musicking, forced and voluntary translocation, Black world-making, women's rights, and feminist thought. That this Black female–authored classical era and these macrohistories are absent from the classical music canon—a canon that took shape through the centuries that encompassed the transatlantic slave trade, the anti-Black regimes that followed, and the continuous remakings of woman-hood—speaks volumes about the concerted efforts to limit the perspectives through which we today see our shared history and to silence voices such as yours, which bear the power to show our collective past in a new light.

I opened *South Side Impresarios* with the groundbreaking moment in which Price became the first Black woman composer to debut with a major national orchestra, which finds a present-day parallel in the way that Price has become the most concertized Black female composer today, experiencing posthumous debuts with high-profile orchestras like the Philadelphia Orchestra and Boston Symphony Orchestra and in prestigious venues such as the Royal Albert Hall and Carnegie Hall.[37] Just as it seemed back in 1933, current directions similarly suggest that "a Black female composer" has been welcomed into the canon—"finally," as Micaela Baranello put it in her 2018 piece for the *New York Times*.[38]

When I was invited as a guest speaker for the televised 2021 BBC Proms in which pianist Jeneba Kanneh-Mason, conductor Kalena Bovell (both descendants of the African diaspora), and Europe's first Black and Minority Ethnic (BAME) orchestra, Chineke! debuted Price's Piano Concerto in One Movement on August 24, I recall the tears that welled up in my eyes as Bovell led the orchestra under her baton through the familiar call-and-response opening in the winds, and as Kanneh-Mason shone with the dazzling cadenza that follows. With that performance, I felt as though we might be on the cusp of change—as if "a new day has dawned for [Black] women" and "a new deal is here," as Elizabeth Lindsay Davis put it almost a century ago. But what I felt continued to warrant as much focus in Price's posthumous narrative were the nested herstories of the Black women in and around her network as well as the aforementioned macrohistories of Black American life embedded in her journey. There-fore, I set out to shift the perspective from one that was less focused on Price being welcomed into the canon to one that was more focused on the spaces in which she was already welcome—that is, the spaces born out of Black female realm-building. I wanted to expand the paradigm through which we, today, understand this history and to reconfigure the landscape to foreground historical Black women's multiplex realities. As a result, I utilized Price's 1933 accomplishment as a point of entry into the herstories behind the history, which would invariably lead to you, the indefatigable Maude Roberts George, and your circle of Race women impresarios.

As a Price scholar and performer, it was necessary for me to peel the layers of the Price narrative to get to the heart of the Black sisterly networks that not only influenced early twentieth-century US concert culture but continue to shape the international concert scene of today. Deepened by my own experience of Sheila Jones's and the Chicago Symphony Orchestra African American Network's advocacy at the start of my career, I knew to look for the pockets of Black institution-building that are typically erased from the narrative once the machines of the predominantly white classical establishment take hold. After all, what does it say of the establishment's attitude to social progress that Grammy Award–winning composer and Sphinx Medal of Excellence recipient Jessie Montgomery holds the position of the 2021–24 Mead Composer-in-Residence of the Chicago Symphony Orchestra yet is only the *second* Black woman to have her music performed by the Chicago Symphony in either the Auditorium Theatre or Orchestra Hall since Price in 1933?[39] Dissociating from narratives that prize delayed white enlightenments, I argue that undergirding past and present-day performances of Price, Margaret Bonds, and other composers of the Black Chicago Renaissance era are the impresarial and organizational foundations that you and your network forged in the realm of music. Your communities and archives made possible the present-day knowability of these historical composers.

Apt, then, is my reflection on your last decade, not solely on the violence that claimed your public voice and the illness that eventually took your life but also on the ways in which you were loved and celebrated and the ways in which you, too, loved and celebrated your Black musical sisterhood. It encompasses moments of great triumph, moments of deep tragedy, and moments of historiographical silence where I lose track of your activity and even the activity of some of the musical Race women around you. But regarding the complication of the latter, I am reminded of Patricia Hill Collins's remarks on the nineteenth-century foremother of Race womanhood, Maria W. Stewart. Of Stewart, Collins writes, "the ideas of this extraordinary woman come to us only in scattered fragments that not only suggest her brilliance but speak tellingly of the fate of countless Black women intellectuals." That I find your fragments at the heart of Black America's burgeoning concert scene, or woven into the fabric of civic life and African American public culture, or nested in the trajectories of some of Chicago's (and the wider nation's) most prominent concert artists and composers, however, tells me something of your agency in how you might have wished for your story—for *this* story—to be told.

You deliberately fashioned your life into a shared narrative that emanated from an unequivocally Black feminist "group-based, collective standpoint."[40] You were one of many protagonists, not only working within a wider network but toward a greater cause. As documented,

> The support and active effort that [you gave] ... never meant one cent to [you] in compensation over the period of years because [you] had always been anxious that the sponsor of artist performance in Chicago should realize the talent and hear the rendition of our people.[41]

Notably, Rae Linda Brown echoed similar sentiments decades after, assuring orchestras, "I am most interested in the opportunity for audiences to hear this music," as she made her own editions of Price's symphonies available to them for rates significantly lower than what is standard or even pro bono on occasion.[42] This gospel of musical giving is your legacy: there is a direct line between Brown's generous collegiality and yours, especially with Brown's work largely having stoked the fire of Price's twenty-first-century revival and yours having fanned the composer's symphonic spark upon her Chicago arrival.

This point of connection between you and Brown underscores the trans- and interhistorical polyphony behind Black women's furtive worldmaking. Yet it is not lost on me that neither you nor Brown lived to see the full fruits of your labor. As a result, what I have sought to disrupt along this lineage is the way in which the covert nature of historical Black women's work can, over time, fall into the cracks of inaudibility, invisibility, and unknowability. I have therefore had to navigate historiographical silences that arise in the wake of these cracks. Yet I also honor your chosen silence around the extent of your activity. As with Brown and the women of your era—known and unknown in my telling of this story—your influence resounds not only in the bold amplification and posthumous resonance of musical Race womanhood but in the strategic pianissimo of your impresarial voice.

Notes

Introduction. Finding Their Place in the Sun

1. "Last Opera in Auditorium Jan. 26," *New York Times*, January 9, 1929, 35.

2. "Black Satin Clothes Seen at Symphony: Many Box Parties at Fair Concert," *Chicago Daily Tribune*, June 16, 1933, 21, Rosenthal Archives of the Chicago Symphony Orchestra Association, Chicago.

3. Unidentified news source but most likely of the white mainstream Chicago press, June 16, 1933, Rosenthal Archives of the Chicago Symphony Orchestra Association, Chicago.

4. Maude Roberts George, "[text cut off] . . . Triumphs in Recital Here: Noted Tenor and Miss Margaret Bond [*sic*] Star with Symphony," *Chicago Defender*, June 17, 1933, Box 5, Series 4, Folder 8.2, Helen Walker-Hill Papers, Center for Black Music Research at Columbia College Chicago.

5. "Gets Fellowship," *Chicago Defender*, June 24, 1933, 4.

6. Nahum Daniel Brascher, "Roland Hayes Concert Shows Progress of Race in Music," *Chicago Defender*, June 24, 1933, 11.

7. Claudia Cassidy, "Roland Hayes Sings for Friends of Music in Auditorium Concert," *Journal of Commerce*, June 16, 1933, Rosenthal Archives of the Chicago Symphony Orchestra Association, Chicago.

8. Claudia Cassidy's acerbic criticism earned her the moniker "Acidy Cassidy." Her obituary in the *New York Times* remarked, "She wrote an energetic, often florid prose, and she took no prisoners." William Grimes, "Claudia Cassidy, 96, Arts Critic; Did Not Mince Words in Chicago: [Obituary (Obit)]," *New York Times*, July 27, 1996, 11.

9. Nettie George Speed, "Society," *Chicago Defender*, November 10, 1928, 5.

10. Barbara Wright-Pryor, "Barbara Wright-Pryor: 'Maude Roberts George . . . President of CMA of which Price Was a Member, Underwrote the Cost of the June 15, 1933 Concert,'" *Africlassical*, April 7, 2014, https://africlassical.blogspot.com/2014/04/barbara-wright-pryor-maude-roberts.html.

11. Unidentified news source but most likely of the white mainstream Chicago press, June 15, 1933, Rosenthal Archives of the Chicago Symphony Orchestra Association, Chicago.

12. Glenn Dillard Gunn, "George Gershwin Is Hailed as Soloist at Friends of Music Concert at the Auditorium Theater: Three of His Compositions Presented," *Chicago Herald and Examiner*, June 15, 1933, Rosenthal Archives of the Chicago Symphony Orchestra Association, Chicago.

13. Amy Absher, *The Black Musician and the White City: Race and Music in Chicago, 1900–1967* (Ann Arbor: University of Michigan Press, 2014), 44; Sandor Demlinger and John Steiner, *Destination: Chicago Jazz* (Stroud, UK: Tempus Publishing, 2003), 33.

14. In their edited collection *Black Women and Music: More than the Blues*, Eileen M. Hayes and Linda F. Williams use "beyond the blues" to emphasize the much-overlooked heterogeneity of Black women's musical experiences and contributions across a wide range of genres and styles. Hayes writes, "As important as examinations of black women's blues are, their positioning in anthologies—particularly in music but also in women's culture anthologies—as the sole representation of black women's musical experience has the unintended effect of muting analytical treatments of black women, race, and gender in opera, gospel music, rock, country, jazz, or, for that matter, electro-acoustic music." Eileen M. Hayes, "New Perspectives in Studies of Black Women and Music," in *Black Women and Music: More than the Blues*, ed. Eileen M. Hayes and Linda F. Williams (Urbana: University of Illinois Press, 2007), 6–7.

15. Hayes, "New Perspectives," 4.

16. Patricia Hill Collins, *Black Feminist Thought: Knowledge, Consciousness, and the Politics of Empowerment* (New York: Routledge, 2009), 5.

17. Teresa L. Reed, "Black Women in Art Music," in Hayes and Williams, *Black Women and Music*, 194.

18. Akwugo Emejulu and Francesca Sobande, "Introduction: On the Problems and Possibilities of European Black Feminism and Afrofeminism," in *To Exist Is to Resist: Black Feminism in Europe*, ed. Akwugo Emejulu and Francesca Sobande (London: Pluto, 2019), 3.

19. I owe this element of my practice to the late Rae Linda Brown and Helen Walker-Hill who, as musicologists, performers, and editors of the scores that shape my recitals, demonstrated the necessary dialogue between research and repertoire. I also draw parallels with the way Tammy L. Kernodle's multifaceted scholarship on Black women's musical activism emerges from both written projects and public performances, as she discusses in "Freedom Singing at the March on Washington with Tammy Kernodle," interview with Will Robin, *Sound Expertise*, podcast audio, April 2021, https://soundexpertise.org/freedom-singing-at-the-march-on-washington-with-tammy-l-kernodle/.

20. Elektra Voyante, "The Poet and Her Song: Analyzing the Art Songs of Florence B. Price" (DMus diss., Indiana University, 2018); Elizabeth Durrant, "Chicago Renaissance Women: Black Feminism in the Careers and Songs of

Florence Price and Margaret Bonds" (MA thesis, University of North Texas, 2021); A. Kori Hill, "Make the Familiar New: New Negro Modernism in the Concertos of Florence B. Price" (PhD diss., University of North Carolina, 2022).

21. Michelle Obama, *Becoming* (London: Viking, 2018), 13.

22. Sheila Anne Jones was promoted to director of the African American Network and retired in 2022. See Stan West, "As the CSO's Sheila Jones Retires, Her Cause Lives On," *Chicago Symphony Orchestra*, January 28, 2022, https://cso .org/experience/article/8051/as-the-csos-sheila-jones-retires-her-cause-li.

23. Baker's programmed chamber operas were *The Baldwin Chronicles: Midnight Ramble* (2019) and *Le Tumulte Noir: Josephine Baker Tribute* (2020); for more about the community-oriented work of the Chicago West Community Music Center, see https://www.cwcmc.org/.

24. Lena James Holt, "The Symphony Concert," *Chicago Defender*, February 9, 1918, 8; Lucy Caplan, "'Strange What Cosmopolites Music Makes of Us': Classical Music, the Black Press, and Nora Douglas Holt's Black Feminist Audiotopia," *Journal of the Society for American Music* 14, no. 3 (2020): 320.

25. Scrapbook, Series II, Box 5, Irene Britton Smith Collection, Center for Black Music Research at Columbia College Chicago.

26. Regarding "philanthropy," I cite Tyrone McKinley Freeman, who defines the term expansively as "voluntary action for the public good" in recognition of the fact that "in the African American experience, philanthropy did not originate in wealth, but rather in resourceful efforts to meet social needs in the face of overwhelming societal constraints and impositions." Tyrone McKinley Freeman, *Madam C. J. Walker's Gospel of Giving: Black Women's Philanthropy during Jim Crow* (Urbana: University of Illinois Press, 2020), 3.

27. See Darlene Clark Hine and John McCluskey Jr., eds., *The Black Chicago Renaissance* (Urbana: University of Illinois Press, 2012).

28. Transcript of Samantha Ege, "A Celebration of Women in Music: Composing the Black Chicago Renaissance," lecture recital, Chicago Symphony Center, Chicago, April 12, 2018.

29. Samantha Ege, "Of Folk, Faith & Fellowship: Exploring Chicago's African-American Women Composers," recital, Chicago Cultural Center, Chicago, April 7, 2019. For the playlist, see "Of Folk, Faith & Fellowship: Exploring Chicago's African-American Women Composers," YouTube, August 21, 2019, https:// www.youtube.com/playlist?list=PLiJRSlJr1IwRXSR6ui6A-OpvdbCC4k3aa.

30. This venue surfaces in the CMA Records. Chicago Music Association Record (1936–40), Center for Black Music Research at Columbia College Chicago.

31. I thank composer and cofounder of the Castle of our Skins concert and educational series Anthony R. Green for a conversation that took place on May 8, 2023, in which he encouraged me to think even more about Coleridge-Taylor as a historical precedent to my work as a Black British scholar and performer who engages deeply with Black concert culture in the United States.

I also cite a presentation by Mark Burford in which he illuminated more of Coleridge-Taylor's activity across the Black Atlantic and his engagements with Black American activists and artists, inspiring more of my thinking about the transatlantic conversations of African-descended practitioners. Mark Burford, "Sorrow Songs and Sisterhood: Samuel Coleridge-Taylor and W. E. B. Du Bois across the Black Atlantic," (paper presented at the American Musicological Society, Society for Ethnomusicology, and Society for Music Theory Joint Annual Meeting, New Orleans, November 11, 2022).

32. Imani Perry, *May We Forever Stand: A History of the Black National Anthem* (Chapel Hill: University of North Carolina Press, 2018), 7–8.

33. Ralph P. Locke and Cyrilla Barr, "Introduction: Music Patronage as a 'Female-Centered Cultural Process,'" in *Cultivating Music in America: Women Patrons and Activists since 1860*, ed. Ralph P. Locke and Cyrilla Barr (Berkeley: University of California Press, 1997), 1, 9.

34. McGinty, "'As Large as She Can Make it,'" 214.

35. Fannie Barrier Williams, "The Woman's Part in a Man's Business," in *The Voice of the Negro* (New York: Negro Universities Press, [1904] 1969), 1:544.

36. Locke and Barr, "Introduction," 2; McGinty, "'As Large as She Can Make It,'" 230.

37. Allyson Hobbs, *A Chosen Exile: A History of Racial Passing in American Life* (Cambridge, MA: Harvard University Press, 2014), 23.

38. Emma Azalia Hackley, "The Musical Progress of the Race during the Last Year," *Indianapolis Freeman*, December 25, 1915, 2, quoted in Juanita Karpf, *Performing Racial Uplift: E. Azalia Hackley and African American Activism in the Postbellum to Pre-Harlem Era* (Jackson: University Press of Mississippi, 2022), 108.

39. I do not want to legitimize white readers using the word "Negro" beyond these exact contexts; this is less about the word's archaism and more about its now derogatory overtones in a white hegemony. And while on the subject of whiteness, I use "white" in lower case to acknowledge its continued function as an antagonistic construction and its evolving, ever-conditional definition as a means to reinforce anti-Black hegemonies and hierarchies in a Eurocentric race-making project.

40. "Negro Spiritual," writes Alisha Lola Jones, is "a widely accepted term for the genre by black music researchers and practitioners." She asserts that the term "precisely marks period language, politics, culture, and historical genre designation" and apprehension to use the term fully "signals white Americans' social anxiety and guilt about this country's racist past and their willful forgetting." Alisha Lola Jones, "Spirituals and the Birth of a Black Entertainment Industry by Sandra Jean Graham (Review)," *Journal of Popular Music Studies* 31, no. 3 (2019): 165.

41. Brittney C. Cooper, *Beyond Respectability: The Intellectual Thought of Race Women* (Urbana: University of Illinois Press, 2017), 15.

42. Mariame Kaba and Essence McDowell, *Lifting as They Climbed: Mapping

a History of Trailblazing Black Women in Chicago (Chicago: Haymarket Books, 2023), 11.

43. Emma Azalia Hackley, *The Colored Girl Beautiful* (Kansas City, MO: Burton Publishing, 1916), 33–36.

44. Tammy L. Kernodle, "Black Women Working Together: Jazz, Gender, and the Politics of Validation," *Black Music Research Journal* 34, no. 1 (2014): 29; emphasis original.

45. Freeman, *Madam C. J. Walker*, 4.

46. The manuscripts recovered in 2009 form the second addendum in the Florence Beatrice Smith Price Papers. See David Priest, "The Long Lost Work of Florence Price Finally Comes Home," *Arkansas Life*, May 24, 2018, https:// arkansaslife.com/22383-2/.

47. Originally published as A. Kori Hill, "To Be Rediscovered When You Were Never Forgotten: Florence Price and the 'Rediscovered' Composer (Tropes of Black Composers, Part One)," *Harry T. Burleigh Society*, November 29, 2018, https://www.burleighsociety.com/blog/2018-11-29/florence -price-part-one. Republished as A. Kori Hill, "To Be Rediscovered When You Were Never Forgotten: Florence Price and Black Composers in the Mainstream," *Litrary Diversty, Substack*, June 11, 2023, https://litrary diversty.substack.com/p/to-be-discovered-when-you-were-never?utm_ source=profile&utm_medium=reader2. See also Douglas W. Shadle, "Plus ça change: Florence B. Price in the #BlackLivesMatterEra," New Music USA, February 20, 2019, https://newmusicusa.org/nmbx/ plus-ca-change-florence-b-price-in-the-blacklivesmatter-era/.

48. Cooper, *Beyond Respectability*, 123.

49. Mia Bay, "The Battle for Womanhood Is the Battle for Race: Black Women and Nineteenth-Century Racial Thought," in *Toward an Intellectual History of Black Women*, ed. Mia Bay, Farah J. Griffin, Martha S. Jones, and Barbara D. Savage (Chapel Hill: University of North Carolina Press, 2015), 77.

50. Alisha Lola Jones, "Lift Every Voice: Marian Anderson, Florence B. Price and the Sound of Black Sisterhood," *NPR*, August 30, 2019, https://www .npr.org/2019/08/30/748757267/lift-every-voice-marian-anderson-florence -b-price-and-the-sound-of-black-sisterh.

51. Hayes, "New Perspectives," 4.

52. Daphne Brooks, *Liner Notes for the Revolution: The Intellectual Life of Black Feminist Sound* (Cambridge, MA: Harvard University Press, 2021), 67–68.

53. Ora Williams, Thelma Williams, Dora Wilson, and Ramona Matthewson, "American Black Women Composers: A Selected Annotated Bibliography," in *All the Women Are White, All the Blacks Are Men, but Some of Us Are Brave: Black Women's Studies*, 2nd ed., ed. Akasha (Gloria T.) Hull, Patricia Bell Scott, and Barbara Smith (New York: Feminist Press, 2015), 298.

54. Naomi André, *Black Opera: History, Power, Engagement* (Urbana: University of Illinois Press, 2018), 16.

Chapter 1. When and Where They Entered

1. "Hackney Concert Musical Treat," *Chicago Defender*, May 1, 1915, 6.

2. I recorded the two-piano arrangement on my album *Black Renaissance Woman: Piano Music by Florence Price, Margaret Bonds, Nora Holt, Betty Jackson King, and Helen Hagan*. Lorelt (Lontano Records Ltd.), 2022, LNT 145. Additionally, on October 20, 2022, I gave the world premiere of a newly orchestrated version by composer and Yale alumna Soomin Kim. I performed as the soloist with the Yale Philharmonia under the baton of conductor Peter Oundjian. The performance took place in Woolsey Hall—the same concert hall where Hagan performed the work with the student orchestra over a century earlier. See Michael Andor Brodeur, "A Pioneering Black Composer Gets Her Due, 110 Years after Her Debut: Samantha Ege and the Yale Philharmonia Will Perform the Orchestra World Premiere of Helen Hagan's 'Piano Concerto in C Minor,'" *Washington Post*, October 22, 2022, https://www.washingtonpost.com/music/2022/10/20/helen-hagan-samantha-ege-yale-music/.

3. "Hackney Concert Musical Treat."

4. "Mrs. David M. Manson Finished Advanced Studies in Music," *Chicago Defender*, July 4, 1914, 4.

5. Faulkner described Manson as "an earnest, serious student of music, who is doing much to aid the people to a better understanding of the true worth and beauty of the best music." Pedro T. Tinsley, director of the Chicago Choral Study Club (whom I elaborate on in chapter 2), noted that "music lovers of the city, and especially members of The Choral Study Club, owe to her a great debt of gratitude inasmuch as she has acquainted us with her literary art, which, but for her love for the work, enthusiasm and enterprise, might never have been heard." Dr. Frank W. Gunsaulus, president of the Armour Institute of Technology, lauded her as "a lady of remarkable ability as a student of literature and music," adding, "her devotion to music and services in this direction have been valuable and suggest a larger field of work." "Testimonials of People Who Know: Mrs. David M. Manson," *Chicago Defender*, September 9, 1911, 6; Nora Holt, "Music: Life Story of Azalia Hackley Evangel of Music, Just Released," *New York Amsterdam News*, September 24, 1949, 22.

6. "Testimonials of People Who Know"; Holt, "Music."

7. George performed Manson's art song "Mother Night" alongside "a varied group of songs in English, German, French and Italian" at a gala concert at Aryan Grotto Temple (on Eighth Street and Wabash Avenue) on July 26, 1923, again suggesting that Manson's style was well situated amid the more canonic repertoire. Maude Roberts George, "News of the Music World," *Chicago Defender*, August 11, 1923, 5.

8. Anna Julia Cooper, "Womanhood: A Vital Element in the Regeneration and Progress of a Race (1886)," in *The Voice of Anna Julia Cooper: Including A Voice from the South and Other Important Essays, Papers, and Letters*, ed.

Charles Lemert and Esme Bhan (Lanham, MD: Rowman & Littlefield, 1998), 63; emphasis original.

9. Alisha Lola Jones, "'When and Where I Enter': Marian Anderson, Florence B. Price, and a Womanist Musical Rebuttal of UnSisterly White Women's Movements" (paper, Center for Research on Race and Ethnicity in Society Speaker Series, Indiana University, Bloomington, March 21, 2019), https://anthropology.indiana.edu/news-events/events-calendar/crres-speaker-series-alisha-jones.html.

10. Tammy L. Kernodle, "'When and Where I Enter': Black Women Composers and the Advancement of a Black Postmodern Concert Aesthetic in Cold War–Era America," in "Colloquy: Shadow Culture Narratives: Race, Gender, and American Music Historiography," *Journal of the American Musicological Society* 73, no. 3 (2020): 771, 776. Additionally, in *Black Women and Music*, the motif appears as the subtitle of the second part of the monograph: "When and Where She Enters: Black Women in Unsung Places." See Eileen M. Hayes and Linda F. Williams, *Black Women and Music: More than the Blues* (Urbana: University of Illinois Press, 2007).

11. "A Scrap Book for Women in Public Life: Maude Roberts George on Musicians Board," *Chicago Defender*, September 21, 1929, 5.

12. "Lena James Holt Takes High Honors at Chicago Musical College," *Chicago Defender*, June 29, 1918, 10.

13. Tyrone McKinley Freeman, *Madam C. J. Walker's Gospel of Giving: Black Women's Philanthropy during Jim Crow* (Urbana: University of Illinois Press, 2020), 17.

14. Patricia Hill Collins, *Black Feminist Thought: Knowledge, Consciousness, and the Politics of Empowerment* (New York: Routledge, 2009), 25; emphasis original.

15. Collins, *Black Feminist Thought*, 13.

16. Hazel V. Carby, *Reconstructing Womanhood: The Emergence of the Afro-American Woman Novelist* (New York: Oxford University Press, 1987), 99.

17. Frances Beale, "Double Jeopardy: To Be Black and Female," in *The Black Woman: An Anthology*, ed. Toni Cade Bambara (New York: New American Library, 1970), 90–100.

18. Michael Kennedy, Joyce Kennedy, and Tim Rutherford-Johnson, eds., *Oxford Dictionary of Music*, 6th ed. (Oxford: Oxford University Press, 2013), 190.

19. For example, see "Nora Holt Ray Bares Divorce Secrets," *Chicago Defender*, February 6, 1926, 1; and "Nora Holt Divorced by Ray: Long Court Battle Ends," *Chicago Defender*, March 29, 1930, 1.

20. Evelyn Brooks Higginbotham, *Righteous Discontent: The Women's Movement in the Black Baptist Church, 1880–1920* (Cambridge, MA: Harvard University Press, 1993), 20.

21. Nora Douglas Holt, "Influence of Lyceums," *Chicago Defender*, October 26, 1918, 12.

22. "Moseley-Lewis Wedding Brilliant Christmas Affair," *Chicago Defender*, December 29, 1917, 5; "Mrs. Cary B. Lewis Joins Defender Staff," *Chicago Defender*, December 15, 1926, 4; "Some Baseball History," *Chicago Defender*, January 30, 1954, 22.

23. Holt, "Influence of Lyceums."

24. Melina Abdullah, "The Emergence of a Black Feminist Leadership Model: African-American Women and Political Activism in the Nineteenth Century," in *Black Women's Intellectual Traditions: Speaking Their Minds*, ed. Kristin Waters and Carol B. Conway (Burlington: University of Vermont Press, 2007), 330.

25. Higginbotham, *Righteous Discontent*, 20.

26. W. E. B. Du Bois, "The Talented Tenth," in *The Negro Problem*, ed. Booker T. Washington, W. E. B. Du Bois, Paul Laurence Dunbar, and Charles W. Chesnutt (New York: James Pott, 1903), 75, 33.

27. See Joy James, *Transcending the Talented Tenth: Black Leaders and American Intellectuals* (New York: Routledge, 1997).

28. Booker T. Washington, ed., *A New Negro for a New Century: An Accurate and Up-to-date Record of the Upward Struggles of the Negro Race* (Chicago: American Publishing House, 1900).

29. Alain Locke, "The New Negro" in *The New Negro: An Interpretation*, edited by Alain Locke (New York: Simon & Schuster, [1925] 1997), 3.

30. Brittney C. Cooper, *Beyond Respectability: The Intellectual Thought of Race Women* (Urbana: University of Illinois Press, 2017), 23.

31. Jane Rhodes, "Pedagogies of Respectability: Race, Media, and Black Womanhood in the Early 20th Century," *Souls: A Critical Journal of Black Politics, Culture, and Society* 18, no. 2–4 (2016): 202.

32. Collins, *Black Feminist Thought*; Angela Davis, *Women, Race & Class* (London: Random House, 1981); bell hooks, *"Ain't I a Woman?": Black Women and Feminism* (New York: Routledge, 1981); Akasha (Gloria T.) Hull, Patricia Bell Scott, and Barbara Smith, eds., *All the Women Are White, All the Blacks Are Men, but Some of Us Are Brave: Black Women's Studies*, 2nd ed. (New York: Feminist Press, 2015); Kimberlé W. Crenshaw, "Demarginalizing the Intersection of Race and Sex: A Black Feminist Critique of Antidiscrimination Doctrine, Feminist Theory and Antiracist Politics," *University of Chicago Legal Forum* (1989): 139–67; Kimberlé W. Crenshaw, "Mapping the Margins: Intersectionality, Identity Politics and Violence against Women of Color," *Stanford Law Review* 43, no. 6 (1991): 1241–99.

33. Higginbotham, *Righteous Discontent*, 67.

34. Williams, "The Club Movement," 379, 378.

35. Cooper, *Beyond Respectability*, 46.

36. Williams, "The Club Movement," 380–81.

37. Alpha Kappa Alpha was founded in 1908 at the historically Black Howard University in Washington, D.C. *Theta Omega Chapter: Alpha Kappa Alpha Sorority, Incorporated* ®, https://thetaomega.com/theta-omega-chapter/theta-omega-history/.

38. Margaret Bonds Promotional Brochure, 1935–36, Box 2, Folder 2, Margaret Bonds Papers, Georgetown University.

39. "Moseley-Lewis Wedding Brilliant Christmas Affair."

40. For recent scholarship on Harrison's experiences in Germany and the broader history of Black concert singers and musicians operating in the region from the 1870s to the 1960s, see Kira Thurman, *Singing like Germans: Black Musicians in the Land of Bach, Beethoven, and Brahms* (Ithaca: Cornell University Press, 2021).

41. Maude Roberts George, "News of the Music World," April 12, 1924, 8.

42. "Marian Anderson Makes Triumph," *Pittsburgh Courier*, November 30, 1929, A2.

43. Williams, "The Club Movement," 384.

44. Cooper, *Beyond Respectability*, 9.

45. Huping Ling, *Chinese Chicago: Race, Transnational Migration and Community since 1870* (Redwood City: Stanford University Press, 2012), 24. See also Cheryl R. Ganz, *The 1933 Chicago World's Fair: A Century of Progress* (Urbana: University of Illinois Press, 2008), 124.

46. St. Clair Drake and Horace Cayton, *Black Metropolis: A Study of Negro Life in a Northern City* (1945; reprint, Chicago: University of Chicago Press, 2015), 12.

47. Robert Bone and Richard A. Courage, *The Muse in Bronzeville: African American Creative Expression in Chicago, 1932–1950* (New Brunswick: Rutgers University Press, 2011), 1.

48. Drake and Cayton, *Black Metropolis*, 12.

49. "The Great Northern Drive Is to Continue," *Chicago Defender*, April 7, 1917, 2.

50. James N. Gregory, *The Southern Diaspora: How the Great Migrations of Black and White Southerners Transformed America* (Chapel Hill: University of North Carolina Press), 126.

51. "Don'ts for Newcomers," *Chicago Defender*, July 14, 1923, 14.

52. Rima Lunin Schultz and Adele Hast, *Women Building Chicago 1790–1990: A Biographical Dictionary* (Bloomington: Indiana University Press, 2001), li.

53. Drake and Cayton, *Black Metropolis*, 60.

54. Darlene Clark Hine, *Hine Sight: Black Women and the Re-Construction of American History* (Bloomington: Indiana University Press, 1994), 99.

55. Saidiya Hartman, *Wayward Lives, Beautiful Experiments: Intimate Stories of Social Upheaval* (New York: Norton, 2019), 173.

56. Wanda A. Hendricks, *Gender, Race, and Politics in the Midwest: Black Club Women in Illinois* (Bloomington: Indiana University Press, 1998), xi.

57. Cooper, "The Status of the Woman in America," , 112.

58. Cooper, "The Status of the Woman," 112.

59. Jones, "'When and Where I Enter,'" 2019.

60. Cooper, "The Status of the Woman," 112.

61. Lilian Serece Williams and Randolph Boehm, eds., *Records of the National Association of Colored Women's Clubs, 1895–1992: Part 1: Minutes*

of National Conventions, Publications, and President's Office Correspondence (Bethesda: University Publications of America, 1994), x.

62. Carby, *Reconstructing Womanhood*, 96.

63. Hendricks, *Gender, Race, and Politics*, xii.

64. See Elizabeth Lindsay Davis, *Lifting as They Climb* (Chicago: National Association of Colored Women, 1933); and Elizabeth Lindsay Davis, *The Story of the Illinois Federation of Colored Women's Clubs, 1900–1922* (Chicago: n.p., 1922).

65. Anne Meis Knupfer, *Toward a Tenderer Humanity and a Nobler Woman-hood: African American Women's Clubs in Turn-of-the-Century Chicago* (New York: New York University Press, 1996), 11.

66. Lawrence Schenbeck elaborates on the schism between Old Settlers and newcomers, particularly as it related to the southern and darker-complected Robert S. Abbott who worked to overcome the colorist and anti-southern sentiments of lighter-complected Chicagoans who vaunted their multigenerational ties to the city. Schenbeck highlights that Black Chicago's Old Settlers were mostly of a lighter skin complexion, which typified the Black aristocratic class across the United States and inevitably shaped intraracial dynamics with the arrival of new settlers in Chicago's South Side at the turn of the century. See Lawrence Schenbeck, *Racial Uplift and American Music, 1878–1943* (Jackson: University Press of Mississippi, 2012), 179–80.

67. "A Scrap Book for Women in Public Life: Miss Merze Tate Wins Foreign Fellowship," *Chicago Defender*, January 16, 1932, 6; "A Scrap Book for Women in Public Life: Mrs. Grace Wilson of Police Scores Policewoman," *Chicago Defender*, September 7, 1929. For recent scholarship on Tate's dynamic life and legacy, see Barbara D. Savage, *Merze Tate: The Global Odyssey of a Black Woman Scholar* (New Haven: Yale University Press, 2023).

68. Charles Hounmenou, "Black Settlement Houses and Oppositional Consciousness," *Journal of Black Studies* 43, no. 6 (2012): 647.

69. Celia Parker Woolley, "Frederick Douglass Center," Wilson Papers, Series 4, 152A Reel 231, Manuscript Division, Library of Congress.

70. Knupfer, *Toward a Tenderer Humanity*, 105.

71. "A Scrap Book for Women in Public Life: Antoinette Tompkins Director of Choir," *Chicago Defender*, August 13, 1932, 6.

72. "A Scrap Book for Women in Public Life: Gertrude S. Jackson a Versatile Musician," *Chicago Defender*, December 5, 1931, 7.

73. Collins, *Black Feminist Thought*, 13.

74. Catherine died in a car accident on June 3, 1958. "A motorist being chased by police crashed into another auto, killing Mrs. Catherine Adams, 31, of 40 W. 78th pl.," reads one of the newspaper clippings held in Box 1 of the Chicago Music Association Collection at Amistad Research Center. Catherine's daughter, Arlene (who was injured and aged six at the time of the accident), is the founder of the Jacksonian Press, which is dedicated to promoting the compositions of Betty Jackson King.

75. "A Scrap Book for Women in Public Life: Gertrude S. Jackson."

76. "A Scrap Book for Women in Public Life: Club History Made by Mrs. A. L. Williams," *Chicago Defender*, August 6, 1932, 7; "Large Assemblage at Reception for Musician," *Chicago Defender*, November 3, 1934, 6.

77. "A Scrap Book for Women in Public Life: Club History Made by Mrs. A. L. Williams."

78. Paula Giddings, *When and Where I Enter: The Impact of Black Women on Race and Sex in America* (New York: Amistad, 2006), 112.

79. Schenbeck, *Racial Uplift*, 182.

80. Mel Tapley, "Nora Holt Dies on the Coast," *New York Amsterdam News*, February 2, 1973, A1.

81. Cheryl A. Wall, "Nora Holt: New Negro Composer and Jazz Age Goddess," in *Women and Migration: Responses in Art and History*, ed. Deborah Willis, Ellyn Toscano, and Kalia Brooks Nelson (Cambridge: Open Book Publishers, 2019), 91–104.

82. Helen Walker-Hill, *From Spirituals to Symphonies: African-American Women Composers and Their Music* (Urbana: University of Illinois Press, 2007), 145. See Harold M. Mayer and Richard C. Wade, *Chicago: Growth of a Metropolis* (Chicago: University of Chicago Press, 1969); Eric Arnesen, *Brotherhoods of Color: Black Railroad Workers and the Struggle for Equality* (Cambridge, MA: Harvard University Press, 2002); and Christopher Robert Reed, *The Rise of Chicago's Black Metropolis, 1920–1929* (Urbana: University of Illinois Press, 2011), 58–59.

83. Hine, *Hine Sight*, 59.

84. Walden University was previously known as Central Tennessee College between 1865 and 1900.

85. Thomas Yenser, "Maude Roberts George," in *Who's Who in Colored America: A Biographical Dictionary of Notable Living Persons of African Descent in America. 1930–1931–1932*, 3rd ed., ed. Thomas Yenser (Brooklyn: Thomas Yenser, 1933), 166.

86. "Miss Irene Hudlin's Debut a Social Triumph," *Chicago Defender*, September 9, 1916, 5.

87. "Maude Roberts George, Local Civic Leader, Dies," *Chicago Defender*, December 11, 1945, 12.

88. "Miss Maude Roberts Has Noted Instructor," *Chicago Defender*, June 6, 1914, 6; "Maude J. Roberts Recital a Triumph in Musical Circle," *Chicago Defender*, February 13, 1915, 6.

89. "Race Woman Honored at Monster Recital," *Chicago Defender*, April 17, 1915, 6; "Roberts Recital March 14," *Chicago Defender*, February 24, 1917, 3; "Maude J. Roberts Touches Musical Hearts of the City," *Chicago Defender*, February 13, 1915, 6.

90. "Maude J. Roberts Touches Musical Hearts of the City."

91. "A Scrap Book for Women in Public Life: Maude Roberts George on Musicians Board."

92. "A Scrap Book for Women in Public Life: Mrs. Clara Hutchison Receives Degree," *Chicago Defender* July 2, 1932, 7.

93. "Clara Hutchison, Retired Teacher, Singer to Be Buried Here Saturday," *Chicago Defender*, February 15, 1964, 1; "Miss Sinclair White Wins Diamond Medal: Pleases an Audience of 5,000 Persons at the Auditorium in Difficult Violin Sections," *Chicago Defender*, June 29, 1912, 1; Nora Douglas Holt, "Diamond and Gold Medal to Local Artists," *Chicago Defender*, June 28, 1919, 16.

94. "A Scrap Book for Women in Public Life: Mrs. Clara Hutchison Receives Degree."

95. Thurman, *Singing like Germans*, 29.

96. "A Scrap Book for Women in Public Life: Irene H. Harrison Is Band Director," *Chicago Defender*, July 9, 1932, 7.

97. See Judith Tick, "Passed Away Is the Piano Girl: Changes in American Musical Life, 1870–1900," in *Women Making Music: The Western Art Tradition, 1150–1950*, ed. Jane Bowers and Judith Tick (Urbana: University of Illinois Press, 1986), 325–48.

98. Ashley D. Farmer, "Shining the Light Just Right: Reconstructing the Life of 'Queen Mother' Audley Moore," *Association of Black Women Historians*, December 4, 2019, http://abwh.org/2019/12/04/shining-the-light-just-right -reconstructing-the-life-of-queen-mother-audley-moore/.

99. "'O, Sing a New Song' Slated for Aug. 25: Represent Africa in Chi Pageant," *Atlanta Daily World*, August 17, 1934, 2.

100. Albert G. Barnett, "Auditions Pageant Thrills Crowd of 60,000: 'O, Sing a New Song' Spectacle Greatest in History," *Chicago Defender*, September 1, 1934, 3.

101. Rae Linda Brown, *The Heart of a Woman: The Life and Music of Florence B. Price* (Urbana: University of Illinois Press, 2020), 154.

102. I borrow the term "piano girl" from Tick's "Passed Away Is the Piano Girl" and reframe it (as chapter 4 of *South Side Impresarios* shows) so as to account for the history of Black piano girls who used their instrument as a tool for empowerment and means to fashion productive livelihoods.

103. Imani Perry explains, "Instructive as well as uplifting, these pageants were forms of political theatre. Through them, black Americans could rehearse their identities as members of a transnational and modern people, with an epic history—one of endurance—while at the same time the participants in each show forged bands with fellow members of the cast who were often neighbors, as the casts were almost always comprised of local talent. Pageants provided occasions to act out the freedom that was being sought. And for both audience and actors they were an opportunity to assert one's worthiness." Imani Perry *May We Forever Stand: A History of the Black National Anthem* (Chapel Hill University of North Carolina Press, 2018), 42.

Chapter 2. She Proclaimed a Chicago Renaissance

1. Lena James Holt, "Roland Hayes Recital," *Chicago Defender*, December 8, 1917, 8.

2. On the back of her "Troubled Water" score, Margaret Bonds writes, "When I was a little girl I never missed a concert of Marian Anderson, Roland Hayes and Abbie Mitchell. I was always thrilled by their singing of Spirituals at the end of each concert. Audiences were thrilled too. (Chicago)." Margaret Bonds, "Troubled Water" score, Cheryl A. Wall Collection of Margaret Bonds and Florence Price Manuscript Scores, Center for Black Music Research at Columbia College Chicago.

3. Holt, "Roland Hayes Recital."

4. Earl Calloway, "Nora Douglas Holt: Became the Defender's Music Critic, Was a Great American Composer, Influenced Black Culture and Organized CMA & NANM," *Chicago Defender*, March 2, 2002, 19; Earl Calloway, "Defender Named Nora Holt the First Female Music Critic in the U.S.," *Chicago Defender*, March 27, 2004, 17.

5. I have not been able to find the original source that Calloway refers to when quoting Holt, but given his position at the *Chicago Defender* and his wider professional network, which included Holt, I regard Calloway's commentary as invaluable insight into the way that Holt conceived of this era.

6. Darlene Clark Hine, introduction to *The Black Chicago Renaissance*, ed. Darlene Clark Hine and John McCluskey Jr. (Urbana: University of Illinois Press, 2012), xv.

7. Hine, "Introduction," xv–xvi, xviii.

8. Helen Walker-Hill, *From Spirituals to Symphonies: African-American Women Composers and Their Music* (Urbana: University of Illinois Press, 2007), 28.

9. St. Clair Drake and Horace R. Cayton used the term "Black Metropolis" in their mid-twentieth-century *Black Metropolis: A Study of Negro Life in a Northern City* (1945; repr., Chicago: University of Chicago Press, 2015).

10. Hine, "Introduction," xvii.

11. Anne Meis Knupfer, *The Chicago Black Renaissance and Women's Activism* (Urbana: University of Illinois Press, 2006), 2.

12. See Steven C. Tracy, ed., *Writers of the Black Chicago Renaissance* (Urbana: University of Illinois Press, 2012); Richard A. Courage and Christopher Reed, *Roots of the Black Chicago Renaissance: New Negro Writers, Artists, and Intellectuals, 1893–1930* (Urbana: University of Illinois Press, 2021); Robert Bone and Richard A. Courage, *The Muse in Bronzeville: African American Creative Expression in Chicago, 1932–1950* (New Brunswick: Rutgers University Press), 94–113.

13. Hine, "Introduction," xv; Samuel A. Floyd Jr., *The Power of Black Music: Interpreting Its History from Africa to the United States* (New York: Oxford University Press, 1995), 100.

14. Samuel A. Floyd Jr., "Music in the Harlem Renaissance: An Overview," in *Black Music in the Harlem Renaissance: A Collection of Essays*, ed. Samuel A. Floyd Jr. (Knoxville: University of Tennessee Press, 1993), 14.

15. Christina Demaitre, "She Has a Musical Mission: Developing Racial Harmony," *Washington Post*, August 14, 1964, Box 5 Series 4, Folder 8.2, Center for Black Music Research at Columbia College Chicago.

16. "The Real Value of Negro Melodies," *New York Herald*, May 21, 1893, 28.

17. Jennifer Lynn Stoever, *The Sonic Color Line: Race and the Cultural Politics of Listening* (New York: New York University Press, 2016), 133.

18. Brian Dolinar, ed. *The Negro in Illinois: The WPA Papers* (Urbana: University of Illinois Press, 2013), 224.

19. W. E. B. Du Bois, *The Souls of Black Folk: Essays and Sketches*, 2nd ed. (Chicago: A. C. McClurg & Co., 1903), 252.

20. See Sandra Jean Graham, *Spirituals and the Birth of a Black Entertainment Industry* (Urbana: University of Illinois Press, 2018), 17–122.

21. Maud Cuney Hare, "The Source," in *International Library of Negro Life and History: The Negro in Music and Art*, ed. Lindsay Patterson (New York: Publishers Company, 1967), 30; Alain Locke, "The Negro Spirituals," in *The New Negro: Voice of the Harlem Renaissance*, ed. Alain Locke (New York: Simon & Schuster, [1925] 1997), 209.

22. Walker-Hill, *From Spirituals to Symphonies*, 24.

23. Recalling her experience seeing Anderson, Hayes, and Mitchell in concert and witnessing their recitals close with Spirituals, Bonds remarked, "So I felt cheated and wanted some Spirituals at the ends of my concerts, too. I learned some settings . . . ." Bonds, "Troubled Water" score; Floyd, *The Power of Black Music*, 102–3.

24. Nahum Daniel Brascher, "Roland Hayes Concert Shows Progress of Race in Music," *Chicago Defender*, June 24, 1933, 11.

25. "Mrs. Bonds, Musician, Dies in New York City," *Chicago Defender*, March 9, 1957, 20; Dolinar, *The Negro in Illinois*, 225; Negro Music and Musicians in Chicago, Illinois Writers Project: Negro in Illinois Collection, Chicago Public Library Digital Collections, https://cdm16818.contentdm.oclc.org/digital/collection/IllWriters/id/9457/rec/1.

26. Some archival sources state Herbert S. Byron, but his obituary says Herbert H. Byron. "Herb H. Byron Musician Is Laid to Rest," *Chicago Defender*, January 24, 1942, 5; Dolinar, *The Negro in Illinois*, 225; Negro Music and Musicians in Chicago, Illinois Writers Project.

27. A. Kori Hill, "Make the Familiar New: New Negro Modernism in the Concertos of Florence B. Price" (PhD diss., University of North Carolina, 2022).

28. Stephanie DeLane Doktor, "How a White Supremacist Became Famous for His Black Music: John Powell and *Rhapsodie nègre (1918)*," *American Music* 38, no. 4 (2020): 400.

29. Teresa L. Reed, "Black Women in Art Music," *Black Women and Music*

More than the Blues, ed. Eileen M. Hayes and Linda F. Williams (Urbana: University of Illinois Press, 2007), 190.

30. Imani Perry, *May We Forever Stand: A History of the Black National Anthem* (Chapel Hill: University of North Carolina Press, 2018), 9.

31. Graham, *Spirituals*, 48.

32. Dolinar, *The Negro in Illinois*, 224.

33. Chicago Choral Study Club, Illinois Writers Project: Negro in Illinois Collection, Chicago Public Library Digital Collections, https://cdm16818 .contentdm.oclc.org/digital/collection/IllWriters/id/9260/rec/1.

34. Dolinar, *The Negro in Illinois*, 224–25.

35. "Mrs. Mattie Johnson Young, Clubwoman, Dies in Chicago," *Chicago Defender*, April 5, 1924, 8.

36. Dolinar, *The Negro in Illinois*, 225

37. "Mrs. Mattie Johnson Young, Clubwoman."

38. "The Choral Study Club of Chicago (Inc.)," *Chicago Defender*, October 4, 1913, 6.

39. Chicago Choral Study Club, Illinois Writers Project.

40. James Monroe Trotter, *Music and Some Highly Musical People* (Boston: Lee and Shepard Publishers, 1878).

41. "Spanish Tenor Lauds Anita Patti-Brown," *Chicago Defender*, December 26, 1914, 4; "Anita Patti Brown a Credit to Her Race," *Chicago Defender*, March 27, 1915, 6; "Umbrian Club Organizer Dies," *Chicago Defender*, August 18, 1945, 6.

42. Nora Douglas Holt, "National Association of Negro Musicians: Chronological History of the N.A.N.M.," *Music and Poetry*, July 1921, 15, Series II, Box 100, Folder 2364, Theodore Charles Stone Collection, Center for Black Music Research at Columbia College Chicago.

43. Samual A. Floyd Jr. wonders whether NANM may have been seen as a "general model" for the "later and much more loosely knit literary movement" spearheaded by Harlem Renaissance figures Alain Locke and Charles Johnson. If true, then this only serves to affirm the strength of Holt's impact. Floyd, "Music in the Harlem Renaissance," 14.

44. Holt, "National Association of Negro Musicians."

45. Quoted in Doris Evans McGinty, ed., *A Documentary History of the National Association of Negro Musicians* (Chicago: Center for Black Music Research, Columbia College Chicago, 2004), 21.

46. Holt, "National Association of Negro Musicians."

47. McGinty, *A Documentary History*, 19.

48. Clara E. Hutchison, The National Association of Negro Musicians, Inc. (1919–1929), Series II, Box 100, Folder 2354, Theodore Charles Stone Collection, Center for Black Music Research at Columbia College Chicago.

49. McGinty, *A Documentary History*, 19.

50. Quoted in McGinty, *A Documentary History*, 61–62.

51. McGinty, *A Documentary History*, 19.

52. Timothy Samuelson writes that the Wabash Avenue YMCA "was an important part of community life in the Black Metropolis. Its large assembly hall was used for a wide variety of civic meetings and community functions. . . . Its educational and social programs became a staple of neighborhood activities, making the Wabash YMCA one of the most heavily utilized public facilities of Chicago's African-American community." Timothy Samuelson, *The Black Metropolis—Bronzeville District* (Chicago: Chicago Department of Planning and Development, 1997), 16.

53. Lynn Abbott and Doug Seroff, *To Do This, You Must Know How: Music Pedagogy in the Black Gospel Quartet Tradition* (Jackson: University Press of Mississippi, 2012), 232.

54. Earl Calloway, "Defender Sparked Holt's Musical Legacy: A Look at Nora Douglas Holt, Former Music Critic for the *Chicago Defender* and Founder of the CMA and NANM," *Chicago Defender*, June 13, 1998, 23.

55. McGinty, *A Documentary History*, 22.

56. Clara E. Hutchison, The National Association of Negro Musicians, Inc. (1919–1929), Series II, Box 100, Folder 2354, Theodore Charles Stone Collection, Center for Black Music Research at Columbia College Chicago.

57. Foreword by George Howard Hutchison in Music Festival & Scholarship Contest of the Chicago Music Association Branch No. 1 of the National Association of Negro Musicians, Inc. Founded 1918. 1949. Box 1 ½ Chicago Music Association: Programs Collection No. 86 Chicago Music Association Collection, 1936–1991, undated, of the Amistad Research Center.

58. Nora Holt, "Musicians Organize National Association," *Chicago Defender*, August 9, 1919, 15.

59. Clara E. Hutchison, The National Association of Negro Musicians, Inc. (1919–1929), Series II, Box 100, Folder 2354, Theodore Charles Stone Collection, Center for Black Music Research at Columbia College Chicago; Foreword by George Howard Hutchison in Music Festival & Scholarship Contest of the Chicago Music Association Branch No. 1 of the National Association of Negro Musicians, Inc. Founded 1918. 1949. Box 1 ½ Chicago Music Association: Programs Collection No. 86 Chicago Music Association Collection, 1936–1991, undated, of the Amistad Research Center.

60. "Clara Hutchison, Retired Teacher, Singer to Be Buried Here Saturday," *Chicago Defender*, February 15, 1964, 3; Foreword by George Howard Hutchison in Music Festival & Scholarship Contest of the Chicago Music Association Branch No. 1 of the National Association of Negro Musicians, Inc. Founded 1918. 1949. Box 1 ½ Chicago Music Association: Programs Collection No. 86 Chicago Music Association Collection, 1936–1991, undated, of the Amistad Research Center.

61. Marian Anderson, *My Lord, What a Morning: An Autobiography by Marian Anderson* (New York: Viking, 1956), 60–61.

62. Holt, "National Association of Negro Musicians."

63. McGinty, *A Documentary History*, 31.

64. McGinty, *A Documentary History*, 26–27.

65. Nora Douglas Holt, "Musical Resume and Prospectus," *Chicago Defender*, October 4, 1919, 12.

66. *The Negro in Chicago, 1779–1927, Volume I* (Chicago: Washington Intercollegiate Club of Chicago, 1927), 4.

67. Suggesting the year of Price's move to be 1927, Goldie M. Walden (in an interview with Price) writes, "Nine years ago she [Price] came to Chicago to devote her time to study and composition, taking up from time to time the latest pedagogical methods." Goldie M. Walden, "Keep Ideals in Front of You; They Will Lead to Victory, Says Mrs. Florence B. Price," *Chicago Defender*, July 11, 1936, 7.

68. See Samantha Ege, "Restaging Respectability: The Subversive Performances of Josephine Baker and Nora Holt in Jazz-Age Paris," *Angelaki: Journal of the Theoretical Humanities* 27, no. 3–4 (2022): 112–24.

69. [Autographed letter signed 1926] October 18, Paris [to] Carl Van Vechten, New York, N.Y. Series I. Correspondence. A–Z Correspondence. Holt, Nora Douglas, Box 14 | 338–345, Carl Van Vechten Papers Relating to African American Arts and Letters. James Weldon Johnson Collection in the Yale Collection of American Literature, Beinecke Rare Book and Manuscript Library.

70. "Nora Holt Opens Chicago's Finest Night Club; Hundreds Attend Debut," *Pittsburgh Courier*, July 9, 1927, 1.

71. Franklin Frazier, "Chicago: A Cross-Section of Negro Life," *Opportunity* 7 (1929): 70–73 and quoted in Walker-Hill, *From Spirituals to Symphonies*, 28.

72. See Lisa Meyerowitz, "The Negro in Art Week: Defining the 'New Negro' through Art Exhibition," *African American Review* 31, no. 1 (1997): 75–89.

73. Cary B. Lewis, "Negro in Art Week in Chicago: Most Delightful Week Chicagoans Have Enjoyed," *Pittsburgh Courier*, November 19, 1927, 5.

74. Lewis, "Negro in Art Week in Chicago"; "Goldie Guy Martin in Recital, May 19," *Chicago Defender*, May 11, 1935, 12; Maude Roberts George, "Music," *Chicago Defender*, December 3, 1927, 6.

75. Lewis, "Negro in Art Week in Chicago."

76. Maude Roberts George, "News of the Music World," *Chicago Defender*, November 19, 1927, 5.

77. The names of the founding cohort included Nellie Bomar (who hosted the meeting at her house), Anna G. Carr, Delia D. Caldwell, Mary Covington, Anna Emanuel, Ruth Allen, Omega J. King, Mable Sanford Lewis, Beatrice Nesbett, and Blanche Thompson. John E. Webb, *Whispers of Love: A History of the R. Nathaniel Dett Club of Music and Allied Arts, 1922–1987* (Chicago: Columbia College, Chicago, 1987), iv, vi, 1, 5. In her "News of the Music World" column, Maude Roberts George later wrote of how the Dett Club "had done some constructive work musically and should continue." Maude Roberts George, "News of the Music World," *Chicago Defender*, May 6, 1933, 15.

78. *The Negro in Chicago, 1779–1927, Volume I*, 88, 138.

Chapter 3. The Black Classical Metropolis

1. Negro in Music program at the Auditorium Theatre during the 1933 Century of Progress Exposition, Rosenthal Archives of the Chicago Symphony Orchestra Association.

2. Liesl Olson, "What Did a 1930s Ballet Say about Cultural Appropriation in Modernist Chicago?" *Chicago Reader*, March 28, 2019, https://www.chicagoreader.com/chicago/ruth-page-katherine-dunham/Content?oid=69265415; Liesl Olson, "She-Devils: Ruth Page, Katherine Dunham, and *La guiablesse*," in *Dancing on the Third Coast: Chicago Dance Histories*, ed. Susan Manning and Lizzie Leopold (Urbana: University of Illinois Press, forthcoming).

3. William Grant Still, *La guiablesse* (Flagstaff: William Grant Still Music, n.d.).

4. Christine-Marie Dunham Pratt in an email to the author on August 20, 2023.

5. Glenn Dillard Gunn, "Ruth Page Stars in Jungle Ballet," *Chicago Herald and Examiner*, June 17, 1933, Rosenthal Archives of the Chicago Symphony Orchestra Association.

6. Herman Devries, "Auditorium Audience Shares Approval of Critic as Shown by Applause," *Chicago American*, June 17, 1933, Rosenthal Archives of the Chicago Symphony Orchestra Association.

7. Olson, "What Did a 1930s Ballet Say?"; Olson, "She-Devils."

8. Martha S. Jones, *All Bound Up Together: The Woman Question in African American Public Culture, 1830–1900* (Chapel Hill: University of North Carolina Press, 2007), 6, 14–15.

9. Jones, *All Bound Up Together*, 5.

10. The Negro Dance Group 1934 program, first page, Ann Barzel dance research collection Series 1: Subject Files, 1890s-2010, Dance-MS-Barzel, Research Special Collections, Newberry Library, Chicago.

11. Gerald Early, ed., *Ain't but a Place: African American Writings about St. Louis* (Saint Louis: Missouri Historical Society Press, 1998), 351.

12. Joanna Dee Das, *Katherine Dunham: Dance and the African Diaspora* (New York: Oxford University Press, 2017), 21–23.

13. Early, *Ain't but a Place*, 351.

14. "Negro Dancers in First Recital of New Program: Spirituals, Folk Themes, Expressed on Concert Stage," *Chicago Daily News*, December 15, 1933, 22; Henry Louis Gates Jr., *The Signifying Monkey: A Theory of African-American Literary Criticism*, 25th anniversary ed. (Oxford: Oxford University Press, 2014), 57.

15. Helen Abbott and Robert Abbott were no longer married at this time, but Helen retained her marital last name and the postdivorce settlement of $50,000 in addition to other acquisitions allowed her to maintain her position

in Black society and continue her impresarial work. "Mrs. Abbott Gets Divorce, $50,000: Demands of Wife Met by Editor," *Pittsburgh Courier*, July 1, 1933, 1.

16. "Dewey Jones to Wed," *Chicago Defender*, April 28, 1928, 8.

17. Doris Evans McGinty, ed., *A Documentary History of the National Association of Negro Musicians* (Chicago: Center for Black Music Research, Columbia College Chicago, 2004), 15.

18. Tyrone McKinley Freeman, *Madam C. J. Walker's Gospel of Giving: Black Women's Philanthropy during Jim Crow* (Urbana: University of Illinois Press, 2020), 113–14.

19. Tammy L. Kernodle, "A Woman's Place: The Importance of Mary Lou Williams' Harlem Apartment," *NPR*, September 12, 2019, https://www.npr .org/2019/09/12/758070439/a-womans-place-the-importance-of-mary-lou -williams-harlem-apartment.

20. Lawrence Schenbeck, *Racial Uplift and American Music, 1878–1943* (Jackson: University Press of Mississippi, 2012), 180–81.

21. Cheryl A. Wall, "Nora Holt: New Negro Composer and Jazz Age Goddess," in *Women and Migration: Responses in Art and History*, ed. Deborah Willis, Ellyn Toscano, and Kalia Brooks Nelson (Cambridge: Open Book Publishers, 2019), 95.

22. Lucy Caplan, "'Strange What Cosmopolites Music Makes of Us,'" *Journal of the Society for American Music* 14, no. 3 (2020): 320, 311.

23. Nora Douglas Holt, "National Association of Negro Musicians: Chronological History of the N.A.N.M.," *Music and Poetry*, July 1921, 15, Series II, Box 100, Folder 2364, Theodore Charles Stone Collection, Center for Black Music Research at Columbia College Chicago; "Lena James Holt Takes High Honors at Chicago Musical College," *Chicago Defender*, June 29, 1918, 10.

24. Bruce Kellner, *The Harlem Renaissance: A Historical Dictionary for the Era* (Westport, CT: Greenwood, 1984), 135.

25. Transcript of Samantha Ege, "A Celebration of Women in Music: Composing the Black Chicago Renaissance" (lecture recital, Chicago Symphony Center, April 12, 2018).

26. John E. Webb, *Whispers of Love: A History of the R. Nathaniel Dett Club of Music and Allied Arts, 1922–1987* (Chicago: Columbia College Chicago, 1987), 3.

27. "Hold Impressive Rites for Neota McCurdy Dyett," *Chicago Defender*, April 2, 1938, 6.

28. "Woman Journalist Succumbs at Home: Mrs. Beulah Mitchell Hill, Long Time Ill, Worked on Defender Staff," *New York Amsterdam News*, February 2, 1935, 2.

29. "Large Assemblage at Reception for Musician," *Chicago Defender*, November 3, 1934, 6. This article lists Martha B. Mitchell Parks as Martha B. Mitchell. Martha B. Mitchell was also a former president of the CMA. The CMA records from 1936–40 show variations on her name, such as Martha

Mitchell Parks, Martha B. Parks, as well as Martha Mitchell. I deduce, however, that these names represent one person and postulate that marriage, or divorce, might be the cause of the variations in name. Mitchell was CMA president ca. 1923, as indicated in Maude Roberts George, "News of the Music World," *Chicago Defender*, August 11, 1923, 5.

30. "Large Assemblage at Reception for Musician."

31. Ted Ston [Theodore Charles Stone], "Heard and Seen," *Chicago Defender*, September 8, 1958, 17.

32. Estella sought a divorce from Majors on the grounds of desertion but was surprised to learn that their marriage had taken place within one year after he divorced his previous wife, Georgia. Bonds was under the impression that Majors had been divorced for a number of years. As a result, Bonds asked for an annulment, which she was granted in 1919, and returned to her maiden name of Bonds. "Court Decision Annuls Marriage of Mrs. Majors," *Chicago Defender*, June 21, 1919, 1; "Margaret Bonds: Lost and Found," Chicago Renaissance Conference, Agnes Scott College, November 7, 1997, Helen Walker-Hill Papers, Series 4, Box 5, Folder 8.3, Center for Black Music Research at Columbia College Chicago.

33. "Margaret Bonds: Lost and Found."

34. Robert W. Bone and Richard A. Courage, *The Muse in Bronzeville: African American Creative Expression in Chicago, 1932–1950* (New Brunswick: Rutgers University Press, 2011), 94.

35. Helen Walker-Hill's interview with Theodore Charles Stone on July 8, 1989 in "Margaret Bonds: Keeper of the Flame," a paper presented at the Harlem Renaissance Conference at the University of Denis Diderot, Paris, January 30, 1998, Helen Walker-Hill Papers. Series 4, Box 5, Folder 8.3, Center for Black Music Research at Columbia College Chicago.

36. "Mrs. Bonds, Musician, Dies in New York City," *Chicago Defender*, March 9, 1957, 20; "Margaret Bonds: Lost and Found."

37. "Margaret Bonds Performs Today at Noon," *California Aggie*, April 22, 1970, Helen Walker-Hill Papers, Series 4, Box 5, Folder 8.2, Center for Black Music Research at Columbia College Chicago; Margaret Bonds, "A Reminiscence," in *International Library of Negro Life and History: The Negro in Music and Art*, ed. Lindsay Patterson (New York: Publishers Company, 1967), 191–92.

38. "Margaret Bonds Performs Today at Noon."

39. Bonds, "A Reminiscence," 192.

40. Berean Baptist Church on Fifty-Second Street and Dearborn was Estella Bonds's religious home where she spent years as its organist, choir director, and Sunday school superintendent. "Mrs. Bonds, Musician, Dies in New York City"; "Margaret Bonds: Lost and Found."

41. Bonds, "A Reminiscence," 192.

42. Eighteenth- to nineteenth-century theologian John Fawcett wrote the words of "Blest Be the Tie that Binds," which was set to music by Swiss composer Hans Georg Nägeli and published in 1828.

43. Transcript of Ege, "A Celebration of Women in Music."

44. Chicago Music Association Record (1936–40), Center for Black Music Research at Columbia College Chicago.

45. Zoe Trodd, "The Black Press and the Black Chicago Renaissance," in *Writers of the Black Renaissance*, ed. Steven C. Tracy (Urbana: University of Illinois Press, 2011), 458.

46. Peter M. Rutkoff and William B. Scott, "Pinkster in Chicago: Bud Billiken and the Mayor of Bronzeville, 1930–1945," *Journal of African American History* 89, no. 4 (2004): 322.

47. Rutkoff and Scott, "Pinkster in Chicago," 326; Chicago Music Association Record (1936–40).

48. Toni Costonie, "Profiles of a Legend: The History of Dr. Marjorie Stewart Joyner," Series 1, Box 1, Folder 13, Biographical materials compiled by Toni Costonie, 1984, Marjorie Stewart Joyner Papers, Chicago Public Library, Woodson Regional Library, Vivian G. Harsh Research Collection of Afro-American History and Literature.

49. Davarian L. Baldwin, *Chicago's New Negroes: Modernity, the Great Migration, and Black Urban Life* (Chapel Hill: University of North Carolina Press, 2007), 86.

50. Chicago Music Association Record (1936–40).

51. "Poro College Moves Plant to Chicago: Entire Block on S. Parkway to House Malone Concern," *Baltimore Afro-American*, August 2, 1930, 18.

52. Chicago Music Association Record (1936–40).

53. Wanda A. Hendricks, *Gender, Race, and Politics in the Midwest: Black Club Women in Illinois* (Bloomington: Indiana University Press, 1998), 29; Elizabeth Lindsay Davis, *The Story of the Illinois Federation of Colored Women's Clubs, 1900–1922* (Chicago: n.p., 1922), 9–10.

54. Patricia Hill Collins, *Black Feminist Thought: Knowledge, Consciousness, and the Politics of Empowerment* (New York: Routledge, 2009), 83–84, 79.

55. Chicago Music Association Record (1936–40).

56. Freeman, *Madam C. J. Walker's Gospel of Giving*, 3, 6–7.

57. Chicago Music Association Record (1936–40).

58. Helen Brascher was married to Nahum Daniel Brascher, a columnist for the *Chicago Defender* and one of the reviewers for the 1933 Negro in Music program.

59. "The Apollo Ensemble: Artists All, and Trained for Service," *Chicago Defender*, October 16, 1937, 17.

60. "Rites for Mrs. Elsie Breeding Observed Here," *Chicago Defender*, January 18, 1936, 2.

61. Rutkoff and Scott, "Pinkster in Chicago," 324.

62. St. Clair Drake and Horace R. Cayton, *Black Metropolis: A Study of Negro Life in a Northern City* (1945; repr., Chicago: University of Chicago Press, 2015), 394–95; Brittney C. Cooper, *Beyond Respectability: The Intellectual Thought of Race Women* (Urbana: University of Illinois Press, 2017), 23.

63. James N. Gregory, *The South Diaspora: How the Great Migrations of Black and White Southerners Transformed America* (Chapel Hill: University of North Carolina Press), 124–26.

64. Other dated correspondence shows that this was Price's address at that time, such as the following archival source: Letter to Maude Wanzer Lane, Correspondence, 1929–1953, MC 988a Series I, Box 1, Folder 1, Florence Beatrice Smith Price Papers Addendum, Special Collections Department, University of Arkansas Libraries, Fayetteville.

65. Rae Linda Brown writes more about Price's Works Progress Administration years (later named Work Projects Administration) in *The Heart of a Woman: The Life and Music of Florence B. Price* (Urbana: University of Illinois Press, 2020), 190–200.

66. Brown, *The Heart of a Woman*, 99.

67. Darlene Clark Hine, introduction to *The Black Chicago Renaissance*, edited by Darlene Clark Hine and John McCluskey Jr. (Champaign: University of Illinois Press, 2012), xvi.

68. Toni Costonie, "Profiles of a Legend: The History of Dr. Marjorie Stewart Joyner."

69. Rae Linda Brown and Wayne Shirley, eds., *Florence Price: Symphonies Nos. 1 and 3* (Middleton, WI: A-R Editions, 2008), xlv.

70. Hine, "Introduction," xvii; Darlene Clark Hine, *Hine Sight: Black Women and the Re-Construction of American History* (Bloomington: Indiana University Press, 1944), 95.

71. Eliza Edmund Hewitt wrote the text for "Will There Be Any Stars in My Crown" in 1897. Johnson Oatman Jr. composed "No, Not One" in 1895.

72. Rae Linda Brown vividly depicts Price's religious life in *The Heart of a Woman*; she elaborates on the intraracial "caste system" that operated in the South Side's churches and interwove complexion, class, and repertoire. Price worshipped with mostly light-complected, well-educated, middle-class congregants; their music drew significantly from a European and Anglo-American canon. "It would be some time before gospel music, with its secularly influenced rhythms, improvisational structure (requiring embellishment of the melody, harmony, and text) and performance in which the congregation participates in call-and-response fashion, would be accepted into the formal worship services of [Price's church], and other, middle-class churches," Brown notes. Brown, *The Heart of a Woman*, 85–86.

73. Correspondence, 1929–1953, MC 988a Series I, Box 1, Folder 12, Florence Beatrice Smith Price Papers Addendum, Special Collections Department, University of Arkansas Libraries, Fayetteville.

74. Schenbeck, *Racial Uplift*, 8.

75. Florence Price to Serge Koussevitzky, September 18, 1941, Box 50, Folder 4, Serge Koussevitzky Archive, Music Division, Library of Congress, Washington, D.C.

76. Art patron Kate Buckingham gave the fountain to the city in 1927 in memory of her brother Clarence Buckingham (a former director of the Art

Institute of Chicago). "Chicago's Buckingham Fountain in Color," *Chicago Daily Tribune*, July 9, 1939, G8; Janice A. Knox and Heather Olivia Belcher, *Then & Now: Chicago's Loop* (Charleston, SC: Arcadia, 2005), 11.

Interlude I.
Race Woman's Guide to the Realm of Music

1. Imani Perry, *May We Forever Stand: A History of the Black National Anthem* (Chapel Hill: University of North Carolina Press, 2018), 11.

2. See Eileen M. Hayes and Linda F. Williams, eds., *Black Women and Music: More than the Blues* (Urbana: University of Illinois Press, 2007).

3. The italicized words appear as "himself" and "man," respectively, in the original text. Ford S. Black, *Colored People's Guide Book for Chicago* (Chicago: White Printer 5106 Dearborn St., 1915–16), 4, in Series I, Subseries 7, Box 100, Folder 2350, Theodore Charles Stone Collection of the Center for Black Music Research at Columbia College Chicago.

4. The names and addresses listed here are gathered from the *Chicago Defender*, the Theodore Charles Stone Collection at the Center for Black Music Research, the Florence Beatrice Smith Price Papers at the University of Arkansas Fayetteville Special Collections, and Mariame Kaba and Essence McDowell, *Lifting as They Climbed: Mapping a History of Trailblazing Black Women in Chicago* (Chicago: Haymarket Books, 2023). I acknowledge that some individuals did not stay put in the addresses given here (Florence Price is one such example) and that some institutions (like the Coleridge-Taylor Music School of Chicago, *Chicago Defender*, and Chicago Musical College) moved to different sites. However, for the purpose of compiling a snapshot in which names of places and people do not appear more than once and for the sake of clarity—that is, not oversaturating this impression of the realm of music—I have aimed to select addresses that adhere most closely to the interwar purview of this book.

Interlude II. *Fantasie Nègre*

1. Helen Walker-Hill, "Black Women Composers in Chicago: Then and Now," *Black Music Research Journal* 12, no. 1 (1992): 9–10.

2. "Mrs. Bonds, Musician, Dies in New York City," *Chicago Defender*, March 9, 1957, 20.

3. Interview with Margaret Bonds, December 28, 1971, Volume/Box: 279.1 and 279.2, Camille Billops and James V. Hatch Archives at Emory University.

4. Price completed *Fantasie Nègre* No. 2 in G minor in March 1932, the exact date is not given on her handwritten score, but it might be assumed that it was prior to March 30, 1932, which was the date that *Fantasie Nègre* No. 3 in F minor was written. The fourth fantasie, *Fantasie Nègre* No. 4 in B minor, completed on April 5, 1932, further suggests a sense of chronological order to the composition of the remaining fantasies for solo piano. For further

details of the works, including how I reconstructed the third fantasie, see Samantha Ege, *Fantasie Nègre: The Piano Music of Florence Price*, LORELT (Lontano Records Ltd.) LNT 144 (2021) and Horace J. Maxile Jr., *"Fantasie Nègre: The Piano Music of Florence Price*, by Samantha Ege (review)," *Journal of the American Musicological Society* 75, no. 2 (2022): 405–9.

5. Kira Thurman, *Singing like Germans: Black Musicians in the Land of Bach, Beethoven, and Brahms* (Ithaca: Cornell University Press, 2021), 26.

6. Kevin Quashie, *Black Aliveness, or A Poetics of Being* (Durham, NC: Duke University Press, 2021), 10–11.

7. Eileen Southern, *The Music of Black Americans: A History*, 3rd ed. (New York: Norton, 1997), 201; Sandra Jean Graham, *Spirituals and the Birth of a Black Entertainment Industry* (Urbana: University of Illinois Press, 2018), 1; Shane White and Graham White, *The Sounds of Slavery: Discovering African American History through Songs, Sermons, and Speech* (Boston: Beacon, 2005), 59.

8. See Samuel A. Floyd Jr., "Ring Shout! Literary Studies, Historical Studies, and Black Music Inquiry," *Black Music Research Journal* 11, no. 2 (1991): 265–87.

9. For more on the vitality, complexity, and multiplicity of African American music, song, and dance in the era of chattel slavery, see Katrina Dyonne Thompson, *Ring Shout, Wheel About: The Racial Politics of Music and Dance in North American Slavery* (Urbana: University of Illinois Press, 2014).

10. Katherine Dunham, Dance MS Barzel Research: Ann Barzel Dance Research Collection, Box 154, Newberry Library, Chicago.

11. "Negro Dancers in First Recital of New Program: Spirituals, Folk Themes, Expressed on Concert Stage," *Chicago Daily News*, December 15, 1933, 22.

12. Liesl Olson, "What Did a 1930s Ballet Say about Cultural Appropriation in Modernist Chicago?" *Chicago Reader*, March 28, 2019, https://www.chicagoreader.com/chicago/ruth-page-katherine-dunham/Content?oid=69265415; and Liesl Olson, "She-Devils: Ruth Page, Katherine Dunham, and *La guiablesse*," In *Dancing on the Third Coast: Chicago Dance Histories*, ed. Susan Manning and Lizzie Leopold (Urbana: University of Illinois Press, forthcoming).

13. A particular detail in the CMA minutes exemplifies the discomfort that some Black female visitors felt with regard to staying at a downtown hotel, leading them to opt for the security of a South Side (i.e., Black-owned) establishment: "First, Mrs George mentioned a Negro woman coming with a delegation from Massachusetts to the Republican Convention, registered at the Stevens Hotel and remained there with her delegation during the convention while some of her more timid sisters domiciled at the Southway and other Southend hotels." Chicago Music Association Record (1936–40), Center for Black Music Research at Columbia College Chicago.

14. "Modern Dancers Praised at Stevens," *Chicago Defender*, December 24, 1932, 12.

15. Thurman, *Singing like Germans*, 23.

16. Alisha Lola Jones, "Lift Every Voice: Marian Anderson, Florence B. Price and the Sound of Black Sisterhood," *NPR*, August 30, 2019, https://www.npr.org/2019/08/30/748757267/lift-every-voice-marian-anderson-florence-b-price-and-the-sound-of-black-sisterh.

17. The program additionally featured ceremonial dances from Ashanti practitioners, songs from the Deep River Quartet, and jazz from the singer and pianist Fletcher Butler. Edward Moore. "Character of Opera Depends on Its Theme," *Chicago Daily Tribune*, October 8, 1933, D3.

18. See Samantha Ege, "Restaging Respectability: The Subversive Performances of Josephine Baker and Nora Holt in Jazz-Age Paris," *Angelaki: Journal of the Theoretical Humanities* 27, no. 3–4 (2022): 112–24.

19. "Negro Dancers in First Recital of New Program: Spirituals, Folk Themes, Expressed on Concert Stage," *Chicago Daily News*, December 15, 1933, 22; Henry Louis Gates Jr., *The Signifying Monkey: A Theory of African-American Literary Criticism*, 25th anniversary ed. (Oxford: Oxford University Press, 2014), 56.

20. "Modern Dancers Praised at Stevens."

21. Olson, "What Did a 1930s Ballet Say?"; Olson, "She-Devils."

22. "Mrs. Bonds, Musician, Dies in New York City."

23. "Modern Dancers Praised at Stevens."

Chapter 4. Movements of a Symphonist

1. Douglas W. Shadle captures the struggle for nineteenth-century American symphonists (largely of European descent) to establish their voice, describing this "symphonic enterprise" as "a winter that never turned into spring." Shadle argues that "ultimately, these composers and their music froze before they could bloom." For further reading, see Douglas W. Shadle, *Orchestrating the Nation: The Nineteenth-Century American Symphonic Enterprise* (New York: Oxford University Press, 2016), 14.

2. Graham became Shirley Graham Du Bois upon her marriage to W. E. B. Du Bois in 1951.

3. Shirley Graham, "Spirituals to Symphonies," *Etude* 54, no. 11 (1936): 692.

4. Although writing on the subject of American music historiography, Richard Crawford reveals how these two camps (i.e., cosmopolitan and provincial) stem as far back as the music-making of eighteenth-century settler Americans in *The American Musical Landscape: The Business of Musicianship from Billings to Gershwin*, updated ed. (Los Angeles: University of California Press, 2000), 7; Graham, "Spirituals to Symphonies," 723.

5. Chicago Music Association Record (1936–40), Center for Black Music Research at Columbia College Chicago.

6. "Writer of 'Tom Tom' and Brother Open Artists' Bureau," *Pittsburgh Courier*, July 18, 1936, A7.

7. "Artists' Bureau Opens Chi Offices," *Pittsburgh Courier*, July 18, 1936, A6.

8. "Writer of 'Tom Tom.'"

9. The artists were violinist Bernard Mason, showman William Allen, and pianists Warner Lawson and Lorenza Jordan Cole—names that likely would have been familiar to CMA members.

10. Chicago Music Association Record (1936–40).

11. "Sepia Composers in Need of Funds," *Atlanta Daily World*, August 27, 1935, 2; "'Musicians Need New Angel' Says Mrs. Maude George," *Pittsburgh Courier*, August 31, 1935, A9.

12. George followed Graham's words with related anecdotes of her own; she "elaborated upon some phases of Miss Graham's remarks and made observations upon her own experiences with talent officials of the Music Division of the WP" (i.e., the Works Progress Administration). Chicago Music Association Record (1936–40).

13. Earl J. Morris, "Graham Artist Bureau 'Broke,'" *Pittsburgh Courier*, September 19, 1936, A7.

14. Graham, "Spirituals to Symphonies," 691.

15. Viola Davis received this award on September 20, 2015. This quotation is extracted from her acceptance speech for which a full transcription is available in Michael Gold, "Viola Davis's Emmy Speech," *New York Times*, September 20, 2015, https://archive.nytimes.com/www.nytimes.com/live/emmys-2015/viola-daviss-emotional-emmys-acceptance-speech/.

16. The history of classically trained Black female jazz musicians is extensive, especially calling to mind pianists such as Lil Hardin Armstrong, Dorothy Donegan, Hazel Scott, and Nina Simone.

17. Ora Williams, Thelma Williams, Dora Wilson, and Ramona Matthewson, "American Black Women Composers: A Selected Annotated Bibliography," in *All the Women Are White, All the Blacks Are Men, but Some of Us Are Brave: Black Women's Studies*, 2nd ed., ed. Akasha (Gloria T.) Hull, Patricia Bell Scott, and Barbara Smith (New York: Feminist Press, 2015), 298–99.

18. Interview with Margaret Bonds, December 28, 1971, Volume/Box 279.1 and 279.2, Camille Billops and James V. Hatch Archives at Emory University.

19. Helen Walker-Hill, *From Spirituals to Symphonies: African-American Women Composers and Their Music* (Urbana: University of Illinois Press, 2007), 27; "Lena James Holt Takes High Honors at Chicago Musical College," *Chicago Defender*, June 29, 1918, 10; Earl Calloway, "Former Defender Critic Holt Was among Nation's Early Music Editors," *Chicago Defender*, March 11, 1995, 23.

20. "Lena James Douglas to Write about Opera and Symphony," *Chicago Defender*, November 3, 1917, 11.

21. Smith, Perry, and Moore studied at the American Conservatory at Fontainebleau under Nadia Boulanger. Margaret Bonds had hoped for a similar experience, but Boulanger was ill-equipped to nurture Bonds's style. Bonds

recalled, "Nadia Boulanger liked 'The Negro Speaks of Rivers.' She liked all of my music. . . . Incidentally, Boulanger refused to take me as a student. She said that I 'had something' but she didn't quite understand what to do with it. She added, however, that whatever it was I was doing 'felt right to her,' and that I should continue to do it, but I shouldn't study with anyone, and I certainly should never study fugue." Of course, Bonds not only studied fugue, but she also wrote them into several of her compositions. Margaret Bonds, "A Reminiscence" in *The Negro in Music and Art*, ed. Lindsay Patterson (New York: Publishers Company, 1967), 192.

22. William Pickens, "Helen E. Hagan," *Baltimore Afro-American*, October 14, 1916, 6.

23. "Helen Hagan, Pianist, Teacher Dies at 73," *New York Amsterdam News*, March 14, 1964, 6; Pickens, "Helen E. Hagan"; "Nora Holt Dead; Music Critic, 89," *New York Times*, January 30, 1974, 38.

24. Kira Thurman, *Singing like Germans: Black Musicians in the Land of Bach, Beethoven, and Brahms* (Ithaca: Cornell University Press, 2021), 43.

25. Pickens, "Helen E. Hagan."

26. Pickens, "Helen E. Hagan"; Etta Augusta Deuce, "Helen Eugenia Hagan: A Type of Negro Womanhood with the Negro's Highest Type of Genius—the Musician," *Philadelphia Tribune*, January 23, 1915, 3; Nora Douglas Holt, "Hagan Piano Recital," *Chicago Defender*, April 24, 1920, 10.

27. Lucy Caplan, "Helen Hagan," in Samantha Ege, *Black Renaissance Woman: Piano Music by Florence Price, Margaret Bonds, Nora Holt, Betty Jackson King, and Helen Hagan*, Lorelt (Lontano Records Ltd.), 2022, LNT 145.

28. Pickens, "Helen E. Hagan."

29. See Samantha Ege, "Nora Douglas Holt's Teachings of a Black Classical Canon," in *The Oxford Handbook of Public Music Theory*, ed. J. Daniel Jenkins (New York: Oxford University Press, 2022), http://doi.org/10.1093/oxfordhb/9780197551554.013.21.

30. Williams et al., "American Black Women Composers," 298.

31. Mia Bay, "The Battle for Womanhood Is the Battle for Race: Black Women and Nineteenth-Century Racial Thought," in *Toward an Intellectual History of Black Women*, ed. Mia Bay, Farah J. Griffin, Martha S. Jones, and Barbara D. Savage (Chapel Hill: University of North Carolina Press, 2015), 77.

32. I have yet to find even the smallest sketches of Martha Bonner's biography. However, traces of Carissa Hardy's activity can be found in the contemporary Black press. She arrived in Chicago by way of Philadelphia, living in the Black Metropolis for a number of years. There, she established her own music school and worked with the CMA's junior division. Like Hagan and Holt, she studied in Paris but with the goal to deepen her pedagogical methods rather than her compositional practice. However, her visit coincided with the beginning of World War II, resulting in her hasty return to Philadelphia. Maude Roberts George, "News of the Music World," *Chicago Defender*, May 28, 1932,

15; Maude Roberts George, "News of the Music World," *Chicago Defender*, October 15, 1932, 15; Sara Neely, "Philadelphia Pianist Escapes European War," *Baltimore Afro-American*, June 1, 1940, 6.

33. Graham, "Spirituals to Symphonies," 736.

34. Rae Linda Brown, *The Heart of a Woman: The Life and Music of Florence B. Price* (Urbana: University of Illinois Press, 2020), 4, quoted in Matkin-Rawn, "'The Great Negro State of the Country': Arkansas's Reconstruction and the Other Great Migration," *Arkansas Historical Quarterly* 72, no. 1 (2013): 5, 26.

35. Dr. Smith was born in 1843 in Camden, Delaware, raised in New Jersey, and worked and studied in New York and Philadelphia before opening his first practice in Chicago. He moved to Arkansas in the 1870s and met Florence Irene soon after his arrival. They married in 1876. Mrs. Smith (born in 1854) hailed from Indianapolis. She belonged to a family of successful, property-owning businessmen. Her sister, Olive Gulliver, also moved to Arkansas, where she met and married the attorney John Gray Lucas (born in 1864). Similarly, John Gray Lucas was a migrant, born in Texas. His parents brought him to Pine Bluff when he was three months old. He completed a bachelor of arts degree at the Industrial University before heading to law school at Boston University for his bachelor of laws. While studying in Boston, he espoused the merits of Arkansas and wondered rhetorically, in an 1889 interview with the *Boston Globe*, why "more colored young men from the North did not make Arkansas their home. It is an inviting field for them and a grand opportunity to make something of themselves." See "J. Gray Lucas Elected President," *Chicago Defender*, October 16, 1915, 4; John William Graves, "John Gray Lucas (1864–1944)," *Encyclopedia of Arkansas*, September 24, 2010, https://encyclopediaofarkansas.net/entries/john-gray-lucas-1700/; J. Clay Smith Jr., *Emancipation: The Making of the Black Lawyer, 1844–1944* (Philadelphia: University of Pennsylvania Press, 1993), 327.

36. *Arkansas Gazette*, February 6, 1889, quoted in Willard B. Gatewood Jr., "Frederick Douglass in Arkansas," *Arkansas Historical Quarterly* 41, no. 4 (1982): 306.

37. Price's handwritten documents in her papers at the University of Arkansas confirm her 1888 birth year. Correspondence, 1929–1953, MC 988a Series I, Box 1, Folder 12, Florence Beatrice Smith Price Papers Addendum, Special Collections Department, University of Arkansas Libraries, Fayetteville.

38. Mildred Denby Green, *Black Women Composers: A Genesis* (Boston: Twayne, 1983), 31; Mary Dengler Hudgins, MC 988, Series I, Folder 6, Box 1, Florence Beatrice Smith Price Collection, Special Collections Department, University of Arkansas Libraries, Fayetteville.

39. Judith Tick, "Passed Away Is the Piano Girl: Changes in American Musical Life, 1870–1900," in *Women Making Music: The Western Art Tradition, 1150–1950*, ed. Jane Bowers and Judith Tick (Urbana: University of Illinois Press, 1986), 325–48.

40. In Tick's chapter, for example, she distinguishes between "black performers" and "women," leaving little space to articulate Black performers as

women, or women as Black performers. The lack of deep engagement with race as it relates to women, and gendered difference as it relates to people of African descent, perpetuates the Black feminist observation that in such discourse, "all the women are white" and "all the blacks are men," in reference to Akasha (Gloria T.) Hull, Patricia Bell Scott, and Barbara Smith, eds., *All the Women Are White, All the Blacks Are Men, but Some of Us Are Brave: Black Women's Studies*, 2nd ed. (New York: Feminist Press, 2015).

41. See Doris Evans McGinty, "'As Large as She Can Make It': The Role of Black Women Activists in Music, 1880–1945," in *Cultivating Music in America: Women Patrons and Activists since 1860*, ed. Ralph P. Locke and Cyrilla Barr (Berkeley: University of California Press, 1997), 214–30; Josephine Wright, "Black Women and Classical Music," *Women's Studies Quarterly* 12, no. 3 (1984): 18–21; and Josephine Wright, "Black Women in Classical Music in Boston during the Late Nineteenth Century: Profiles of Leadership," in *New Perspectives on Music: Essays in Honor of Eileen Southern*, ed. Josephine Wright (Sterling Heights, MI: Harmonie Park Press, 1992), 373–407.

42. Candace Bailey, *Unbinding Gentility: Women Making Music in the Nineteenth-Century South* (Urbana: University of Illinois Press, 2021), 2.

43. Lucy Caplan points out Bailey's comparatively undertheorized approach to nineteenth-century Black women in her review of *Unbinding Gentility*. Although Bailey writes that her work will "hopefully inspire further research on Black women and other women of color," Caplan suggests that Bailey's "important and laudable aspirations . . . raise questions about whether the archival methods relied on here are the most effective ones through which to engage these women's histories." For Caplan, "it would be helpful to see [Saidiya] Hartman's ideas about critical fabulation and historical narrative engaged more fully here, as well as those of other scholars in Black studies, including Black music studies, who theorize the limits of the archive and advance other analytic possibilities." Bailey, *Unbinding Gentility*, 49; Lucy Caplan, "Unbinding Gentility: Women Making Music in the Nineteenth-Century South by Candace Bailey (Review)," *Women and Music: A Journal of Gender and Culture* 26 (2022): 179. For Bailey's more recent work, see Candace Bailey, "Black Women and the Cultural Performance of Music in Mid-Nineteenth Century Natchez," *American Nineteenth Century History* (2024), https://doi.org/10.1080/14664658.2024.2303867.

44. Correspondence, 1929–1953, MC 988a Series I, Box 1, Folder 1, Florence Beatrice Smith Price Papers Addendum, Special Collections Department, University of Arkansas Libraries, Fayetteville.

45. Pickens, "Helen E. Hagan."

46. Holt graduated from Kansas State College with a bachelor of science degree. Around 1914, she pursued further academic study at the historically Black Western University at Quindaro, Kansas. Given her parents' connection to the institution, Western University was familiar territory for the young Holt and an appropriate environment for a woman of her social standing, for

Western University, as Helen Walker-Hill describes, "cultivated the ideals of racial uplift in its female students—respectability, refinement, competency, and responsibility." Helen Walker-Hill, "Western University at Quindaro, Kansas (1865–1943) and Its Legacy of Pioneering Musical Women," *Black Music Research Journal* 26, no. 1 (2006): 24, 12.

47. General Correspondence, #112–6, Folder 170, Washington Conservatory of Music, Digital Howard, Howard University.

48. Mary Dengler Hudgins, MC 988, Series I, Folder 6, Box 1, Florence Beatrice Smith Price Collection, Special Collections Department, University of Arkansas Libraries, Fayetteville.

49. William Grant Still, "My Arkansas Boyhood," *Arkansas Historical Quarterly* 26, no. 3 (1967): 285–87.

50. Josephine Wright, "Black Women and Classical Music," *Women's Studies Quarterly* 12, no. 3 (1984): 19.

51. Wright, "Black Women in Classical Music in Boston during the Late Nineteenth Century," 373–409.

52. The Grant Hagan Society at Yale University honors these two pioneering African American women and provides an important intellectual, creative, and pastoral space for students of color. See Grant Hagan Society, https://campuspress.yale.edu/granthagan/.

53. "New England Conservatory of Music," *Journal of Education* 50, no. 6 (1899): 106.

54. Maud Cuney Hare, *Norris Wright Cuney: A Tribune of the Black People* (New York: Crisis Publishing, 1913), 131–34.

55. Fannie Barrier Williams, "A Northern Negro's Autobiography," *Independent* 57 (1906): 91–96, https://search.alexanderstreet.com/view/work/bibliographic_entity%7Cbibliographic_details%7C2757427.

56. Interview with Margaret Bonds, December 28, 1971, Volume/Box: 279.1 and 279.2, Camille Billops and James V. Hatch Archives at Emory University.

57. Williams, "A Northern Negro's Autobiography."

58. Correspondence, 1929–1953, MC 988a Series I, Box 1, Folder 12, Florence Beatrice Smith Price Papers Addendum, Special Collections Department, University of Arkansas Libraries, Fayetteville.

59. Although Florence Irene's views on race have been published elsewhere (namely in Rae Linda Brown's *The Heart of a Woman*), Robinson was reluctant to have this be publicly known, adding in her exchange with Hudgins, "This should not be included but it gives you insight into the background of my mother." I therefore reproduce this quotation with the view that its position in the archives and Brown's book now place it in the public record. Mary Dengler Hudgins, MC 988, Series I, Folder 6, Box 1, Florence Beatrice Smith Price Collection, Special Collections Department, University of Arkansas Libraries, Fayetteville.

60. See Allyson Hobbs, *A Chosen Exile: A History of Racial Passing in American Life* (Cambridge, MA: Harvard University Press, 2014).

61. Correspondence, 1929–1953, MC 988a Series I, Box 1, Folder 1), Florence Beatrice Smith Price Papers Addendum, Special Collections Department, University of Arkansas Libraries, Fayetteville.

62. "Composer Wins Noteworthy Prizes for Piano Sonata," *Chicago Defender*, May 4, 1935, 25.

63. Correspondence, 1929–1953, MC 988a Series I, Box 1, Folder 1, Florence Beatrice Smith Price Papers Addendum, Special Collections Department, University of Arkansas Libraries, Fayetteville.

64. For more on the nineteenth-century formation of Boston's Black classical scene and the influence of African American women alongside their male counterparts, see James Monroe Trotter, *Music and Some Highly Musical People* (Boston: Lee and Shepard, 1878), 288–98; Maud Cuney Hare, "Chapter X: Musical Pioneers," *Negro Musicians and Their Music* (Washington, DC: Associated Publishers, 1936), 197–238; and Wright, "Black Women in Classical Music in Boston during the Late Nineteenth Century," 373–409.

65. "Composer Wins Noteworthy Prizes for Piano Sonata."

66. Florence Price to Serge Koussevitzky, July 5, 1843, Box 50, Folder 4, Serge Koussevitzky Archive, Music Division, Library of Congress, Washington, D.C.

67. Quoted in Richard Crawford, "Edward MacDowell: Musical Nationalism and an American Tone Poet," *Journal of the American Musicological Society* 49, no. 3 (1996): 556.

68. Quoted in Joseph Horowitz, *Wagner Nights: An American History* (Berkeley: University of California Press, 1994), 166; Joseph Horowitz, "Dvořák and Boston," *American Music* 19, no. 1 (2001): 11.

69. Quoted in Horowitz, "Dvořák and Boston," 11.

70. Etta Augusta Deuce, "Helen Eugenia Hagan: A Type of Negro Womanhood with the Negro's Highest Type of Genius—the Musician," *Philadelphia Tribune*, January 23, 1915, 3.

71. Tammy L. Kernodle in Samantha Ege, "Florence Price and the Black Female Fellowship," *BBC Sounds* [radio], March 6, 2022.

72. Upon returning to the South, Price's prospects differed greatly from the masses of lower-class Black women, tethered through their labor to the lands and homes of white Arkansans. Their work demanded a physical strain, manual effort, and psychological weight that Price (and others of her social stature) would never know.

73. "Helen Hagan, Pianist, Teacher Dies at 73."

74. Rae Linda Brown and Wayne Shirley, eds., *Florence Price: Symphonies Nos. 1 and 3* (Middleton, WI: A-R Editions, 2008), xx.

75. Clark University, "The Clark University Catalogue, 1911–1912," retrieved March 15, 2020, https://radar.auctr.edu/islandora/object/auc.004.cc.catalogs%3A0018.

76. Mary Dengler Hudgins, MC 988, Series I, Folder 6, Box 1, Florence Beatrice Smith Price Collection, Special Collections Department, University of Arkansas Libraries, Fayetteville.

77. "Mrs. J. Gray Lucas Attends Theatre," *Chicago Defender*, March 11, 1911, 1.

78. Booker T. Washington, "Industrial Education for the Negro," in *The Negro Problem*, ed. Booker T. Washington, W. E. B. Du Bois, Paul Laurence Dunbar, and Charles W. Chesnutt (New York: James Pott, 1903), 7–29.

79. Smith, *Emancipation*, 327; William H. Davis, *National Negro Business League: Annual Report of the Sixteenth Session and the Fifteenth Anniversary Convention* (Nashville: African M. E. Sunday School Union, 1915), 137.

80. For a detailed contemporary account, see Ida B. Wells-Barnett, "The Arkansas Race Riot," (N.p., 1920).

81. O. A. Rogers Jr., "The Elaine Race Riots of 1919," *Arkansas Historical Quarterly* 19 (1960): 143.

82. Wells-Barnett, "The Arkansas Race Riot."

83. Grif Stockley, "Elaine Massacre," *Encyclopedia of Arkansas*, last modified August 18, 2023, http://www.encyclopediaofarkansas.net/encyclopedia/entry-detail.aspx?entryID=1102.

84. Goldie M. Walden, "Keep Ideals in Front of You; They Will Lead to Victory, Says Mrs. Florence B. Price," *Chicago Defender*, July 11, 1936, 7.

85. Sandra T. Dougherty, Florence Beatrice Smith Price, Series IV, Box 75, Folder 1620, Theodore Charles Stone Collection, Center for Black Music Research at Columbia College Chicago.

86. Darlene Clark Hine, *Hine Sight: Black Women and the Re-Construction of American History* (Bloomington: Indiana University Press, 1994), 90, 103.

87. Price was a victim of domestic violence. Rae Linda Brown documents a particularly harrowing event that took place on February 19, 1930: "Thomas was totally out of control. He threw his wife to the floor where he choked and beat her. He threatened to kill her and this time he meant it. Pulling out his gun, he started to chase her but Florence ran from their home to the safety of a friend." Brown, *The Heart of a Woman*, 99–100.

88. A discussion with A. Kori Hill on June 26, 2019, brought this visit to my attention.

89. "Mrs. Price Returns Home," *Chicago Defender*, September 7, 1918, 11.

90. "J. Gray Lucas Elected President."

91. Julie A. Golia writes even more broadly of the Woman's Page "in daily American newspapers between 1895 and 1935," explaining that while they have "long been dismissed as frivolous and banal," they nonetheless "fostered experimental and participatory features even as they reinforced traditional gender norms." Julie A. Golia, "Courting Women, Courting Advertisers: The Woman's Page and the Transformation of the American Newspaper, 1895–1935," *Journal of American History* 103, no. 3 (2016): 606. See also Kimberly Voss, "Diversity Essay: The Women's Pages at American Black Newspapers," *Journalism History*, June 27, 2022, https://journalism-history.org/2022/06/27/diversity-essay-the-womens-pages-at-american-black-newspapers/.

92. News of Holt's accomplishments were situated amid other reports on the Woman's Page of racial uplift that included Alice Dunbar-Nelson's

leading involvement in the city's "monster parade and pageant" in celebration of Flag Day and Mme. M. Calloway Byron's stunning operatic display at the Quinn Chapel African Methodist Episcopal Church on the Near South Side (as reviewed by Holt herself). "Prominent Woman Responsible for Flag Day Celebration," *Chicago Defender*, June 29, 1918, 10; Lena James Holt, "M. Calloway-Byron Stirs Musical Chicago with Operatic Program," *Chicago Defender*, June 29, 1918, 10.

93. "Lena James Holt Takes High Honors."

94. Estella Bonds was occasionally identified as Mrs. Estella Bond-Majors [*sic*] prior to the 1919 annulment of her marriage.

95. Second Annual All Colored Composer's Program at Orchestra Hall, April 23, 1915, Rosenthal Archives of the Chicago Symphony Orchestra Association.

96. "Lena James Holt Takes High Honors."

97. Walker-Hill, *From Spirituals to Symphonies*, 26.

98. Doris Evans McGinty notes, "New York, a city in which many musicians lived and worked, was ideal for a meeting of NANM, and attendance at this meeting increased dramatically from that of the 1919 meeting in Chicago." In Doris Evans McGinty, ed., *A Documentary History of the National Association of Negro Musicians* (Chicago: Center for Black Music Research, Columbia College Chicago, 2004), 80.

99. McGinty, *A Documentary History*, 74–75, 78.

100. NANM, Minutes of the Second Annual Meeting of the National Association of Negro Musicians, New York City, July 1920, pp. 10–11. MC 988a, Series 1, Box 5, Item 10, Florence Beatrice Smith Price Papers Addendum, Special Collections Department, University of Arkansas Libraries, Fayetteville; McGinty, *A Documentary History*, 88.

101. Juanita Karpf examines how Hackley navigated chronic illness, noting, "Determined and stoic, Hackley expended considerable effort to maintain a public image of seeming vitality. Yet, in actuality, she endured the uneasy life of a disabled person, especially owing to her unreliable hearing acuity." See, Juanita Karpf, *Performing Racial Uplift: E. Azalia Hackley and African American Activism in the Postbellum to Pre-Harlem Era* (Jackson: University Press of Mississippi, 2022), 151.

102. McGinty, *A Documentary History*, 77–78, 81.

103. NANM, Minutes of the Second Annual Meeting of the National Association of Negro Musicians, New York City, July 1920 pp. 18, 4–5. MC 988a, Series 1, Box 5, Item 10, Florence Beatrice Smith Price Papers Addendum, Special Collections Department, University of Arkansas Libraries, Fayetteville.

Chapter 5. Seizing the World Stage

1. "Chicago the New Babel: Prof. Buck Finds 40 Tongues Are Spoken Here," *Chicago Tribune*, February 11, 1903, 13; "Cosmopolitan Chicago," *Chicago Daily Tribune*, August 1, 1893, 4.

2. "Cosmopolitan Chicago."

3. See Anna R. Paddon and Sally Turner, "African Americans and the World's Columbian Exposition," *Illinois Historical Journal* 88, no. 1 (1995): 19–36.

4. Ida B. Wells, Frederick Douglass, Irvine Garland Penn, and Ferdinand Barnett, *The Reason Why the Colored American Is Not in the World's Columbian Exposition*, Manuscript/Mixed Material, https://www.loc.gov/item/mfd.25023.

5. Dewey R. Jones, "Race Represented as World's Fair Opens in Blaze of Glory," *Chicago Defender*, June 3, 1933, 1.

6. Chicago Music Association Record (1936–40), Center for Black Music Research at Columbia College Chicago.

7. Shaping these ideas are Michelle M. Wright, *Physics of Blackness: Beyond the Middle Passage Epistemology* (Minneapolis: University of Minnesota Press, 2015) and Michelle M. Wright, "On Epiphenomenal Temporality: Black German Identities and Quantum Physics in the African Diaspora" (lecture, ICI Berlin, February 26, 2018, https://www.ici-berlin.org/events/michelle-m-wright/).

8. Alisha Lola Jones, "Lift Every Voice: Marian Anderson, Florence B. Price and the Sound of Black Sisterhood," *NPR*, August 30, 2019, https://www.npr.org/2019/08/30/748757267/lift-every-voice-marian-anderson-florence-b-price-and-the-sound-of-black-sisterh.

9. Cheryl R. Ganz, *The 1933 Chicago World's Fair: A Century of Progress* (Urbana: University of Illinois Press, 2012), 115.

10. Elizabeth Lindsay Davis, foreword to *Lifting as They Climb* (Chicago: National Association of Colored Women, 1933), 7.

11. *Official Guide Book of the Fair Chicago: 1933 A Century of Progress* (Chicago: A Century of Progress, 1933), 8 and 10. Chicago was the second largest city in the United States behind New York and the fourth largest in the world behind London and Tokyo.

12. Ganz, *The 1933 Chicago World's Fair*, 107, 115.

13. Alain Locke, "Famous Musicians Give Lie to VA. Critic: There Is Real Negro Music, Artists Say," *Baltimore Afro-American*, February 4, 1933, 11; "John Powell's Assertion that There Is No Real American Negro Music Disproved by Eminent Musicians and Critics," *New Journal and Guide*, January 28, 1933, 8.

14. Stephanie DeLane Doktor, "How a White Supremacist Became Famous for His Black Music: John Powell and *Rhapsodie nègre (1918)*," *American Music* 38, no. 4 (2020): 397.

15. Lucy Caplan, "'Strange What Cosmopolites Music Makes of Us': Classical Music, the Black Press, and Nora Douglas Holt's Black Feminist Audiotopia," *Journal of the Society for American Music* 14, no. 3 (2020): 320.

16. Doktor, "How a White Supremacist," 397, 401, 420.

17. Ganz, *The 1933 Chicago World's Fair*, 112.

18. "Wanamaker Offers Cash for Prize Musical Compositions," *Chicago Defender*, March 26, 1932, 3.

19. "Sepia Composers in Need of Funds," *Atlanta Daily World*, August 27, 1935, 2; "'Musicians Need New Angel' Says Mrs. Maude George," *Pittsburgh Courier*, August 31, 1935, A9.

20. Maude Roberts George, "News of the Music World," October 1, 1932, 15.

21. Doris Evans McGinty, *A Documentary History of the National Association of Negro Musicians* (Chicago: Center for Black Music Research, Columbia College Chicago, 2004), 38; Maude Roberts George, "Wanamaker Awards Given in Music," *Chicago Defender*, October 1, 1932, 2. In the first year of the contest, the panel comprised Burleigh, Diton, and Clarence Cameron White alongside two white practitioners: official Wanamaker organist, Charles M. Courboin, and music editor of the *Philadelphia Ledger*, Samuel Le Clar. For the 1932 contest, the judges were once again an integrated group, comprising J. Rosamond Johnson and Melville Charlton and white composers Frank Black and William T. Timmings, band directors Edward B. Cullen and Arthur A. Rosander, and educator George P. Spangler.

22. "R. Wanamaker Announces Rules in Contest," *Chicago Defender*, February 19, 1927, 5.

23. Samuel A. Floyd Jr., *The Power of Black Music: Interpreting Its History from Africa to the United States* (New York: Oxford University Press, 1995), 103.

24. Writing on the subject of Black culture-making in the interwar years, Lisa Meyerowitz rightly highlights that "the shadow of white patronage explicitly or implicitly meant that artists could explore a subject only to the extent that their patron would accept." Meyerowitz's observations therefore invite us to consider how much autonomy African-descended composers actually had with regard to the aesthetic character of their Wanamaker submissions. Lisa Meyerowitz, "The Negro in Art Week: Defining the 'New Negro' through Art Exhibition," *African American Review* 31, no. 1 (1997): 83.

25. McGinty, *A Documentary History*, 38.

26. "Prizes for Negro Composers: Rodman Wanamaker Offers $1,000 for Musicians of the Colored Race," *New York Amsterdam News*, March 2, 1927, 8.

27. For more on musical Signifyin(g), see Floyd, *The Power of Black Music*, 95.

28. Quoted in Notes on 3 × 5 index cards by Florence Price Robinson concerning her mother, Florence Price, n.d., MC 988, Box 1, Series 1, Folder 11, Florence Beatrice Smith Price Collection, Special Collections Department, University of Arkansas Libraries, Fayetteville.

29. Margaret Bonds, "A Reminiscence," in *The Negro in Music and Art*, ed. Lindsay Patterson (New York: Publishers Company, 1967), 192.

30. Maude Roberts George, "News of the Music World," *Chicago Defender*, October 15, 1932, 15; Florence Price to Serge Koussevitzky, July 5, 1943, Box 50, Folder 4, Serge Koussevitzky Archive, Music Division, Library of Congress, Washington, D.C.

31. Bonds, "A Reminiscence," 192.

32. Linda Ruth Holzer, "Selected Solo Piano Music of Florence B. Price (1887–1953)" (DMus diss., Florida State University, 1995), 9.

33. Florence Beatrice Price Box 75 Folder 1620 Theodore Charles Stone Collection, Center for Black Music Research at Columbia College Chicago.

34. Teresa L. Reed, "Black Women in Art Music," in *Black Women and Music: More than Blues*, eds. Eileen M. Hayes and Linda F. Williams (Urbana: University of Illinois Press, 2007), 179, 190.

35. James V. Hatch was a white archivist of Black artistry who alongside his wife, the African American artist and filmmaker Camille Billops, amassed a vast collection of materials (including interviews) that sought to reflect the depth and breadth of Black creative life in their contemporary United States. These materials now form the Camille Billops and James V. Hatch Archives at the Stuart A. Rose Manuscript, Archives, and Rare Book Library at Emory University.

36. See Samantha Ege and Chelsea M. Daniel, "Black Excellence on the Airwaves: Nora Holt and the American Negro Artist Program," *Sounding Out*, February 24, 2020, https://soundstudiesblog.com/2020/02/24/black -excellence-on-the-airwaves-nora-holt-and-the-american-negro-artist -program/; Samantha Ege, "Nora Douglas Holt's Teachings of a Black Classical Canon," in *The Oxford Handbook of Public Music Theory*, ed. J. Daniel Jenkins (New York: Oxford University Press, 2022), http://doi.org/10.1093/ oxfordhb/9780197551554.013.21.

37. See Rae Linda Brown, *The Heart of a Woman: The Life and Music of Florence B. Price* (Urbana: University of Illinois Press, 2020), 101.

38. Volume/Box 279.1 and 279.2 Camille Billops and James V. Hatch archives at Emory University.

39. "Chi Takes All Wanamaker Prizes," *Baltimore Afro-American*, October 1, 1932, 4.

40. "Chicago Women Capture Wanamaker Music Prizes," *Norfolk Journal and Guide*, October 1, 1932, 11.

41. "$750 Prizes Result of Injury: 2 Chicago Women Get All the Cash Given in Music Contest," *Atlanta Daily World*, October 2, 1932, A1.

42. "Chicago Women Win Prizes for Negro Composers," *Washington Tribune*, September 30, 1932, 3.

43. "Chicago Women Win $1,000 Prizes in Rodman Wanamaker Memorial Contest," *New York Age*, October 1, 1932, 7.

44. Maude Roberts George, "News of the Music World," *Chicago Defender*, October 8, 1932, 15.

45. George, "Wanamaker Awards Given in Music."

46. Maude Roberts George, "News of the Music World," *Chicago Defender*, June 3, 1933, 15.

47. Maude Roberts George, "News of the Music World," *Chicago Defender*, May 13, 1933, A3.

48. Chicago Music Association Record (1936–40).

49. Maude Roberts George, "[Excerpt lost in newspaper clipping] Triumphs in Recital Here: Noted Tenor and Miss Margaret Bond [*sic*] Star with Symphony," *Chicago Defender*, June 17, 1933, located in Helen Walker-Hill Papers, Series 4, Box 5, Folder 8.2, Center for Black Music Research at Columbia College Chicago.

50. Brown, *The Heart of a Woman*, 115.

51. Robert S. Abbott, "The Week: This Is Progress, About Communism, Real Mixture," *Chicago Defender*, June 24, 1933, 11.

52. Nahum Daniel Brascher, "Roland Hayes Concert Shows Progress of Race in Music," *Chicago Defender*, June 24, 1933, 11.

53. Barbara Wright-Pryor, "Barbara Wright-Pryor: 'Maude Roberts George . . . President of CMA of which Price Was a Member, Underwrote the Cost of the June 15, 1933 Concert,'" *Africlassical*, April 7, 2014, https://africlassical .blogspot.com/2014/04/barbara-wright-pryor-maude-roberts.html.

54. "Sepia Composers in Need of Funds"; "'Musicians Need New Angel.'"

55. Chicago Music Association Record (1936–40).

56. Marian Anderson brochure, Series 2, Box 2, Chicago Music Association Collection, Amistad Research Center, New Orleans.

57. Abbott, "The Week."

58. Anna Julia Cooper, "The Status of the Woman in America (1892)," in *The Voice of Anna Julia Cooper: Including* A Voice from the South *and Other Important Essays, Papers, and Letters*, ed. Charles Lemert and Esme Bhan (Lanham, MD: Rowman & Littlefield, 1998), 112.

59. Marian Anderson, *My Lord, What a Morning: An Autobiography by Marian Anderson* (New York: Viking, 1956), 184–85.

60. Marian Anderson brochure, Series 2, Box 2, Chicago Music Association Collection, Amistad Research Center, New Orleans.

61. Leslie Heaphy, "Daniel Gardner Burley: Musician, Journalist and Activist," *Black Ball: A Negro Leagues Journal* 2, no. 2 (2009): 4.

62. Dan Burley, "Backdoor Stuff," *New York Amsterdam News*, April 15, 1939, 20.

63. I borrow "envoices" from Alisha Lola Jones who uses it to describe how, "as Anderson envoiced Price's composition in particular, she provided a musical rebuttal to the concert domains that predominantly comprised white male decision makers, an exclusionist industry bolstered by unsisterly white women patrons that stemmed from a joint colonial past of chattel slavery plantation hierarchy. And these are barriers that African American women still face in the concert music industry and in their homes today." Jones also notes that "several individuals and black organizations made that 1939 recital possible through unmarked, free labor. Sustained by a web of black women-inclusive networks—black churches, black women's clubs, Howard University, the NAACP [National Association for the Advancement of Colored People] and the National Association for Negro Musicians—Anderson ascended the stage voicing Florence B. Price's composition as the 'final say' on that landmark moment." Jones, "Lift Every Voice."

Conclusion. In Honor of Mrs. Maude Roberts George

1. Rae Linda Brown, *The Heart of a Woman: The Life and Music of Florence B. Price* (Urbana: University of Illinois Press, 2020), 238.

2. Guthrie P. Ramsey Jr., *Who Hears Here? On Black Music, Pasts and Present* (Oakland: University of California Press, 2022), 58.

3. Maude Roberts George, "Women in Music," in Elizabeth Lindsay Davis, *Lifting as They Climb* (Chicago: National Association of Colored Women, 1933), 416.

4. Chicago Music Association Record (1936–1940), Center for Black Music Research at Columbia College Chicago.

5. Farrah Jasmine Griffin, *Harlem Nocturne: Women Artists & Progressive Politics during World War II* (New York: Basic Civitas, 2013), 125.

6. Christina Demaitre, "She Has a Musical Mission: Developing Racial Harmony," *Washington Post,* August 14, 1964, Box 5 Series 4, Folder 8.2, Center for Black Music Research at Columbia College Chicago; Nora Holt, "Music Appreciation, Non-professional," *Chicago Defender,* November 2, 1918, 12. See also Samantha Ege, "Nora Douglas Holt's Teachings of a Black Classical Canon," in *The Oxford Handbook of Public Music Theory,* ed. J. Daniel Jenkins (New York: Oxford University Press, 2022), http://doi.org/10.1093/oxfordhb/9780197551554.013.21.

7. Tammy L. Kernodle, "'I Wish I Knew How It Would Feel to Be Free': Nina Simone and the Redefining of the Freedom Song of the 1960s," *Journal of the Society for American Music* 2, no. 3 (2008): 297.

8. Many of these compositions remain unlocated and therefore unseen by Bonds musicologists and performers, which therefore contributes to the tragically vast body of Black women's unheard canons. Demaitre, "She Has a Musical Mission."

9. Paula Giddings, *When and Where I Enter: The Impact of Black Women on Race and Sex in America* (New York: Amistad, 2006), 116–17; Olga Idris Davis, "'I Rose and Found My Voice': Claiming 'Voice' in the Rhetoric of Ida B. Wells," in *Black Women's Intellectual Traditions: Speaking Their Minds,* ed. Kristin Waters and Carol B. Conway (Burlington: University of Vermont Press, 2007), 314; Melina Abdullah, "The Emergence of a Black Feminist Leadership Model: African American Women and Political Activism in the Nineteenth Century," in *Black Women's Intellectual Traditions: Speaking Their Minds,* ed. Kristin Waters and Carol B. Conway (Burlington: University of Vermont Press, 2007), 334; Joy James, "Shadowboxing: Liberation Limbos—Ida B. Wells," in Waters and Conway, *Black Women's Intellectual Traditions,* 350–52.

10. Demaitre, "She Has a Musical Mission."

11. Demaitre, "She Has a Musical Mission."

12. Carter G. Woodson established Negro History Week in 1926, which took place in the second week of February so as to purposefully encompass the birthdays of Abraham Lincoln and Frederick Douglass. It appears that the CMA started their celebrations early!

13. For the full score of the solo-piano suite and insightful note on its performance history from editor Louise Toppin, see Louise Toppin, ed., *Rediscovering Margaret Bonds: Spiritual Suite for Piano* (Fayetteville, AR: Classical Vocal Reprints, 2020).

14. It was a particularly sweet victory for Bonds to branch into symphonic writing, as in her own words, "Florence Price had told me I would never be able to write for orchestra. . . . Some of these giants will decide that you can't [do] this." Despite the closeness of the Bonds and Price matriarchs, this anecdote is a necessary reminder of the tensions that inevitably exist across generations and of how Bonds's voice, though an extension of Black Chicago Renaissance aesthetics, ventures into a postmodernist identity that is at once in conversation with and distinct from Price's aesthetic. Volume/Box 279.1 and 279.2 Camille Billops and James V. Hatch archives at Emory University.

15. "All Margaret Bonds Concert," Series 1, Box 1, Chicago Music Association Collection, Amistad Research Center, New Orleans.

16. "Judge George's Widow Shot by Son: Judge George's Widow Wounded by Her Son," *Chicago Defender*, October 26, 1940, 1.

17. "Maude Roberts George Shot: Bullet Fired by Son thru Mistake," *Pittsburgh Courier*, October 26, 1940, 1.

18. "Drop Charge in Shooting of Mrs. George: State Secures Leave to Reopen Case in Event Findings Warrant," *Chicago Defender*, December 21, 1940, 7.

19. Journalist Natalie Y. Moore writes, "The blanket Chicago South Side image in many white minds equals pathological ghetto. Reporters often enable that stereotype by only covering crime when they deign to venture to the South Side." As a result, I am cautious not to perpetuate this stereotype in how I approach George's incident. Natalie Y. Moore, *The South Side: A Portrait of Chicago and American Segregation* (New York: Picador, 2016), 14.

20. Kira Thurman makes this salient point as she discusses the tragedy of Draylen William Mason, a seventeen-year-old Black boy and classically trained double bassist, who was murdered on March 12, 2018. A white male domestic terrorist, named Mark Anthony Conditt, left a package bomb outside of Mason's home in Austin, Texas, killing Mason in the explosion. As I write my second iteration of this concluding chapter and meditate on Thurman's observations that "many musicians in the past made the mistake of thinking that classical music could save us from white supremacy," my thoughts are also enveloped in the near fatal shooting of the sixteen-year-old Black boy Ralph Yarl, an award-winning clarinetist and bassoonist. On April 13, 2023, Yarl (from Kansas City, Missouri) went to collect his siblings, mistakenly knocked on the door of the wrong house, and was shot twice—once in the arm and once in the head—by its inhabitant, a white eighty-four-year-old male named Andrew Lester. (Lester claimed that Yarl was attempting to break into his home.) Yarl was refused help from three different households until someone agreed to act. And even then, the severely injured teenager was treated with hostility, as if he had committed a crime; he was made to lie on the ground with his hands up while the resident called for emergency help. Kira Thurman,

"Singing against the Grain: Playing Beethoven in the #BlackLivesMatter Era," *Point Magazine*, September 29, 2018, https://thepointmag.com/examined-life/singing-against-grain-playing-beethoven-blacklivesmatter-era/.

21. This was not an unfamiliar position for Race women. Throughout this book, we see instances of Black women who were nominally middle to upper class even if their finances told a different story, such as Florence Price around the Wanamaker era, the young Gertrude Smith Jackson upon the death of her mother, or the Bonds family who were not particularly well-off despite the immense material and communal support they offered those around them. In her book *Harlem Nocturne*, Farrah Jasmine Griffin describes how the family of author Ann Petry were "solidly middle class—in status if not always financially." It is a description that extends to the dynamic here among some of Chicago's Black culturati. Griffin, *Harlem Nocturne*, 82.

22. Darlene Clark Hine writes, "Because of the interplay of racial animosity, class tensions, gender role differentiation, and regional economic variations, black women as a rule developed a politics of silence, and adhered to a cult of secrecy, a culture of dissemblance, to protect the sanctity of the inner aspects of their lives." Although Hine relates her concept of the culture of dissemblance to the sexual violence that historical Black women suffered in the United States, she acknowledges that the concept "exists in an even more complex fashion among black women who endured the combination of race, gender, and class oppression"; we see its complex presence in George's own experience of violence, regardless of who pulled the trigger. Hine, "Rape and the Inner Lives of Black Women: Thoughts on the Culture of Dissemblance," in *Hine Sight: Black Women and the Re-Construction of American History* (Bloomington: Indiana University Press, 1994), 41, 37.

23. Elaborating on the nature of this liminal space, Kira Thurman writes, "Held up as symbols of racial advancement, used to denigrate others who cannot or will not make the same aesthetic choices, or denounced as Uncle Toms, black classical musicians inhabit a liminal space." For George and numerous others, however, this liminal space becomes a source of power through which to reconfigure the wider cultural landscape that seeks to contain it. Thurman, "Singing against the Grain."

24. "Maude Roberts George, Local Civic Leader, Dies," *Chicago Defender*, December 11, 1943, 12.

25. Brittney C. Cooper, *Beyond Respectability: The Intellectual Thought of Race Women* (Urbana: University of Illinois Press, 2017), 123.

26. The complete list of artists are as follows: Mme. Neal Hawkins Buckner; Mrs. Gertrude Harrison; Louise Cowan Harris; the Impromptu Quartette consisting of Anna Hocker, Della Ridgway, Pearl Pitts, and Effie Jones; Mme. Azalia Hackley; Mme. Anita Patti Brown; Mme. M. Calloway Byron; Mme. Clara Williams; Mme. Florence Cole Talbert; Mme. Antoinette Garnes; Marian Anderson; Mme. Lillian Evanti; Hazel Harrison; Maud Cuney Hare; Mme. Abbie Mitchell; Lillian LeMon; Pauline James Lee; Dr. Mildred Bryant

Jones; Florence B. Price; Camille Nickerson; Shirley Graham; and Mrs. Martin. George, "Women in Music," 416–20.

27. Jennifer Stoever, *The Sonic Color Line: Race and the Cultural Politics of Listening* (New York: New York University Press, 2016); Kira Thurman, *Singing like Germans: Black Musicians in the Land of Bach, Beethoven, and Brahms* (Ithaca: Cornell University Press, 2021), 43.

28. George, "Women in Music," 416–20.

29. Kimberly Wallace-Sanders, introduction to *Skin Deep, Spirit Strong: The Black Female Body in American Culture*, ed. Kimberly Wallace-Sanders (Ann Arbor: University of Michigan Press, 2002), 2–3.

30. George, "Women in Music," 416–20.

31. For a wider history of Race women's internationalism, see Imaobong D. Umoren, *Race Women Internationalists: Activist-Intellectuals and Global Freedom Struggles* (Oakland: University of California Press, 2018).

32. In a CMA meeting that took place on December 15, 1936, Theodore Charles Stone "called attention to a new and comprehensive volume on Negro Musicians and their Music by Maud Cuney Hare," read the minutes. George then "announced that the Hare book was published after Miss Hare's death and the preface gives credit to Dr. Clarence Cameron White for collaboration in completing it." Chicago Music Association Record (1936–1940), Center for Black Music Research at Columbia College Chicago.

33. Maude Roberts George, "Women Contributors to the World of Music: Short Sketches of Women in Music," *Chicago Defender*, December 17, 1938, 17.

34. "Appreciation Testimonial by C.N.D.A.C.: Mrs. Maude R. George Is Honored," *Chicago Defender*, October 7, 1933, 6.

35. Clarence Lee's role under Martha B. Mitchell is mentioned in Maude Roberts George, "News of the Music World," *Chicago Defender*, August 15, 1931, 15.

36. I am indebted to Anthony E. Philpott whose personal archives identify the names of those in the photograph labeled fig. 33.

37. "At Last! Music by Florence Price Performed by the Boston Symphony Orchestra," *Women's Philharmonic Advocacy*, March 22, 2019, https://wophil.org/at-last-music-by-florence-price-performed-by-the-boston-symphony-orchestra/; Sarah Fritz and A. Kori Hill, "Clara Schumann and Florence Price Get Their Due at Carnegie Hall," *New York Times*, October 27, 2022, https://www.nytimes.com/2022/10/27/arts/music/clara-schumann-florence-price-philadelphia-orchestra.html.

38. Micaela Baranello, "Welcoming a Black Composer into the Canon. Finally" [originally titled, "Once Overlooked, Now Rediscovered"], *New York Times*, February 9, 2018, https://www.nytimes.com/2018/02/09/arts/music/florence-price-arkansas-symphony-concerto.html.

39. Founded by Aaron P. Dworkin, Sphinx Organization certainly intersects with the aims of NANM and its affiliated branches, as well as the Chicago West Community Music Center and Chineke!, to uplift classical musicians from

underrepresented communities. Citing Jessie Montgomery's professiona
website, "Since 1999, Jessie has been affiliated with The Sphinx Organiza
tion, which supports young African-American and Latinx string players anc
has served as composer-in-residence for the Sphinx Virtuosi, the Organiza
tion's flagship professional touring ensemble. She was a two-time laureat
of the annual Sphinx Competition and was awarded their highest honor, th
Sphinx Medal of Excellence." Jessie Montgomery, "About," *Jessie Montgom
ery*, https://www.jessiemontgomery.com/about/; Kyle MacMillan, "Jessi
Montgomery Named as the CSO's Next Composer-in-Residence," *Chicag
Symphony Orchestra*, April 20, 2021, https://cso.org/experience/article/3598
jessie-montgomery-named-as-the-csos-next-comp.

40. Patricia Hill Collins, *Black Feminist Thought: Knowledge, Consciousness
and the Politics of Empowerment* (New York: Routledge, 2009), 4–5, 28.

41. Chicago Music Association Record (1936–1940), Center for Black Musi
Research at Columbia College Chicago.

42. Carlene J. Brown, afterword to *The Heart of a Woman*, 240.

Bibliography

Abbott, Lynn, and Doug Seroff. *To Do This, You Must Know How: Music Pedagogy in the Black Gospel Quartet Tradition.* Jackson: University Press of Mississippi, 2012.

Abdullah, Melina. "The Emergence of a Black Feminist Leadership Model: African-American Women and Political Activism in the Nineteenth Century." In *Black Women's Intellectual Traditions: Speaking Their Minds*, edited by Kristin Waters and Carol B. Conway, 328–45. Burlington: University of Vermont Press, 2007.

Absher, Amy. *The Black Musician and the White City: Race and Music in Chicago, 1900–1967.* Ann Arbor: University of Michigan Press, 2014.

Anderson, Marian. *My Lord, What a Morning: An Autobiography by Marian Anderson.* New York: Viking, 1956.

André, Naomi. *Black Opera: History, Power, Engagement.* Urbana: University of Illinois Press, 2018.

Arnesen, Eric. *Brotherhoods of Color: Black Railroad Workers and the Struggle for Equality.* Cambridge, MA: Harvard University Press, 2002.

"At Last! Music by Florence Price Performed by the Boston Symphony Orchestra." *Women's Philharmonic Advocacy*, March 22, 2019. https://wophil.org/at-last-music-by-florence-price-performed-by-the-boston-symphony-orchestra/.

Austin, Addell P. "The 'Opportunity' and 'Crisis' Literary Contests, 1924–1927." *CLA Journal* 31, no. 2 (1988): 235–46.

Bailey, Candace. "Black Women and the Cultural Performance of Music in Mid-Nineteenth Century Natchez." *American Nineteenth Century History* (2024). https://doi.org/10.1080/14664658.2024.2303867.

Bailey, Candace. *Unbinding Gentility: Women Making Music in the Nineteenth-Century South.* Urbana: University of Illinois Press, 2021.

Baldwin, Davarian L. *Chicago's New Negroes: Modernity, the Great Migration, and Black Urban Life*. Chapel Hill: University of North Carolina Press, 2007.

Bambara, Toni Cade, ed. *The Black Woman: An Anthology*. New York: New American Library, 1970.

Baranello, Micaela. "Welcoming a Black Composer into the Canon. Finally [originally titled, 'Once Overlooked, Now Rediscovered']." *New York Times*, February 9, 2018. https://www.nytimes.com/2018/02/09/arts/music/florence-price-arkansas-symphony-concerto.html.

Bay, Mia. "The Battle for Womanhood Is the Battle for Race: Black Women and Nineteenth-Century Racial Thought." In *Toward an Intellectual History of Black Women*, edited by Mia Bay, Farah J. Griffin, Martha S. Jones, and Barbara D. Savage, 75–92. Chapel Hill: University of North Carolina Press, 2015.

Bay, Mia, Farah J. Griffin, Martha S. Jones, and Barbara D. Savage, eds. *Toward an Intellectual History of Black Women*. Chapel Hill: University of North Carolina Press, 2015.

Beale, Frances. "Double Jeopardy: To Be Black and Female." In *The Black Woman: An Anthology*, edited by Toni Cade Bambara, 109–22. New York: New American Library, 1970.

Biographical and Historical Memoirs of Pulaski, Jefferson, Lonoke, Faulkner, Grant, Saline, Perry, Garland and Hot Springs Counties, Arkansas. Chicago: Goodspeed Publishing, 1889.

Bonds, Margaret. "A Reminiscence." In *The Negro in Music and Art*, edited by Lindsay Patterson, 191–93. New York: Publishers Company, 1967.

Bone, Robert W., and Richard A. Courage. *The Muse in Bronzeville: African American Creative Expression in Chicago, 1932–1950*. New Brunswick: Rutgers University Press, 2011.

Bowers, Jane, and Judith Tick, eds. *Women Making Music: The Western Art Tradition, 1150–1950*. Urbana: University of Illinois Press, 1986.

Brodeur, Michael Andor. "A Pioneering Black Composer Gets Her Due, 110 Years after Her Debut: Samantha Ege and the Yale Philharmonia Will Perform the Orchestra World Premiere of Helen Hagan's 'Piano Concerto in C Minor.'" *Washington Post*, October 20, 2022. https://www.washingtonpost.com/music/2022/10/20/helen-hagan-samantha-ege-yale-music/.

Brooks, Daphne. *Liner Notes for the Revolution: The Intellectual Life of Black Feminist Sound*. Cambridge, MA: Harvard University Press, 2021.

Brown, Rae Linda. *The Heart of a Woman: The Life and Music of Florence B. Price*. Urbana: University of Illinois Press, 2020.

Brown, Rae Linda, and Wayne Shirley, eds. *Florence Price: Symphonies Nos. 1 and 3*. Middleton, WI: A-R Editions, 2008.

Burford, Mark. "Sorrow Songs and Sisterhood: Samuel Coleridge-Taylor and W. E. B. Du Bois across the Black Atlantic." Paper presented at the American Musicological Society, Society for Ethnomusicology, and Society for Music Theory Joint Annual Meeting, New Orleans, November 11, 2022.

Caplan, Lucy. "'Strange What Cosmopolites Music Makes of Us': Classical Music, the Black Press, and Nora Douglas Holt's Black Feminist Audiotopia." *Journal of the Society for American Music* 14, no. 3 (2020): 308–36.

Caplan, Lucy. "Unbinding Gentility: Women Making Music in the Nineteenth-Century South by Candace Bailey (Review)." *Women and Music: A Journal of Gender and Culture* 26 (2022): 175–80.

Carby, Hazel V. *Reconstructing Womanhood: The Emergence of the Afro-American Woman Novelist.* New York: Oxford University Press, 1987.

Chicago West Community Music Center. https://www.cwcmc.org/.

Collins, Patricia Hill. *Black Feminist Thought: Knowledge, Consciousness, and the Politics of Empowerment.* New York: Routledge, 2009.

Cooper, Anna Julia. "The Status of the Woman in America (1892)." In *The Voice of Anna Julia Cooper: Including* A Voice from the South *and Other Important Essays, Papers, and Letters*, edited by Charles Lemert and Esme Bhan, 109–17. Lanham, MD: Rowman & Littlefield, 1998.

Cooper, Anna Julia. "Womanhood: A Vital Element in the Regeneration and Progress of a Race (1886)." In *The Voice of Anna Julia Cooper: Including* A Voice from the South *and Other Important Essays, Papers, and Letters*, edited by Charles Lemert and Esme Bhan, 53–71. Lanham, MD: Rowman & Littlefield, 1998.

Cooper, Brittney C. *Beyond Respectability: The Intellectual Thought of Race Women.* Urbana: University of Illinois Press, 2017.

Courage, Richard A., and Christopher Reed. *Roots of the Black Chicago Renaissance: New Negro Writers, Artists, and Intellectuals, 1893–1930.* Urbana: University of Illinois Press, 2021.

Crawford, Richard. *The American Musical Landscape: The Business of Musicianship from Billings to Gershwin.* Updated ed. Los Angeles: University of California Press, 2000.

Crawford, Richard. "Edward MacDowell: Musical Nationalism and an American Tone Poet." *Journal of the American Musicological Society* 49, no. 3 (1996): 528–60.

Crenshaw, Kimberlé W. "Demarginalizing the Intersection of Race and Sex: A Black Feminist Critique of Antidiscrimination Doctrine, Feminist Theory and Antiracist Politics." *University of Chicago Legal Forum* (1989): 139–67.

Crenshaw, Kimberlé W. "Mapping the Margins: Intersectionality, Identity Politics and Violence against Women of Color." *Stanford Law Review* 43, no. 6 (1991): 1241–99.

Das, Joanna Dee. *Katherine Dunham: Dance and the African Diaspora.* New York: Oxford University Press, 2017.

Davis, Angela. *Women, Race & Class.* London: Random House, 1981.

Davis, Elizabeth Lindsay. Foreword to *Lifting as They Climb*, by Elizabeth Lindsay Davis, 7. Chicago: National Association of Colored Women, 1933.

Davis, Elizabeth Lindsay. *Lifting as They Climb.* Chicago: National Association of Colored Women, 1933.

Davis, Elizabeth Lindsay. *The Story of the Illinois Federation of Colored Women's Clubs, 1900–1922*. Chicago: n.p., 1922.

Davis, Olga Idris. "'I Rose and Found My Voice': Claiming 'Voice' in the Rhetoric of Ida B. Wells." In *Black Women's Intellectual Traditions: Speaking Their Minds*, edited by Kristin Waters and Carol B. Conway, 309–27. Burlington: University of Vermont Press, 2007.

Davis, William H. *National Negro Business League: Annual Report of the Sixteenth Session and the Fifteenth Anniversary Convention*. Nashville: African M. E. Sunday School Union, 1915.

Demlinger, Sandor, and John Steiner. *Destination: Chicago Jazz*. Stroud, UK: Tempus Publishing, 2003.

Doktor, Stephanie DeLane. "How a White Supremacist Became Famous for His Black Music: John Powell and *Rhapsodie nègre (1918)*," *American Music* 38, no. 4 (2020): 395–427.

Dolinar, Brian, ed. *The Negro in Illinois: The WPA Papers*. Urbana: University of Illinois Press, 2013.

Drake, St. Clair, and Horace R. Cayton. *Black Metropolis: A Study of Negro Life in a Northern City*. 1945. Reprint, Chicago: University of Chicago Press, 2015.

Du Bois, W. E. B. *The Souls of Black Folk: Essays and Sketches*. 2nd ed. Chicago: A. C. McClurg, 1903.

Du Bois, W. E. B. "The Talented Tenth." In *The Negro Problem*, edited by Booker T. Washington, W. E. B. Du Bois, Paul Laurence Dunbar, and Charles W. Chesnutt, 33–75. New York: James Pott, 1903.

Durrant, Elizabeth. "Chicago Renaissance Women: Black Feminism in the Careers and Songs of Florence Price and Margaret Bonds." MA thesis, University of North Texas, 2021.

Early, Gerald, ed. *Ain't but a Place: African American Writings about St. Louis*. Saint Louis: Missouri Historical Society Press, 1998.

Edmondson, Jacqueline, ed. *Music in American Life: An Encyclopedia of the Songs, Styles, Stars and Stories That Shaped Our Culture*. Santa Barbara: Greenwood, 2013.

Ege, Samantha. "Nora Douglas Holt's Teachings of a Black Classical Canon." In *The Oxford Handbook of Public Music Theory*, edited by J. Daniel Jenkins. New York: Oxford University Press, 2022. http://doi.org/10.1093/oxfordhb/9780197551554.013.21.

Ege, Samantha. "Restaging Respectability: The Subversive Performances of Josephine Baker and Nora Holt in Jazz-Age Paris." *Angelaki: Journal of the Theoretical Humanities* 27, no. 3–4 (2022): 112–24.

Ege, Samantha. "The Art of the Black Feminist Scholar-Performer." *American Music* 40, no. 4 (2022): 487–91.

Ege, Samantha, and Chelsea M. Daniel, "Black Excellence on the Airwaves: Nora Holt and the American Negro Artist Program." *Sounding Out*, February 24, 2020. https://soundstudiesblog.com/2020/02/24/black-excellence-on-the-airwaves-nora-holt-and-the-american-negro-artist-program/.

Emejulu, Akwugo, and Francesca Sobande. "Introduction: On the Problems and Possibilities of European Black Feminism and Afrofeminism." In *To Exist Is to Resist: Black Feminism in Europe*, edited by Akwugo Emejulu and Francesca Sobande, 3–9. London: Pluto, 2019.

Emejulu, Akwugo, and Francesca Sobande. *To Exist Is to Resist: Black Feminism in Europe*. London: Pluto, 2019.

Farmer, Ashley D. "Shining the Light Just Right: Reconstructing the Life of 'Queen Mother' Audley Moore." *Association of Black Women Historians*, December 4, 2019. http://abwh.org/2019/12/04/shining-the-light-just-right-reconstructing-the-life-of-queen-mother-audley-moore/.

Floyd, Samuel A., Jr. "Ring Shout! Literary Studies, Historical Studies, and Black Music Inquiry." *Black Music Research Journal* 11, no. 2 (1991): 265–87.

Floyd, Samuel A., Jr. *The Power of Black Music: Interpreting Its History from Africa to the United States*. New York: Oxford University Press, 1995.

Floyd, Samuel A., Jr., ed. *Black Music in the Harlem Renaissance: A Collection of Essays*. Knoxville: University of Tennessee Press, 1995.

Floyd, Samuel A., Jr. "Music in the Harlem Renaissance: An Overview." In *Black Music in the Harlem Renaissance: A Collection of Essays*, edited by Samuel A. Floyd Jr., 1–27. Knoxville: University of Tennessee Press, 1993.

Freeman, Tyrone McKinley. *Madam C. J. Walker's Gospel of Giving: Black Women's Philanthropy during Jim Crow*. Urbana: University of Illinois Press, 2020.

Fritz, Sarah, and A. Kori Hill. "Clara Schumann and Florence Price Get Their Due at Carnegie Hall." *New York Times*, October 27, 2022. https://www.nytimes.com/2022/10/27/arts/music/clara-schumann-florence-price-philadelphia-orchestra.html.

Ganz, Cheryl R. *The 1933 Chicago World's Fair: A Century of Progress*. Urbana: University of Illinois Press, 2008.

Gates, Henry Louis, Jr. *The Signifying Monkey: A Theory of African-American Literary Criticism*. 25th anniversary ed. Oxford: Oxford University Press, 2014.

Gatewood, Willard B., Jr. "Frederick Douglass in Arkansas." *Arkansas Historical Quarterly* 41, no. 4 (1982): 303–15.

George, Maude Roberts. "Women in Music." In Elizabeth Lindsay Davis, *Lifting as They Climb*, 416–20. Chicago: National Association of Colored Women, 1933.

Giddings, Paula. *When and Where I Enter: The Impact of Black Women on Race and Sex in America*. New York: Amistad, 2006.

Gold, Michael. "Viola Davis's Emmy Speech." *New York Times*, September 20, 2015. https://archive.nytimes.com/www.nytimes.com/live/emmys-2015/viola-daviss-emotional-emmys-acceptance-speech/.

Golia, Julie A. "Courting Women, Courting Advertisers: The Woman's Page and the Transformation of the American Newspaper, 1895–1935." *Journal of American History* 103, no. 3 (2016): 606–28.

Graham, Sandra Jean. *Spirituals and the Birth of a Black Entertainment Industry*. Urbana: University of Illinois Press, 2018.

Graham, Shirley. "Spirituals to Symphonies." *Etude* 54, no. 11 (1936): 691–92, 723, 736.

Gregory, James N. *The Southern Diaspora: How the Great Migrations of Black and White Southerners Transformed America*. Chapel Hill: University of North Carolina Press, 2005.

Green, Mildred Denby. *Black Women Composers: A Genesis*. Boston: Twayne, 1983.

Griffin, Farah Jasmine. *Harlem Nocturne: Women Artists & Progressive Politics during World War II*. New York: Basic Civitas, 2013.

Hackley, Emma Azalia. *The Colored Girl Beautiful*. Kansas City, MO: Burton, 1916.

Hare, Maud Cuney. "Chapter X: Musical Pioneers." In *Negro Musicians and Their Music*, 197–238. Washington, DC: Associated Publishers, 1936.

Hare, Maud Cuney. *Negro Musicians and Their Music*. Washington, DC: Associated Publishers, 1936.

Hare, Maud Cuney. *Norris Wright Cuney: A Tribune of the Black People*. New York: Crisis Publishing, 1913.

Hare, Maud Cuney. "The Source." In *International Library of Negro Life and History: The Negro in Music and Art*, edited by Lindsay Patterson, 19–30. New York: Publishers Company, 1967.

Hartman, Saidiya. *Wayward Lives, Beautiful Experiments: Intimate Stories of Social Upheaval*. New York: Norton, 2019.

Hayes, Eileen M. "New Perspectives in Studies of Black Women and Music." In *Black Women and Music: More than the Blues*, edited by Eileen M. Hayes and Linda F. Williams, 1–20. Urbana: University of Illinois Press, 2007.

Hayes, Eileen M., and Linda F. Williams, eds. *Black Women and Music: More than the Blues*. Urbana: University of Illinois Press, 2007.

Heaphy, Leslie. "Daniel Gardner Burley: Musician, Journalist and Activist." *Black Ball: A Negro Leagues Journal* 2, no. 2 (2009): 4–9.

Hendricks, Wanda A. *Gender, Race, and Politics in the Midwest: Black Club Women in Illinois*. Bloomington: Indiana University Press, 1998.

Higginbotham, Evelyn Brooks. *Righteous Discontent: The Women's Movement in the Black Baptist Church, 1880–1920*. Cambridge, MA: Harvard University Press, 1993.

Hill, A. Kori. "Make the Familiar New: New Negro Modernism in the Concertos of Florence B. Price." PhD diss., University of North Carolina, 2022.

Hill, A. Kori. "To Be Rediscovered When You Were Never Forgotten: Florence Price and Black Composers in the Mainstream." *Litrary Diversty, Substack*, June 11, 2023. https://litrarydiversty.substack.com/p/to-be-discovered-when-you-were-never?utm_source=profile&utm_medium=reader2.

Hill, A. Kori. "To Be Rediscovered When You Were Never Forgotten: Florence Price and the 'Rediscovered' Composer (Tropes of Black Composers,

Part One)." *Harry T. Burleigh Society*, November 29, 2018. https://www
.burleighsociety.com/blog/2018-11-29/florence-price-part-one.

Hine, Darlene Clark. *Hine Sight: Black Women and the Re-Construction of
American History*. Bloomington: Indiana University Press, 1994.

Hine, Darlene Clark. Introduction to *The Black Chicago Renaissance*, edited by
Darlene Clark Hine and John McCluskey Jr., xv–xxxiii. Urbana: University
of Illinois Press, 2012.

Hine, Darlene Clark, and John McCluskey Jr., eds. *The Black Chicago Renaissance*. Urbana: University of Illinois Press, 2012.

Hisama, Ellie. *Gendering Musical Modernism: The Music of Ruth Crawford,
Marion Bauer, and Miriam Gideon*. Cambridge: Cambridge University Press,
2001.

Hobbs, Allyson. *A Chosen Exile: A History of Racial Passing in American Life*.
Cambridge, MA: Harvard University Press, 2014.

Holly, Ellistine Perkins. "Black Concert Music in Chicago, 1890 to the 1930s."
Black Music Research Journal 10, no. 1 (1990): 141–49.

Holzer, Linda Ruth. "Selected Solo Piano Music of Florence B. Price (1887–
1953)." DMus diss., Florida State University, 1995.

hooks, bell. *"Ain't I a Woman?": Black Women and Feminism*. New York: Routledge, 1981.

Horowitz, Joseph. "Dvořák and Boston." *American Music* 19, no. 1 (2001): 3–17.

Horowitz, Joseph. *Wagner Nights: An American History*. Berkeley: University
of California Press, 1994.

Hounmenou, Charles. "Black Settlement Houses and Oppositional Consciousness." *Journal of Black Studies* 43, no. 6 (2012): 644–66.

Hull, Akasha (Gloria T.), Patricia Bell Scott, and Barbara Smith, eds. *All the
Women Are White, All the Blacks Are Men, but Some of Us Are Brave: Black
Women's Studies*. 2nd ed. New York: Feminist Press, 2015.

Jackson, Barbara Garvey. "Florence Price, Composer." *Black Perspective in
Music* 5, no. 1 (1977): 30–43.

James, Joy. "Shadowboxing: Liberation Limbos—Ida B. Wells." In *Black
Women's Intellectual Traditions: Speaking Their Minds*, edited by Kristin
Waters and Carol B. Conway, 346–62. Burlington: University of Vermont
Press, 2007.

James, Joy. *Transcending the Talented Tenth: Black Leaders and American Intellectuals*. New York: Routledge, 1997.

Jones, Alisha Lola. "Lift Every Voice: Marian Anderson, Florence B. Price and
the Sound of Black Sisterhood." *NPR*, August 30, 2019. https://www.npr
.org/2019/08/30/748757267/lift-every-voice-marian-anderson-florence
-b-price-and-the-sound-of-black-sisterh.

Jones, Alisha Lola. "Spirituals and the Birth of a Black Entertainment Industry
by Sandra Jean Graham (Review)." *Journal of Popular Music Studies* 31 no.
3 (2019): 163–66.

Jones, Alisha Lola. "'When and Where I Enter': Marian Anderson, Florence B.

Price, and a Womanist Musical Rebuttal of UnSisterly White Women's Movements." Paper presented at the Center for Research on Race and Ethnicity
in Society Speaker Series, Indiana University, Bloomington, March 21, 2019.
https://anthropology.indiana.edu/news-events/events-calendar/crres
-speaker-series-alisha-jones.html.

Jones, Martha S. *All Bound Up Together: The Woman Question in African American Public Culture, 1830–1900*. Chapel Hill: University of North Carolina
Press, 2007.

Kaba, Mariame, and Essence McDowell. *Lifting as They Climbed: Mapping
a History of Trailblazing Black Women in Chicago*. Chicago: Haymarket
Books, 2023.

Karpf, Juanita, *Performing Racial Uplift: E. Azalia Hackley and African American Activism in the Postbellum to Pre-Harlem Era*. Jackson: University Press
of Mississippi, 2022.

Kellner, Bruce. *The Harlem Renaissance: A Historical Dictionary for the Era*.
Westport, CT: Greenwood, 1984.

Kennedy, Michael, Joyce Kennedy, and Tim Rutherford-Johnson, eds. *Oxford
Dictionary of Music*. 6th ed. Oxford: Oxford University Press, 2013.

Kernodle, Tammy L. "A Woman's Place: The Importance of Mary Lou Williams' Harlem Apartment." *NPR*, September 12, 2019. https://www.npr
.org/2019/09/12/758070439/a-womans-place-the-importance-of-mary
-lou-williams-harlem-apartment.

Kernodle, Tammy L. "Black Women Working Together: Jazz, Gender, and the
Politics of Validation." *Black Music Research Journal* 34, no. 1 (2014): 27–55.

Kernodle, Tammy L. "'I Wish I Knew How It Would Feel to Be Free': Nina
Simone and the Redefining of the Freedom Song of the 1960s." *Journal of
the Society for American Music* 2, no. 3 (2008): 295–317.

Kernodle, Tammy L. "'When and Where I Enter': Black Women Composers
and the Advancement of a Black Postmodern Concert Aesthetic in Cold
War–Era America." In "Colloquy: Shadow Culture Narratives: Race, Gender,
and American Music Historiography." *Journal of the American Musicological Society* 73, no. 3 (2020): 770–77.

Knox, Janice A., and Heather Olivia Belcher. *Then & Now: Chicago's Loop*.
Charleston, SC: Arcadia, 2005.

Knupfer, Anne Meis. *The Chicago Black Renaissance and Women's Activism*. Chicago: University of Illinois Press, 2006.

Knupfer, Anne Meis. *Toward a Tenderer Humanity and a Nobler Womanhood*.
New York: New York University Press, 1997.

Lemert, Charles, and Esme Bhan, eds. *The Voice of Anna Julia Cooper: Including A Voice from the South and Other Important Essays, Papers, and Letters*.
Lanham, MD: Rowman & Littlefield, 1998.

Ling, Huping. *Chinese Chicago: Race, Transnational Migration and Community
since 1870*. Redwood City: Stanford University Press, 2012.

Locke, Alain. "The Negro Spirituals." In *The New Negro: Voice of the Harlem*

Renaissance, edited by Alain Locke, 199–213. New York: Simon & Schuster, [1925] 1997.

Locke, Alain. "The New Negro." In *The New Negro: An Interpretation*, edited by Alain Locke, 3–16. New York: Simon & Schuster, [1925] 1997.

Locke, Alain, ed. *The New Negro: An Interpretation*. New York: Simon & Schuster, [1925] 1997.

Locke, Ralph P., and Cyrilla Barr, eds. *Cultivating Music in America: Women Patrons and Activists since 1860*. Berkeley: University of California Press, 1997.

Locke, Ralph P., and Cyrilla Barr. "Introduction: Music Patronage as a 'Female-Centered Cultural Process.'" In *Cultivating Music in America: Women Patrons and Activists since 1860*, edited by Ralph P. Locke and Cyrilla Barr, 1–23. Berkeley: University of California Press, 1997.

MacMillan, Kyle. "Jessie Montgomery Named as the CSO's Next Composer-in-Residence." *Chicago Symphony Orchestra*, April 20, 2021. https://cso.org/experience/article/3598/jessie-montgomery-named-as -the-csos-next-comp.

Manning, Susan, and Lizzie Leopold. *Dancing on the Third Coast: Chicago Dance Histories*. Urbana: University of Illinois Press, forthcoming.

Matkin-Rawn, Story. "'The Great Negro State of the Country': Arkansas's Reconstruction and the Other Great Migration." *Arkansas Historical Quarterly* 72, no. 1 (2013): 1–41.

Maxile, Horace J., Jr. "*Fantasie Nègre: The Piano Music of Florence Price*, by Samantha Ege (Review)." *Journal of the American Musicological Society* 75, no. 2 (2022): 405–9.

Mayer, Harold M., and Richard C. Wade. *Chicago: Growth of a Metropolis*. Chicago: University of Chicago Press, 1969.

McGinty, Doris Evans. "'As Large as She Can Make It': The Role of Black Women Activists in Music, 1880–1945." In *Cultivating Music in America: Women Patrons and Activists since 1860*, edited by Ralph P. Locke and Cyrilla Barr, 214–30. Berkeley: University of California Press, 1997.

McGinty, Doris Evans, ed. *A Documentary History of the National Association of Negro Musicians*. Chicago: Center for Black Music Research, Columbia College Chicago, 2004.

Meyerowitz, Lisa. "The Negro in Art Week: Defining the 'New Negro' through Art Exhibition." *African American Review* 31, no. 1 (1997): 75–89.

Montgomery, Jessie. "About." *Jessie Montgomery*. https://www.jessie montgomery.com/about/.

Moore, Natalie Y. *The South Side: A Portrait of Chicago and American Segregation*. New York: Picador, 2016. "New England Conservatory of Music." *Journal of Education* 50, no. 6 (1899): 106.

The Negro in Chicago, 1779–1927, Volume I. Chicago: Washington Intercollegiate Club of Chicago, 1927.

The Neume: 1906. Boston: New England Conservatory of Music, 1906.

"New England Conservatory of Music." *Journal of Education* 74, no. 6 (1911): 149.

Obama, Michelle. *Becoming*. London: Viking, 2018.

Official Guide Book of the Fair Chicago: 1933 A Century of Progress. Chicago: A Century of Progress, 1933.

Oja, Carol A. *Making Music Modern: New York in the 1920s*. New York: Oxford University Press, 2000.

Olson, Liesl. "She-Devils: Ruth Page, Katherine Dunham, and *La guiablesse*." In *Dancing on the Third Coast: Chicago Dance Histories*, edited by Susan Manning and Lizzie Leopold. Urbana: University of Illinois Press, forthcoming.

Paddon, Anna R., and Sally Turner. "African Americans and the World's Columbian Exposition." *Illinois Historical Journal* 88, no. 1 (1995): 19–36.

Patterson, Lindsay, ed. *International Library of Negro Life and History: The Negro in Music and Art*. New York: Publishers Company, 1967.

Perry, Imani. *May We Forever Stand: A History of the Black National Anthem*. Chapel Hill: University of North Carolina Press, 2018.

Priest, David. "The Long Lost Work of Florence Price Finally Comes Home." *Arkansas Life*, May 24, 2018. https://arkansaslife.com/22383-2/.

Quashie, Kevin. *Black Aliveness, or A Poetics of Being*. Durham, NC: Duke University Press, 2021.

Ramsey, Guthrie P., Jr. *Who Hears Here? On Black Music, Pasts and Present*. Oakland: University of California Press, 2022.

Reed, Christopher Robert. *The Rise of Chicago's Black Metropolis, 1920–1929*. Urbana: University of Illinois Press, 2011.

Reed, Teresa L. "Black Women in Art Music." In *Black Women and Music: More than the Blues*, edited by Eileen M. Hayes and Linda F. Williams, 179–96. Urbana: University of Illinois Press, 2007.

Rhodes, Jane. "Pedagogies of Respectability: Race, Media, and Black Womanhood in the Early 20th Century." *Souls: A Critical Journal of Black Politics, Culture, and Society* 18, no. 2–4 (2016): 201–14.

Rogers, O. A., Jr. "The Elaine Race Riots of 1919." *Arkansas Historical Quarterly* 19 (1960): 142–50.

Rutkoff Peter M., and William B. Scott. "Pinkster in Chicago: Bud Billiken and the Mayor of Bronzeville, 1930–1945." *Journal of African American History* 89, no. 4 (2004): 316–30.

Samuelson, Timothy. *The Black Metropolis—Bronzeville District*. Chicago: Chicago Department of Planning and Development, 1997.

Savage, Barbara D. *Merze Tate: The Global Odyssey of a Black Woman Scholar*. New Haven: Yale University Press, 2023.

Schenbeck, Lawrence. *Racial Uplift and American Music, 1878–1943*. Jackson: University Press of Mississippi, 2012.

Schultz, Rima Lunin, and Adele Hast. *Women Building Chicago 1790–1990: A Biographical Dictionary*. Bloomington: Indiana University Press, 2001.

Shadle, Douglas W. *Orchestrating the Nation: The Nineteenth-Century American Symphonic Enterprise*. New York: Oxford University Press, 2016.

Shadle, Douglas W. "Plus ça change: Florence B. Price in the #BlackLivesMatterEra." *New Music USA*, February 20, 2019. https://newmusicusa.org/nmbx/plus-ca-change-florence-b-price-in-the-blacklivesmatter-era/.

Smith, J. Clay, Jr. *Emancipation: The Making of the Black Lawyer, 1844–1944*. Philadelphia: University of Pennsylvania Press, 1993.

Southern, Eileen. *The Music of Black Americans: A History*. 3rd ed. New York: Norton, 1997.

Southern, Eileen, ed. *Readings in Black American Music*. New York: Norton, 1972.

Still, William Grant. *La guiablesse*. Flagstaff: William Grant Still Music, n.d.

Still, William Grant. "My Arkansas Boyhood." *Arkansas Historical Quarterly* 26, no. 3 (1967): 285–93.

Stockley, Grif. "Elaine Massacre." *Encyclopedia of Arkansas*, last modified May 30, 2018. http://www.encyclopediaofarkansas.net/encyclopedia/entry-detail.aspx?entryID=1102.

Stoever, Jennifer. *The Sonic Color Line: Race and the Cultural Politics of Listening*. New York: New York University Press, 2016.

Theta Omega Chapter: Alpha Kappa Alpha Sorority, Incorporated ®. https://thetaomega.com/theta-omega-chapter/theta-omega-history/.

Thompson, Katrina Dyonne. *Ring Shout, Wheel About: The Racial Politics of Music and Dance in North American Slavery*. Urbana: University of Illinois Press, 2014.

Thurman, Kira. "Performing Lieder, Hearing Race: Debating Blackness, Whiteness, and German Identity in Interwar Central Europe." *Journal of the American Musicological Society* 72 no. 3 (2019): 825–65.

Thurman, Kira. "Singing against the Grain: Playing Beethoven in the #BlackLivesMatter Era." *Point Magazine*, September 29, 2018. https://thepointmag.com/examined-life/singing-against-grain-playing-beethoven-blacklivesmatter-era/.

Thurman, Kira. *Singing like Germans: Black Musicians in the Land of Bach, Beethoven, and Brahms*. Ithaca: Cornell University Press, 2021.

Tick, Judith. "Passed Away Is the Piano Girl: Changes in American Musical Life, 1870–1900." In *Women Making Music: The Western Art Tradition, 1150–1950*, edited by Jane Bowers and Judith Tick, 325–48. Urbana: University of Illinois Press, 1986.

Toppin, Louise, ed. *Rediscovering Margaret Bonds: Spiritual Suite for Piano*. Fayetteville, AR: Classical Vocal Reprints, 2020.

Tracy, Steven C., ed. *Writers of the Black Chicago Renaissance*. Urbana: University of Illinois Press, 2011.

Trodd, Zoe. "The Black Press and the Black Chicago Renaissance." In *Writers of the Black Renaissance*, edited by Steven C. Tracy, 448–64. Urbana: University of Illinois Press, 2011.

Trotter, James Monroe. *Music and Some Highly Musical People*. Boston: Lee and Shepard, 1878.

Umoren, Imaobong D. *Race Women Internationalists: Activist-Intellectuals and Global Freedom Struggles.* Oakland: University of California Press, 2018.

Voss, Kimberly. "Diversity Essay: The Women's Pages at American Black Newspapers." *Journalism History*, June 27, 2022. https://journalism-history .org/2022/06/27/diversity-essay-the-womens-pages-at-american-black -newspapers/.

Voyante, Elektra. "The Poet and Her Song: Analyzing the Art Songs of Florence B. Price." DMus diss., Indiana University, 2018.

Walker-Hill, Helen, ed. *Black Women Composers: A Century of Piano Music (1893–1990).* Bryn Mawr: Hildegard Publishing, 1992.

Walker-Hill, Helen. "Black Women Composers in Chicago: Then and Now." *Black Music Research Journal* 12, no. 1 (1992): 1–23.

Walker-Hill, Helen. *From Spirituals to Symphonies: African–American Women Composers and Their Music.* Urbana: University of Illinois Press, 2007.

Walker-Hill, Helen. "Western University at Quindaro, Kansas (1865–1943) and Its Legacy of Pioneering Musical Women." *Black Music Research Journal* 26, no. 1 (2006): 7–37.

Wall, Cheryl A. "Nora Holt: New Negro Composer and Jazz Age Goddess." In *Women and Migration: Responses in Art and History*, edited by Deborah Willis, Ellyn Toscano, and Kalia Brooks Nelson, 91–104. Cambridge: Open Book Publishers, 2019.

Wall, Cheryl A. *On Freedom and the Will to Adorn: The Art of the African American Essay.* Chapel Hill: University of North Carolina Press, 2019.

Wallace-Sanders, Kimberly, ed. *Skin Deep, Spirit Strong: The Black Female Body in American Culture.* Ann Arbor: University of Michigan Press, 2002.

Washington, Booker T., ed. *A New Negro for a New Century: An Accurate and Up-to-date Record of the Upward Struggles of the Negro Race.* Chicago: American Publishing House, 1900.

Washington, Booker T. "Industrial Education for the Negro." In *The Negro Problem*, edited by Booker T. Washington, W. E. B. Du Bois, Paul Laurence Dunbar, and Charles W. Chesnutt, 7–29. New York: James Pott, 1903.

Waters, Kristin, and Carol B. Conway, eds. *Black Women's Intellectual Traditions: Speaking Their Minds.* Burlington: University of Vermont Press, 2007.

Webb, John E. *Whispers of Love: A History of the R. Nathaniel Dett Club of Music and Allied Arts, 1922–1987.* Chicago: Columbia College Chicago, 1987.

Wells, Ida B., Frederick Douglass, Irvine Garland Penn, and Ferdinand Barnett. *The Reason Why the Colored American Is Not in the World's Columbian Exposition.* Manuscript/Mixed Material. https://www.loc.gov/item/mfd.25023.

Wells-Barnett, Ida B. "The Arkansas Race Riot." N.p., 1920.

West, Stan. "As the CSO's Sheila Jones Retires, Her Cause Lives On." *Chicago Symphony Orchestra*, January 28, 2022. https://cso.org/experience/article/ 8051/as-the-csos-sheila-jones-retires-her-cause-li.

White, Shane, and Graham White. *The Sounds of Slavery: Discovering African*

American History through Songs, Sermons, and Speech. Boston: Beacon, 2005.

Williams, Fannie Barrier. "A Northern Negro's Autobiography." *Independent* 57 (1906): 91–96. https://search.alexanderstreet.com/view/work/bibliographic_entity%7Cbibliographic_details%7C2757427.

Williams, Fannie Barrier. "The Club Movement among Colored Women of America." In *A New Negro for a New Century: An Accurate and Up-to-date Record of the Upward Struggles of the Negro Race*, edited by Booker T. Washington, 379–405. Chicago: American Publishing House, 1900.

Williams, Fannie Barrier. "The Woman's Part in a Man's Business." In *The Voice of the Negro*, 1:543–47. New York: Negro Universities Press, [1904] 1969.

Williams, Lilian Serece, and Randolph Boehm, eds. *Records of the National Association of Colored Women's Clubs, 1895–1992: Part 1: Minutes of National Conventions, Publications, and President's Office Correspondence*. Bethesda: University Publications of America, 1994.

Williams, Ora, Thelma Williams, Dora Wilson, and Ramona Matthewson. "American Black Women Composers: A Selected Annotated Bibliography." In *All the Women Are White, All the Blacks Are Men, but Some of Us Are Brave: Black Women's Studies*, 2nd ed., edited by Akasha (Gloria T.) Hull, Patricia Bell Scott, and Barbara Smith, 297–306. New York: Feminist Press, 2015.

Wintz, Cary D., and Paul Finkelman, eds. *Encyclopedia of the Harlem Renaissance: A–J*. New York: Routledge, 2004.

Wintz, Cary D., and Paul Finkelman, eds. *Encyclopedia of the Harlem Renaissance: K–Y*. New York: Routledge, 2004.

Wright, Josephine. "Black Women and Classical Music." *Women's Studies Quarterly* 12, no. 3 (1984): 18–21.

Wright, Josephine. "Black Women in Classical Music in Boston during the Late Nineteenth Century: Profiles of Leadership." In *New Perspectives on Music: Essays in Honor of Eileen Southern*, edited by Josephine Wright, 373–409. Sterling Heights, MI: Harmonie Park Press, 1992.

Wright, Josephine, ed. *New Perspectives on Music: Essays in Honor of Eileen Southern*. Sterling Heights, MI: Harmonie Park Press, 1992

Wright, Michelle M. *Physics of Blackness: Beyond the Middle Passage Epistemology*. Minneapolis: University of Minnesota Press, 2015.

Wright, Michelle M. "On Epiphenomenal Temporality: Black German Identities and Quantum Physics in the African Diaspora." Paper presented at the ICI Berlin, February 26, 2018. https://www.ici-berlin.org/events/michelle-m-wright/.

Wright-Pryor, Barbara. "Barbara Wright-Pryor: 'Maude Roberts George . . . President of CMA of which Price Was a Member, Underwrote the Cost of the June 15, 1933 Concert.'" *Africlassical*, April 7, 2014. https://africlassical.blogspot.com/2014/04/barbara-wright-pryor-maude-roberts.html.

Yenser, Thomas. "Maude Roberts George." In *Who's Who in Colored America: A Biographical Dictionary of Notable Living Persons of African Descent in America. 1930–1931–1932*, 3rd ed., edited by Thomas Yenser, 166. Brooklyn: Thomas Yenser, 1933.

Index

Hutchison, 56; legacy of, 68–69, 70, 186; mixed heritage of, 15–16; one-drop rule and, 15–16; works (*see* Coleridge-Taylor, Samuel, works)
Coleridge-Taylor, Samuel, works: *Bon-Bon Suite,* 72; *Hiawatha's Wedding Feast,* 4, 72; "On-Away, Awake Beloved," 4, 61–62; *24 Negro Melodies,* op. 59, 25, 93
Coleridge-Taylor Music School of Chicago, 68–69, 70, 86
Collins, Patricia Hill, 7–13, 33–34, 217
colorism/racial passing, 14–15, 159–60, *161,* 162, 166, 228n66, 240n72, 248–49n59
Cook, Will Marion, 25
Cooper, Anna Julia: as foremother of intellectual Race womanhood, 28–31, 33, 46; "when and where I enter" motif, 28–31, 33, 41
Cooper, Brittney C., 16–17, 41; "Great Race Man Narrative," 37–38
Cosmopolitan School of Music (Indiana), 212
Costonie, Toni, 106
counterpoint: as musical term, 33–34; in organizing by Race women, 31–35, 48–57
Creole cultures, 69, 83, 85, 163, 212–13
The Crisis, 83
Crossing Borders Music, 12–13
Cullen, Countee, 93

dance: Ballet Night, 88–91; *Fantasie Nègre* in E minor for piano (F. Price) ballet performances, 134–38, 207; intersections between Black concert music and, 93–96; Negro Dance Group program, 91–97
Das, Joanna Dee, 92–93
Davis, Elizabeth Lindsay, 1, 83, 178–79, 201, 211–13, 216
Davis, Viola, 145, 244n15
Dawson, Charles Clarence, 57–60
Dawson, Mary Cardwell, 82, 173, *174, 175*
Dawson, William Levi, 70, 141, 173, *174; Negro Folk Symphony,* 16,

141–42, 144; as teacher of Margaret Bonds, 102
Debussy, Claude, "Golliwog's Cake-walk," 93–94, 135
Demaitre, Christina, 205
Denton, Grace, 5
Dett, Robert Nathaniel, 25, 173, 181; *In the Bottoms Suite* for solo piano, 148; Canadian background of, 15; "Juba Dance," 148; and NANM, 82, 171, *175;* and the National Association of Negro Music Teachers, 75, 76; R. Nathaniel Dett Club of Music and Allied Arts, 7, 86, 97–98, 100, 101, 235n77
Deuce, Etta Augusta, 148
Devries, Herman, 54, 89–91, 195
D'Indy, Vincent, 147
Diton, Carl Rossini, 172–73
Doktor, Stephanie DeLane, 69, 181
Dolinar, Brian, 71
Donizetti, Gaetano: "Una Furtiva Lagrima," 62
Dorsey, Thomas A., 65
Dougherty, Sandra T., 189
Douglass, Frederick, 155, 176–77
Douglass League of Women Voters, 52
Drake, St. Clair, 42, 45, 63, 64–65, 90, 110, 231n9
Du Bois, W. E. B.: Negro Spirituals and, 67; Talented Tenth, 37, 38, 67, 164, 205
Dunbar, Paul Laurence, 26, 70; "The Sand Man" (poem), 149
Duncan, George W., 73
Dunham, Katherine, 58; Ballet Night and, 88–91; *Fantasie Nègre* in E minor for piano (F. Price) and, 134–38, 207; Negro Dance Group program, 91–97
Durrant, Elizabeth, 8
Du Sable, Jean Baptiste Point, 180
Dyett, Neota L. McCurdy, 100, 101, 125–26

Ege, Samantha: as BBC Proms speaker, 216; "A Celebration of Women in Music," 10–11; notes on terminology, 14–17; "Of Folk, Faith,

SAMANTHA EGE is an award-winning researcher and musicologist, internationally recognized concert pianist, and popular public speaker.

The University of Illinois Press
is a founding member of the
Association of University Presses.

———————————————

Composed in 10.5/13 Mercury Text
with Avenir display
by Jim Proefrock
at the University of Illinois Press
Manufactured by Sheridan Books, Inc.

University of Illinois Press
1325 South Oak Street
Champaign, IL 61820-6903
www.press.uillinois.edu